UNDERSTANDING CHINA'S ECONOMY

UNDERSTANDING CHINA'S ECONOMY

Gregory C. Chow

Princeton University

World Scientific
Singapore • New Jersey • London • Hong Kong

Published by

World Scientific Publishing Co. Pte. Ltd.
P O Box 128, Farrer Road, Singapore 9128
USA office: Suite 1B, 1060 Main Street, River Edge, NJ 07661
UK office: 73 Lynton Mead, Totteridge, London N20 8DH

Library of Congress Cataloging-in-Publication Data

Chow, Gregory C., 1929–
    Understanding China's economy / Gregory C. Chow.
       p.   cm.
    Includes bibliographical references and indexes.
    ISBN 9810218419 -- ISBN 9810218583 (pbk.)
    1. China--Economic conditions--1976–   2. China--Economic
policy--1976– I. Title.
HC427.92.C4783   1994
330.951'05--dc20   94-19947
                                            CIP

Printed in Singapore.

PREFACE

This book represents a record of the authors's effort to understand and to help improve the Chinese economy from the early 1980s to 1994. An attempt to understand the Chinese economy was made in the author's book, *The Chinese Economy* (Harper & Row, 1985, and World Scientific, 1988). Since the publication of that book the author has made further attempts as recorded in this book.

A reader wishing to understand the Chinese economy may benefit from the observations and the economic analyses reported here. The book describes and evaluates China's economic reforms since 1978 (Part I), examines the prospects for future growth (Part II), sets forth the basic tools and data for studying the Chinese economy (Part III), and presents microeconomic analyses (Part IV) as well as macroeconomic analyses (Part V) for the Chinese economy. It represents only the author's effort and is not a text covering the research on the Chinese economy completed by many other scholars. The coverage of the important topics, though incomplete, is sufficient to provide the reader a coherent picture of the Chinese economy. The reader will find interesting facts, ideas and analytical methods for understanding China's economy.

The Economics Department of Princeton University has provided a stimulating and congenial environment for me to pursue my interests in the Chinese economy, in addition to my other interests in economics. The Center for International Studies at Princeton has provided support for a part of the research. I would like to thank my colleagues at the State Commission on Education and the State Commission on Restructuring the Economic System of the State Council of China, with whom I have cooperated to improve economics education and the economic system in China. From these colleagues I have learned a great deal about economics in action. I am grateful to all the publishers cited who have granted permission to reproduce previous published material, and especially to Dr. K. K. Phua, World Scientific Publishing, for his enthusiasm and effort in getting this book published, and to Yew Kee Chiang for an excellent job in editing the manuscript. I would also like to thank Pia Ellen and Cynthia Cohen for excellent typing of various drafts of the manuscript.

The following publishers have given permission to reprint material previously published. I would like to acknowledge with thanks: Chapter 1 from *Science*, vol. 235 (1987); Chapter 2 from *Urban Land and Housing Reform in Socialist and Formerly Socialist Countries*, George Tolley ed., University of Chicago; Chapter 3 from *China Economic Review*, vol. 4, no. 2 (1993); Chapter 4, section on Economics Education was originally published as "Economics Education and Economic Reform in China" in *Proceedings of the American Philosophical Society*, vol. 133, 1 (1989), section on Economics Exchanges with the United States contains reports of the American Economic Association's Committee on U.S.–China Exchanges from the May issues of *The American Economic Review* (1982–1994); Chapter 5 from *China Economic Review*, vol. 1, no. 2 (1989); Chapter 7 from *International Economic Insights*, vol. II, no. 3 (1991); Chapter 10 from *The American Statistician*, vol. 40, no. 3 (1986); Chapter 12 from *Journal of Economic Education*, vol. 19, (1988), reprinted with permission of the Helen Dwight Reid Educational Foundation, published by Heldref Publications, 1319 18th Street, N.W., Washington, DC 20036-1802; Chapter 14 from *Academia Economic Papers*, vol. 20, no. 2, Part I (1992); Chapter 15 from *Journal of Economic Dynamics and Control*, vol. 4 (1982); Chapter 16 from *The Quarterly Journal of Economics* (1993); Chapter 17 from *Journal of Political Economy*, vol. 93 (1985); Chapter 18 from *Journal of Comparative Economics*, vol. 11 (1987).

Gregory C. Chow
Princeton, New Jersey
April 1994

"$" in this book refers to the U.S. dollar unless otherwise stated.

CONTENTS

Contents

PART V - MODELING GROWTH AND FLUCTUATIONS   **191**

INTRODUCTION

In the early 1990s the world began to recognize that China's economy is dynamic and rapidly growing and that rapid growth is likely to continue for some time. This recognition is partly reflected in the tremendous expansion of foreign capital flowing into China and in the increase in the Hang Seng index of Hong Kong stock prices from approximately 3,000 in January 1989 to about 10,000 in January 1994. Many people must believe that economic development in China will be fast enough, and the political institution stable enough, to assure the continued increase in profits of companies in Hong Kong, a city to become part of China after July 1, 1997. If one projects an average annual rate of growth of 8.5% (as compared with 9.5% real growth in China between 1977 and 1988 and about 13% in 1992) the economy will be 7.69 times after 25 years, while a 2.5% annual growth amounts to 1.85 times. If in 1995, per capita output of China were one-fortieth of that of the U.S., so that total output would be about one-ninth, in 2020, using the above growth rates for the two countries, China's output will be $(1/9) \times 7.69/1.85$ or about 46% of that of the U.S. China will soon be a major economic power if it is not already one today. This book represents the author's attempts over the past ten years to understand the Chinese economy.

The book is divided into five parts. Part I deals with economic reform. Chapter 1 begins with a description of the Chinese economic institutions before reforms began in 1978. It summarizes the major elements of economic reform up to 1986, discusses the important reform issues as of that time and comments on prospects of further reform. This Chapter serves as an introduction to Chinese economic institutions and the reform process. Chapter 2 characterizes the reform process, compares it with the reform process in Taiwan and discusses one aspect of reform, namely that of urban housing. Chapter 3 reviews the success story of China's economic reform up to 1993 and explains how and why China succeeded. Chapter 4 is concerned with economics education in China which affects the Chinese economic system in the long-run. It also includes annual reports on economics exchanges with the United States from 1981 to 1993 which reveal important changes in the economic education in China during these years. Chapter 5 is a personal account of aspects of the modernization of economics education by the State Education Commission and the design of economic reform by the State Commission for Restructuring the

Economic System as the author has worked with both Commissions since the 1980s.

Part II discusses prospects of economic growth beginning with Chapter 6 which contains the author's optimistic view as of June 1989, soon after the tragic incident of Tiananmen Square, when many other people were pessimistic about China's economic future. Such optimistic views were again expressed a little later in an article published in May 1991 which constitutes Chapter 7. China's growth and integration into the world economy is the subject of Chapter 8 where the author also comments on the role the United States can play as a world economic leader. Chapter 9 evaluates the possibility of serious inflation in China in the 1990s from the perspective of January 1994 as inflation is a serious issue for China's economic stability and growth.

Part III serves as an introduction to a more formal economic analysis of the Chinese economy. It begins by an evaluation of the quality of official economic data from China in Chapter 10. The chapter originally appeared in 1986 when many scholars questioned the usefulness of these data for research purposes. Part of the answer comes later when these data are actually used for economic research in Chapters 16, 17 and 18. Chapter 16 in particular raises the same question again and provides an answer with reference to a particular study of China's economic growth through capital formation. Chapter 11 reports on the economic research in China as of the mid-1980s for the purpose of providing information to foreign scholars who might be interested in using research results from China or in cooperative research with Chinese economists. Chapter 12 illustrates with several examples how modern tools of economic analysis can be applied to understand the Chinese economy. Many scholars in the mid-1980s questioned the usefulness of these tools, in view of the different cultural and institutional setting in China from those of the western developed economies for which the tools had been originally invented. This chapter also prepares the ground work for the use of these tools in Parts IV and V of the book.

Part IV begins with a study of some aspects of China's socialist economy and an evaluation of its economic performance as compared with capitalism in Chapter 13. Many economists in the western world do not believe that a socialist economy can work well. The question is how well. Although economists have granted that socialism can rely on market forces, as the Chinese economic system has demonstrated in practice, some believe that private ownership is essential for economic efficiency. If socialism is characterized by the importance of public ownership, then would it be able to function efficiently? The apparently efficient working of Chinese enterprises (known as township and village enterprises) which are owned by the government at the provincial and local levels or owned collectively provides a partial answer to this question in practice. Further theoretical studies of this issue are needed. Weitzman and Xu (1993) is a preliminary theoretical analysis of this question.

Chapter 14 is a formal but elementary analysis of economic behavior of Chinese individuals and enterprises using microeconomic theory. It contains a model of state enterprises before economic reform and compares it with a model after certain reforms in order to assess the effect of these reforms. It demonstrates an important point concerning the method of economic analysis which is applicable to different institutional settings. Economic units are assumed to maximize certain objective subject to constraints on resources. When the institutions change, the objective and the constraints may change, but the method is equally applicable. Chapter 15 is concerned with a method of government planning in China using an econometric model based on Chinese economic institutions as of the early 1980s. Some of the tools described can be adopted for use in planning after China's economy becomes more market-oriented. This chapter is technical and would appeal only to specialists.

Finally, macroeconomic growth and fluctuations are treated in Part V. Chapter 16 provides estimates of Cobb–Douglas production functions for China's aggregate economy and for its five sectors using data from 1952 to 1980. The five sectors are agriculture, industry, construction, transportation and commerce as the classification is used in Chinese official statistics modeled after the former Soviet Union. The author constructed the capital stock data for the five sectors used in this study. The estimated production functions are used to project into the 1980s to measure the successes of economic reform in the five sectors in enhancing output in the 1980s, more than what could be accounted for by the increases in inputs through the production functions. The estimated functions can also be used to measure the economic impact of major events in the sample period, including the Great Leap Forward Movement of 1958–1961 and the Cultural Revolution of 1966–1976. A major finding of the study is that there was no technological improvement in the Chinese economy from 1952 to 1980, with increases in outputs accounted for entirely by increases in labor and capital inputs.

Chapter 17 is a simple model of macroeconomic fluctuations consisting of a consumption function and an investment function. Consumption is a function of income and lagged consumption. Investment is determined by the accelerations principle, which postulates that investment depends on the change in (and not the level of) income and lagged investment. Such a model was known to explain the annual data well for the United States and other developed market economies. It is interesting to note how well such a model can explain the Chinese national income data from 1952 to 1982.

Chapter 18, the last chapter, is a simple model to explain the price level and inflation in China from 1952 to 1983, using as the key variable the ratio of money supply (measured by currency in circulation) to real output. This variable is derived from the quantity theory of money. Some might question the adequacy of such a variable in explaining inflation in China because prices of many products were subjected to government control during the sample period and there was allegedly suppressed inflation in China. It is the author's opinion that market forces still worked to a significant extent despite government efforts to control prices. One set of evidence is provided in Sec. 5.3 of Chapter 16. In spite of government price fixing, prices of industrial products declined substantially from 1952 to 1980 relative to prices of agricultural products simply because of the relative increases in the supply of industrial products. Similar explanations based on the forces of demand and supply can explain the relative prices of the five sectors, as given in Sec. 5.3 of Chapter 16. Furthermore, the data in Chapter 18, and discussion in Chapter 9, reveal that the three important inflation episodes of 1960–61, 1985 and 1988 could be explained by the increase in the ratio of money supply to real output, the first due to reduction in output and the second and third due to rapid increases in money supply. The inflation of 1993 is no exception. Based on this variable, the model incorporates a dynamic relationship between the current price level and past price levels as well as current and past ratios of money supply to output. Modeling and estimating such a dynamic relationship make the chapter technical for the general reader. The resulting model explains the Chinese data well up to 1984, but fails to track the inflation record in the late 1980s (results not reported in this book). How to improve or modify the model to account for the rapid changes in Chinese monetary and market institutions remains an interesting topic of research. The reader may refer to a recent book by Gang Yi (1994) which deals with monetary reform in China and contains studies on China's inflation.

In summary, the studies in this book have resulted from the author's attempts to understand the Chinese economy. The author has observed, participated in and reported on the reform process (Part I); has evaluated the prospects of future economic growth and stability (Part II); has examined basic data and tools for economic analysis (Part III) and has studied microeconomic behavior (Part IV) as well as macroeconomic fluctuations and growth (Part V). Many scholars have contributed to our understanding of the Chinese economy, and much more remains to be studied and understood. It is hoped that the reader will enjoy and benefit from reading the discussions and studies reported in this book.

References

Weitzman, Martin L. and Xu, Chenggang, 1993, "Chinese Township Village Enterprises as Vaguely Defined Cooperatives," presented at China (Hainan) Institute for Reform and Development, July.

Yi, Gang, 1994, *Money, Banking, and Financial Markets in China*, Westview Press: Boulder/San Francisco/Oxford.

Part I
Economic Reform

CHAPTER 1

DEVELOPMENT OF A MORE MARKET-ORIENTED ECONOMY IN CHINA*†

Before 1978 in China, the economic institutions for agriculture and industry operated essentially under a centrally planned system. The reasons for a change toward a more market-oriented economy and the key elements of economic reform are discussed. Today the major issues being deliberated by the leading economic offficials include reform of the price system, the administrative structure of state-owned enterprises, the banking system and macroeconomic control mechanisms, and foreign trade and investment.

The transformation of the economy of the People's Republic of China from a planned to a more market-oriented economy is one of the most significant developments in world history during the last quarter of the 20th century. What the Chinese economic system was like before 1979, why reforms were introduced, what their essential elements are, and what issues are currently being addressed by reform officials are questions to be addressed in this article. The Chinese economy is a complicated entity with many dimensions, but only those aspects pertinent to the transition to a more market-oriented economy will be discussed here.

1.1. Economic Institutions Before the Reforms

A market economy differs from a centrally planned one in three important ways. Major economic resources are privately owned rather than owned by the state. Prices are determined by the market forces of demand and supply rather than by administrative orders. Economic decisions concerning consumption, production, distribution, and investment are decentralized, being made by private citizens or individual enterprises rather than by central command. Although most actual economies have characteristics of both market and planned economies, these two prototypes serve as convenient devices for understanding them.

*Originally published in *Science*, vol. 235, 16 January 1987, pp. 295–299. Copyright 1987 by the AAAS.

†The author would like to acknowledge with thanks the helpful comments of two referees on an earlier draft and the financial support of The Garfield Foundation in the preparation of this article.

Agriculture in China in the two decades before 1978 operated essentially as in a centrally planned economy. In the early 1950s land was confiscated from the landlords and redistributed to the peasants. In the mid-1950s, the peasants were organized into cooperatives. In 1958, Chairman Mao Zedong started the Great Leap Forward Movement and reorganized the cooperatives into communes. Formally, a commune is not a state enterprise but a collective economic and political unit. Its land is owned collectively by its members. However, in the two decades from 1958 to 1978, communes were operated by administrative controls. There were 53,300 communes in China in 1979, which were divided into 699,000 brigades, the latter being further divided into 5,154,000 production teams (*Statistical Yearbook of China 1981*). A production team often consisted of a traditional village. On average, there were 157 persons per team in 1979, and most farming was performed by a team, whereas larger scale construction work was done by a brigade.

Although team members officially owned the land, they had no control over its use. Commune authorities, following directions from the central government, determined what to produce on each piece of land. An assigned quota of the output had to be delivered to the government procurement department at a centrally fixed procurement price, the remaining output being left for distribution by the commune to its members. Members received incomes in money and in kind proportional to the numbers of work points earned, which equaled the numbers of days the team worked. Members followed orders and made no economic decisions. However, in varying degrees, some features of a market economy existed in rural China between 1958 and 1978. These included small private plots for the farmers and some rural markets where agricultural products were traded. A major objective of central procurement of agricultural products was to provide adequate supplies of essential food products to the urban residents under a system of rationing; among items rationed were food grain, vegetable oil, meat, sugar, and cotton cloth.

After the People's Republic of China was established in 1949, the new government took over industrial enterprises belonging to the previous government of the Republic of China. Private enterprises were tolerated for a brief period of several years. They soon became joint ventures. Then owners and managers were forced to surrender control to the new government, with some managers remaining to administer the enterprises under new directions. For the key industries, methods of central planning were adopted from the Soviet Union. The First Five-Year Plan was started in 1953. The government managed various state enterprises through some 20 ministries in the State Council. A State Planning Commission was established to direct and coordinate these ministries. Targets were planned in terms of output, and some important inputs and financial indices were transmitted to the enterprises. Under a system of material balancing used in the Soviet Union, important material inputs required were centrally distributed to the enterprises through a bureau of material supplies. Products of state enterprises were distributed by the state, with prices determined by a price commission. The bulk of the profits of state enterprises was surrendered to the state, providing a major source of government revenue. Funds required for capital construction and expansion had to be approved by the state and constituted an important part of government expenditures.[a]

Since enterprises obtained their inputs through central allotment, surrendered their outputs for central distribution, and had no control over their profits, they did not respond to prices. The main concern of enterprise managers was to obtain through skillful negotiations more than sufficient material and labor inputs to fulfill the production targets. They tended to understate the productive capacity of their enterprise in order to reduce output targets, and to overstate the input requirements in order to ensure their fulfillment. Inefficiencies and wastes occurred under this system, as partly reflected in the underutilization of productive capacity and the large stockpiling of inventories in Chinese state enterprises (Zhou, 1982). However, central planning, as described above, did not cover Chinese industry entirely — only major products were centrally distributed. Many smaller enterprises were operated by provincial and local governments (Chow, 1985, pp. 50–51).

From the 1950s on, the Chinese economic system did not remain static but was subject to two very serious political disturbances. One was the Great Leap Forward Movement from 1958 to 1961. The rapid formation of agricultural communes from April to September 1958 was itself a serious political disturbance. The second Five-Year Plan (1958–1962) was severely interrupted. Mistaken agricultural and industrial policies of the Great Leap caused famines and the curtailment of industrial output.[b] The other disturbance was the Cultural Revolution of 1966 to 1976. Having lost political power in the early 1960s as a result of the failure of the Great Leap, Mao attempted to regain political control by appealing directly to the Chinese youth to engage in a Cultural Revolution. Economic planning and agricultural production were disrupted. Intellectuals and social groups other than the peasants and workers were victimized. Higher education practically ceased, with total enrollment reduced form 674,000 in 1965 to 48,000 in 1970 (*Statistical Yearbook of China 1984*, p. 483). However, to the extent that the economic system functioned, its main characteristics were as described in the last two paragraphs.

1.2. Major Elements of Economic Reform

Mao died in 1976. The Chinese people as well as many party leaders had been extremely dissatisfied with the affairs prevailing during the Cultural Revolution and the new situation called for a drastic change in political leadership and economic

---

[a]Starting with the Cultural Revolution in the late 1960s, enterprises and local authorities began to keep a significant portion of their depreciation funds and used them to finance large amounts of investment.

[b]An official index of national income in 1952 prices was reduced from 202.1 in 1959 to 130.9 in 1962, and the annual death rate increased from 10.80 per thousand in 1957 to 25.43 per thousand in 1960 (6, pp. 30 and 83). A. J. Coale [*Rapid Population Change in China, 1952–1982* (National Academy Press, Washington, DC, 1984), p. 7] states that "the peak death rate in 1960 is about 35 [per thousand] ... . Excess deaths (those above a linear trend) from 1958 to 1963 are about 16 million when based on the understated official figures and about 27 million when adjusted for understatment."

policy. Two years later, Deng Xiaoping became the leader of China, having removed the political leaders responsible for the more extreme policies of the Cultural Revolution. More liberal economic policies were introduced because the Chinese leaders and economic officials, after experimenting with the commune system and central economic planning for more than two decades, recognized their deficiencies. They had begun to appreciate some virtues of a market economy, which had existed to a small extent throughout the previous 25 years. Their recognition was further enhanced by the successful experience of economic development in the neighboring economies of Hong Kong, Singapore, Taiwan, and South Korea. The open-door policy of Deng permitted them to learn more about the successful development of these and other economies.

Inefficiencies of Chinese agriculture under the Commune system were well recognized. Farmers were more knowledgeable about what crops to plant with their land than political leaders and economic planners. Farm workers had no incentive to work hard under the work-point system because they were not rewarded for their labors. There was a brief period in Chinese agriculture, after the land reform in the early 1950s, when farm households owned land and were able to sell products in the market. Reform of the commune system occurred initially in 1978 and 1979 when commune leaders in some regions recognized that they could fulfill their output quotas for delivery to the government procurement departments by reorganizing the commune internally following and improving upon practices in the 1950s. In essence, each farm household was assigned a piece of land and was held responsible for delivering a given quantity of a certain product to satisfy the procurement requirement. After fulfilling the delivery quota, the farm household would be free to keep products for its own consumption or sale in the market at market prices. This "responsibility system" is similar to private farming in a market economy, with each farm household leasing its land and paying the delivery quota as rent. Under this system the farm household has control over the land it uses and can choose what to produce and how to market its products as is the case in a market economy. This system was officially adopted by the Fourth Plenum of the Eleventh Central Committee of the Communist Party in September 1979. The rapid increase in agricultural output and in the incomes of the farmers in the years following have provided support for this responsibility system.

Elements of urban reform were adopted by the Chinese People's Congress in September 1980. In the opening session of that congress, Vice Premier Yao Yilin, chairman of the State Planning Commission, announced that experiments of more autonomous state enterprises and market competition would be greatly expanded in the following 2 years. Industrial reforms had begun in late 1978 with six pilot enterprises in Sichuan Province. By the end of June 1980, 6600 industrial enterprises that had been allowed to make certain output, marketing, and investment decisions through partial profit retention had produced in value 45 percent of the output of all state-owned industrial enterprises. By the end of 1981 some 80 percent of state-owned industrial enterprises were involved. The major elements of the industrial reforms include (i) a certain autonomy regarding the use of retained profits, production planning, sales of output, experimentation with new products, and capital expansion; (ii) adoption of features of an "economic responsibility system" by assignment of identifiable tasks to lower level units and payment to them according to productivity; (iii) increase in the role of markets; (iv) the streamlining of the administrative system at local levels for enterprises under local control; and (v) the encouragement of the establishment of collectively owned enterprises (Chow, 1984, pp. 148–151).

Reform in the industrial sector has turned out to be more difficult than in the agricultural sector. It is much easier to make small farm households behave like private enterprises in a market economy than to make large state enterprises so behave for four types of reasons. First, ideologically, members of the Communist Party of China believe in the ownership and the control of the means of production by the state. They are unwilling to surrender control of large state enterprises to nongovernment individuals and allow them to keep substanial profits for themselves, as in the case of small farms. Second, politically, government bureaucrats are unwilling to give up their power and vested interests by allowing the state enterprises to operate independently. Economic ministries tend to hold on to their control over the operations of the state enterprises. The bureau of material supplies tends to retain its control over the distribution of major material inputs. Third, economically, large industrial enterprises are more dependent on factors outside their control than are small household farms. Given a piece of land, a farm household can produce as it pleases, subject to climatic conditions. A large industrial enterprise needs the supplies of equipment and of material inputs produced by other enterprises. The entire system of pricing and distribution of industrial products and material inputs has to be changed to provide more autonomy to the state enterprises. Fourth, administratively, the efficient operation of a large industrial enterprise is much more difficult than operation of a small farm. Chinese managers often do not have sufficient knowledge and experience to run a modern enterprise as an independent entity. Even with additional training, managers and administrators of state enterprises are reluctant to give up their old habits of dependence on the economic ministries. The mode of operation of a large economic organization is difficult to change, as it is true for a large American corporation and more so for a large country like China.

Four years after the adoption of the urban reform decisions by the National People's Congress in September 1980 only limited progress in industrial efficiency had been achieved.[c] Observing this limited progress in the urban industrial sector and stimulated by further success in the agricultural sector, the Twelfth Central Committee of the Chinese Communist Party at its Third Plenary Session on 20

---

[c] I reported on a production function of Chinese state-owned industrial enterprises using data up to 1981 (*4*, pp. 123–126). The same production function fits the post-sample data from 1982, 1983, and 1984 very well, showing that there is no increase in industrial efficiency (see Sec. 12.1).

October 1984 adopted a major proposal to achieve overall reform of the economic structure. Economic reforms in China in the late 1980s will be based on this major decision. Implementation is to be formulated and carried out to a significant extent during the Seventh Five-Year Plan of 1986 to 1990.

Seven key elements of the Decision of 20 October 1984 concerning reform of the economic system are to (i) give individual state enterprises autonomy in decisions regarding production, supply, marketing, pricing, investment, and personnel as independent profit-seeking economic units; (ii) reduce the scope of central planning and, except for certain major products, change the method from mandatory planning to guidance planning; (iii) allow prices of more products to be determined by the forces of demand and supply rather than by central control; (iv) develop macroeconomic control mechanisms through the use of taxes, interest rates, and monetary policy under an improved financial and banking system; (v) establish various forms of economic responsibility systems within individual enterprises to promote efficiency and encourage differential wage rates to compensate for different kinds of work and levels of productivity; (vi) foster the development of individual and collective enterprises as supplements to the state enterprises; and (vii) expand foreign trade and investment as well as technological exchanges. An often-quoted slogan to capture the essential characteristics of the reform is, "Invigorate the microeconomic units. Control by macroeconomic means."

1.3. Current Issues

To design a structure of a "socialist economy with Chinese characteristics" and to facilitate its implementation, a State Commission for Restructuring the Economic System was formed in the State Council in 1982, with Premier Zhao Ziyang as chairman.[d] I will discuss some of the issues currently being studied by the members of this commission following the October 1984 decision.

It is well recognized by the leading economic reform officials that price reform is basic to other components of the decision on economic reform of October 1984. If input prices do not reflect the scarcity of the resources and output prices do not reflect the usefulness of the product, it is not economically beneficial to allow the state enterprises to seek more profits. Large profits do not mean economic efficiency if the input prices are set too low and output prices are set too high. The price of an input will measure its cost to society (termed the opportunity cost) if potential users are allowed to bid for it in the market. The price of an output will measure its benefit to society when users express their willingness to pay for it in the market. To ensure that autonomous state enterprises can perform their cost and profit calculations correctly, prices have to be determined by conditions of

---

[d]Premier Zhao has a good sense of economic reasoning as I learned from our extensive conversations on 5 June 1984. On 15 July 1985, the Premier asked me to invite economists from abroad to work with the Economic Restructuring Commission on problems of economic reform (see *The People's Daily*, 6 July 1984, p. 1; *ibid.*, 16 July 1985, p. 1; *ibid.*, 1 July 1986, p. 1).

demand and supply. What steps should be taken to achieve such a system of prices is a crucial question. In particular, the prices of steel, oil, coal, and electricity are set too low and need to be adjusted upward and perhaps set free eventually.

Concerning the second component of the Decision of October 1984, central planning will remain an important part of the Chinese economic system even though its scope will be reduced. The continued building of an economic infrastructure will be accomplished by central planning. Output targets for certain important industrial products will likely be set by mandatory planning in the sense of being compulsory rather than by guidance planning in the sense of being suggestive. Even in the fulfillment of mandatory output targets, the Chinese economic planner can beneficially use a set of market prices and respect the autonomy of state enterprises. The mandatory products would have to be paid for at prices agreed upon by negotiations with producers. At the beginning of this article, a centrally planned economy was distinguished from a market economy in that the former does not rely on prices to play an important role in the allocation of resources. This characteristic of Soviet-style central planning is being changed in China. State enterprises will obtain more of their material inputs from other enterprises directly rather than through central distribution and will sell more of their products directly to other enterprises or to consumers. Market prices will play a more important role, as has already occurred for agricultural products.

The remaining components of the 1984 decision on economic reform also depend on the functioning of market prices. The development of macroeconomic control devices through the uses of taxes, interest rates, and monetary policy will be effective and economically efficient in regulating the behavior of industrial enterprises and individual banks only if physical, human, and financial resources are appropriately priced. The encouragement of differential wage rates to reflect labor productivity is a step to improve the pricing of labor services. Individual and collective enterprises can function efficiently only if prices are determined by the forces of demand and supply, and many enterprises are already functioning in this manner. Foreign trade will be beneficial only if domestic prices reflect the relative scarcity of economic resources.

Besides price reform, three other sets of problems receive the attention of the Chinese economic reformers. First, they need to formulate a set of rules for state enterprises so that these can operate more efficiently. Second, they need to design macroeconomic mechanisms and institutions to regulate the microeconomic units. Third, they need to improve the operations of foreign trade and foreign investment.

So far state enterprises have been given some autonomy in the purchase of inputs and in the sale of outputs. They are also allowed to retain a part of their profits for distribution to the workers in the form of bonuses and for reinvestment. They are allowed to borrow from banks to finance their investments in lieu of obtaining funds through central appropriation. This increase in autonomy, however, has not led to marked increases in economic efficiency.[e] Large profits may have resulted from inappropriate prices. Retained profits have been distributed to workers in the form of large bonuses without regard to labor productivity. Often large-scale capital constructions have been undertaken with the use of retained profits or bank loans without regard to the economic worth of the projects. In short, what will ensure responsible behavior on the part of state enterprise managers once they are given more power? They may lack sufficient incentive if they are not allowed to share a part of the profits of the enterprise. They may undertake unprofitable and risky investments if they are not penalized for the losses. Chinese economic reformers recognize that state ownership may be divorced from state management. Managers of state enterprises could be made responsible to some independent boards of directors. Shares of the enterprises may be held by fairly independent government agencies, by workers, by managers, and by other economic units. Shareholders may help elect members of the board of directors. These and other possible arrangements for the management of state enterprises are being considered.

The development of a macroeconomic control mechanism for the execution of monetary policy depends on the institution of a new banking system. Under central planning before 1979, the banking system in China did not exercise much economic power. Essentially it served as the treasury for the government, keeping deposits from the Finance Ministry and from state enterprises, issuing currencies and extending loans to state enterprises as they were needed and were approved by the economic planning authorities. In 1983 and 1984, the banking system was reorganized. The former People's Bank was subdivided so as to separate its central banking macroeconomic control element, now under the People's Bank, from its commercial banking element, now called the Industrial and Commercial Bank. Other banks include the Agricultural Bank, the People's Construction Bank, the People's Insurance Company, and the Bank of China, the last dealing with foreign transactions. The People's Bank was given more power in regulating money supply and controlling interest rates. The specialized banks were given authority to extend credits to state and collective enterprises at their own discretion. However, an effective mechanism of monetary control by the central bank is yet to be developed. A set of rules for the improved operations of the individual banks has yet to be formulated. How can the previously passive banks be made to operate effectively in attracting savings from the economy and channeling them for profitable investments? What kind of reserve requirement or what other regulatory scheme should be introduced for the central bank to control total money supply and bank credits? These are among the most important questions being studied.

Concerning foreign trade and investment, by what mechanism or set of rules should the exchange rate of the Chinese currency be determined? The People's Bank has the authority to set the official exchange rate for the Chinese yuan. The yuan was devalued three times from 1.9 yuan per one U.S. dollar in 1981 to 3.7 yuan in

---

[e]See footnote c on page 11.

July 1986, mainly to make the official exchange rate closer to the market rate. In the past foreign exchange was tightly controlled; all uses by enterprises, universities and individuals had to be approved centrally although an unofficial market for foreign exchange has existed. Some relaxation of foreign exchange control has taken place in recent years as exporting has been partly decentralized, and exporters are allowed to keep a part of their foreign exchange earnings, which constitute an additional supply of foreign exchange. The setting of an exchange rate closer to the market rate will reduce the shortage of foreign exchange as shortage will cease to exist if the price of U.S. dollars is allowed to rise freely. Hence there will be less need for strict control of foreign exchange in China. How should foreign investment be further promoted? Bureaucracy, red tape, the lack of a sound legal system, unreasonable profit-sharing arrangements, high and nonuniform costs of labor and materials, difficulty in profit remittance, problems in managing Chinese labor, and unexpected changes in policy and terms of agreements are among the obstacles to foreign investors. How can these conditions be improved? How can the special economic zones be made more attractive to foreign investors and more beneficial to the growth of the Chinese economy?

As the Chinese economic reformers are seeking answers to these questions, they are experimenting with reform proposals deemed to have a good chance of success. Reforms are introduced partly by trial and error. For example, the initial reform of state enterprises was carried out by experimentation with a selected number of them. When mistakes are found they will be corrected. One serious mistake was the granting of power to individual banks in extending loans to investors before the establishment of an effective mechanism to limit the total supply of money and credit. The result was a tremendous increase in credit and an increase in currency in circulation by 50 percent from 52.98 billion yuan at the end of 1983 to 79.21 billion yuan at the end of 1984 (*Statistical Yearbook of China 1985*). To correct the mistake, credit was greatly tightened in 1985, partly by administrative control, assigning credit quotas to banks and limiting the withdrawal of deposits. A second mistake was the loosening of imports in 1984 and 1985, including the import of a great number of foreign cars into Hainan Island, resulting in a large reduction of foreign exchange reserves from 16.3 billion U.S. dollars on 1 October 1984 to 11.3 billion on 31 March 1985. To stop the drain in foreign exchange, use of reserves was greatly tightened later in 1985 and 1986. Many foreign investors suffered as a result since foreign exchanges were required in the operation of joint ventures. For example, the production of jeeps by a joint venture with American Motors practically ceased because of the unavailability of foreign exchange to buy parts. In the course of Chinese economic reforms, continued experimentation will be inevitable. The reformers are realizing that it is costly to correct large mistakes. They are learning to proceed more cautiously.

I have confined my discussion mainly to economic issues with which the Chinese economic reform are currently concerned in restructuring the economy toward a more market-oriented one. Major economic problems outside the scope of the restructuring process include urban–rural economic disparities, population control policy, and policy to improve the transportation infrastructure. Other important problems that have received the attention of economic reform officials but are beyond the scope of my discussion include the functioning of the special economic zones, the liberalization of domestic commerce and trade, reforming the labor policy of "eating from the same big pot" and restricting labor mobility, the design of an appropriate legal system underlying the economic institutions, and improving the political system. In addition, the official endorsement of the study of post-Marxian, modern economics at Chinese universities will have an impact in the long run on the development of a more market-oriented economy in China.[f]

1.4. The Future

What are the prospects for Chinese economic reforms? There are forces to push them forward as well as forces to hold them back. Among the former are an enlightened leadership, strong popular support, pressure of competition on state enterprises from collective enterprises and joint ventures, and assistance and influence from many overseas Chinese and foreigners. In spite of many unfavorable conditions in China, many foreigners have helped and will continue to help China. Among the forces holding back the reforms are ideological resistance, vested interests, bureaucracy, inertia inherent in economic organizations, and the lack of education among the middle management personnel in government and in state enterprises. The existing labor policy of providing jobs to most, if not all, laborers without regard to performance and the lack of labor mobility are major obstacles to reform. The prospects for reform that I have noted previously (Chow, 1985, p. 68) appear essentially valid today:

... The tendency in China is for government enterprises to be allowed to operate more like profit-maximizing enterprises in a market economy and for the private sector to expand. However, the desire on the part of the planning authority to exercise direct control rather than to use only financial means for economic planning, the resistance of a middle-level administrative bureaucracy, and the inertia in the economic and political system will limit the expansion of market forces. Precisely how far the reforms toward adopting features of a market economy will go in the next decade is difficult to predict. However, it appears safe to say that in absolute terms the market elements will be much more important in 1994 than in 1984, but will still fall short of being the major means used by the Chinese government to achieve its planning objectives. In the meantime, we may observe oscillations in the trend toward a market-oriented economy because the Chinese leaders are in the process of experimenting with and learning about the working of a market economy.

---

[f]In October 1983 two officials of the Chinese Ministry of Education discussed with me possible ways to modernize economic education in China. This led first to three summer workshops in 1984, 1985, and 1986 on microeconomics, macroeconomics, and econometrics, respectively, and also to the sending of Chinese graduate students to American and Canadian universities to study economics. Sixty-three students entered schools in the fall of 1985, and more are to follow. By 1985, some students of the 1984 summer microeconomics workshop had begun to teach applied economics courses at their universities. Now modern economics is offficial in China.

Reform toward a more market-oreinted economy will continue in China. The degree of success may be uncertain, but there is no turning back to a system of central control in agriculture and in industry operating within closed doors. Substantial economic growth will continue even if structural reforms progress slowly. The Chinese economy was able to grow between 1952 and 1979 in spite of the adverse conditions of inefficient central planning and two very serious political disturbances. It can only be expected to grow faster under the more favorable economic and political conditions of the 1980s.

References

Chow, G. C., 1985, *The Chinese Economy*, New York: Harper & Row; 2nd edn., 1987, Singapore: World Scientific.

Statistical Yearbook of China 1981, State Statistical Bureau 1982, Beijing: p. 133.

Statistical Yearbook of China 1984, State Statistical Bureau 1985, Beijing.

Statistical Yearbook of China 1985, State Statistical Bureau 1986, Beijing: p. 526.

Zhou, S., 1982, in *Zhongguo Jingji Jiegou Wenti Yanjiu* (Studies of the problems of China's economic structure), Ma, H. and Sun, S., eds., Beijing: People's Publishing Society, vol. 1, pp. 23–55.

CHAPTER 2

CHINA'S REFORM PROCESS AND
ITS IMPLICATIONS FOR HOUSING*

2.1. Introduction

The purpose of this paper is to characterize the process of economic reform in China since 1978 as a background for understanding the reform of urban housing.

Let us begin by pointing out certain important characteristics of the Chinese society as of 1992 which might be relevant for our discussion. First, although China is ruled by a communist party, it functions differently from the way a Communist country functions as the word communist is generally understood. For example, over sixty percent of the output of China is produced by profit-seeking units, including almost all of agriculture, which accounts for about 35 percent of national income in 1990, about 40 percent of industry, which accounts for 46 percent of national income, and over 40 percent of the remaining three sectors of construction, transportation and commerce. It practices an open-door policy, sending students to study in Western countries, attempting to expand international trade and encouraging foreign investment. The American press and the American public would cheer if the Chinese Communist Party were to change its name to something more pleasing to their ears, but in reality China has done much better than some other formerly socialist countries whose political leaders have changed the name without changing the substance.

Secondly, the Chinese leadership is more pragmatic than ideological. During the years of reform in the 1980s, the officials of the State Commission for Restructuring the Economy in the State Council, which is responsible for economic reform, openly declared that they should learn the methods of capitalism, and that they would adopt anything useful in the capitalist system while practicing "socialism with Chinese characteristics." In the 14th Congress of the Communist Party of China on October 12, 1992, both Secretary General Jiang Zemin and Prime Minister Li Peng declared that Chinese socialism should embrace market economy rather than

---

*Originally appeared in *Urban Land and Housing Reform in Socialist and Formerly Socialist Countries*, ed., George Tolley, University of Chicago.

central planning as its main economic institution, after Deng Xiaoping had said earlier in the year that socialism should not be identified with central planning.

Thirdly, although there are gross inefficiencies in Chinese state enterprises and much corruption in China, the economic institutions as of 1992 are already providing sufficient opportunities for the Chinese people to engage in economic activities for profit so that the economy can be expected to enjoy fairly rapid growth, say over 7 percent per year, for at least one decade even without much further institutional reforms. That the imperfect Chinese economic institutions are capable of generating substantial growth has been demonstrated by historical experience from the late 1970s on.

Fourthly, although political factors play some role in economic development, the political situation in China as of 1992 is such that, short of something unexpected, whoever succeeds Deng as the next political leader will not seriously hamper the fairly rapid economic growth in the 1990s. Economic momentum, supported by vested interests of the mass of the people benefitting from the reforms already instituted and by the vast majority of party leaders and government officials, will continue to push the economy forward despite a change in political leadership.

How did China get to its present economic structure and what are the characteristics of its reform process?

2.2. Historical Background and Characteristics of the Reform Process

Officially, economic reform began at the Third Session of the Central Committee of the 11th Congress of the Communist Party in 1978, when Deng Xiaoping became the political leader after the death of Mao Zedong in 1976. The second annual session of the Fifth National People's Congress in June 1979 endorsed the reform policy adopted by the Party Congress towards a more market-oriented economy. The historical situation was ripe for reform since the Chinese people as well as the political leadership were extremely dissatisfied with the state of affairs during the Cultural Revolution of 1966–1976. People wanted a change. Economic officials had learned from past experiences the difficulties and shortcomings of central planning. The success story of the economic development of Taiwan was another impetus. In the meantime, the failure of the communist system based on collective farming had convinced Chinese farmers and local leaders in certain Chinese provinces to return to private farming by assigning land to individual farm households. After paying a fixed amount of produce to the commune for delivery to the state agricultural procurement agencies, the farm households could keep the remainder of the output for consumption or sale in rural markets as is practiced in private farming. Such a household responsibility system was officially adopted by the Fourth Plenum of the Eleventh Central Committee of the Communist Party in September 1979. Elements of urban reform to allow for more autonomy and initiative to state enterprises were adopted in 1980.

Five important factors appear to have contributed to the apparent success of China's economic reform, as partly measured by the 9.5 percent average rate of annual growth in real output between 1978 and 1988. First, the historical circumstances after the Cultural Revolution prepared the people and the political leadership to undertake the reform. Secondly, the private farming institutions of early 1958 prior to collectivization still remained in 1978 to reassert themselves once the communist system of collective farming was abolished. Thirdly, the resourcefulness of the Chinese people in farming, light industry and trade was given opportunity to manifest itself in promoting economic growth. Fourthly, the political structure remained intact during the economic reform process, providing direction and leadership for economic reform. Fifthly, a policy of gradualism, rather than shock treatment, has allowed economic institutions to change step by step, and prevented the disruption in economic activities caused by sudden changes in institutions. For example, price reform was gradual. Privatization of housing was gradual partly to prevent the possible discontent due to redistribution of housing benefits to the consumers. The state enterprises were allowed to continue, although changes in operation guidelines to increase profits rather than to fulfill assigned output targets by the central planning authority were introduced. Perhaps a sixth factor could be added, i.e., the able leadership of Deng Xiaoping and Zhao Ziyang, the former providing general directions while the latter implemented the reform process effectively — not without policy errors including a loose monetary policy responsible for the two-digit inflation in 1988–1989.

One of the two additional landmarks in the reform process was the resolution of the 12th Central Committee of the Chinese Communist Party at its Third Plenary Session on October 20, 1984. Seven key elements of the decision of 20 October 1984 concerning reform of the economic system are to

  (i) give individual state enterprises autonomy in decisions regarding production, supply, marketing, pricing, investment, and personnel as independent profit-seeking economic units;

 (ii) reduce the scope of central planning and, except for certain major products, change the method from mandatory planning to guidance planning;

(iii) allow prices of more products to be determined by the forces of demand and supply rather than by central control;

(iv) develop macroeconomic control mechanisms through the use of taxes, interest rates, and monetary policy under an improved financial and banking system;

 (v) establish various forms of economic responsibility systems within individual enterprises to promote efficiency and encourage differential wage rates to compensate for different kinds of work and levels of productivity;

(vi) foster the development of individual and collective enterprises as supplements to the state enterprises;

(vii) expand foreign trade and investment as well as technological exchanges.

An often-quoted slogan to capture the essential characteristics of the reform is, "Invigorate the microeconomic units. Control by macroeconomic means."

The second was when the Fourteenth Congress of the Communist Party in October 1992 openly endorses the adoption of a market economy as a main goal of practicing "socialism with Chinese characteristics."

2.3. Reform Policies Similar to Those of Taiwan

It is interesting to note that several economic policies adopted by the leadership of Mainland China during its reform process were similar to those adopted by the government of Taiwan over two decades earlier.

The first common feature in the growth process of both parts of China is the reduction of government intervention and the encouragement of private initiative. The optimal role that the government should play in each economy is a controversial question which I do not need to address in this descriptive essay. In both parts of China, to initiate the development process, the government had a set of fairly well-defined policy guidelines. In each case the government reduced its intervention and allowed more private initiatives to assert themselves. In Taiwan in the early 1950s, the idea of a command economy was shared by the leadership of the government of President Chiang Kaishek, including one of his important economic officials K. Y. Yin, Vice Chairman of the Taiwan Production Board, 1951–1954, and Minister of Economic Affairs, 1955. Partly through the persuasion of economists T. C. Liu and S. C. Tsiang, Yin began to appreciate the efficient working of the market mechanism. He reduced the scope of government control, initiated policies to liberalize imports, lowered the exchange rate of the Taiwan currency and encouraged exports (see Scott, 1979, pp. 314–345). In the case of the Chinese Mainland, the command economy modeled after the Soviet Union was modified in the late 1970s (see Chow, 1985, pp. 114–116 and 148–154). Economic reform began with the privatization of agriculture, the increase in rural markets and the open-door policy, followed by urban reform to allow more autonomy of state enterprises and the establishment of individual and collective enterprises. Premier Zhao Ziyang deserved much credit in fostering the working of market-oriented economic institutions. Essentially, by giving to the Chinese people freedom and economic opportunities, however incomplete, the governments of both regions of China succeeded in developing the Chinese economy.

Economic liberalization took place in Taiwan through government encouragement of private investment in the form of providing financial services of government banks, the establishment of a stock market, tax exemptions for certain industries, relaxing controls over the establishment of factories, and appropriately adjusting the prices of government-produced commodities and services (see Li, 1976, pp. 9–11). An important step in economic reform in the Mainland was the decision of the Central Committee of the Communist Party of 20 October 1984 concerning reform of the economic system. The key elements in this decision include granting individual state enterprises autonomy in decisions regarding production, supply, marketing, pricing, investment and personnel as independent profit-seeking economic units, reducing the scope of central planning, allowing prices of more products to be determined by the forces of demand and supply rather than by central control and fostering the development of individual and collective enterprises as supplements to state enterprises (see Chow, 1987, p. 297).

The second common element is the importance of the agricultural sector in the early stage of the growth process. In both Taiwan and the Mainland, the increase in agricultural productivity was achieved mainly by redistributing land to the farmers. In Taiwan, from 1953 to 1957, through the sale of public land to tenant farmers and the redistribution of private tenanted land to the tenant-cultivators, the percentage of total farm families which were owner-farmers increased from 36 in 1949 to 60 in 1957. Owner-farmers and part owner-farmers owned more than 83% of total farmland in 1957 (see Kuo, 1983, p. 27). I n the Mainland, through the assignment of the rights of land use to individual farm households under the household responsibility system beginning in 1978 and the abolishment of the communist system of collective farming in the early 1980s, almost all the households in China's rural areas had switched to the system of essentially private farming by 1983 (see Lin, 1988, p. S201). I use the term private farming because although the Chinese farmers do not own the land, they have the rights to use the land and, to a large extent, to transfer its use to others. They can sell all the outputs to the markets for profits after surrendering a fixed amount of the product to the government procurement agent at below market prices, which amounts to paying a fixed rental for using the land. The incentives are similar to those under private farming. In both parts of China, agricultural productivity increased and there were shifts in output from grain to the more profitable cash crops. See Kuo (1983, Chapter 3) for the case of Taiwan and Chow (1993, Table XI). The latter reference reports an increase in total agricultural productivity from an index of 1.01 in 1980 to 1.436 in 1985, which are estimates of the multiplicative factor in a Cobb–Douglas production function for the agriculture sector in the Chinese Mainland.

A third common feature is the promotion of exports as an important component of the development strategy. The Taiwan experience is partly contained in the following quotation from a speech by K. T. Li in 1968 (see Li, 1976, pp. 20–21).

> The growth of many of our industries in Taiwan has been made possible because of the development of overseas markets. Several examples may be cited. In 1966, the cotton textile industry exported 66% of its output; the glass industry, 47%; and the plastics industry, 44%. The ratio for cement was 39% and for steel products, 22%. In such heavily-export-oriented industries as sugar, canned products and plywood, the ratios were higher than 90%. Thus, without the overseas markets, the present scales of these industries would not have been attainable.

> Taiwan's total exports rose from US$169.9 million in 1960 to US$569.4 million in 1966 at an average annual growth rate of 22%. Indeed, the

prosperity of the export sector has been a major cause behind the rapid growth of the economy.

The increase in exports accounted for 30% of the growth of the gross domestic product (GDP) in 1960. Its contribution rose to 42% in 1966. In the Mainland, through the encouragement of joint ventures, the decentralization of the control of exports from the central government to provincial and local levels, and the promotion of private and collective enterprises mentioned above, exports as fraction of national income increased from 5.3% in 1977 to 15.1% in 1988 and 20.7% in 1990 (see *Statistical Yearbook of China 1991*, pp. 32 and 615).

The fourth element is the government's emphasis on the stability of the general price level. The governments of both regions learned from the bitter experience of hyperinflation in China prior to the establishment of the People's Republic of China in 1949, as inflation was recognized to be an important factor contributing to the collapse of the government of the Republic of China in the Mainland. Much effort was made to restore price stability in Taiwan in the early 1950s. From 1961 to 1972, the consumer price index in Taiwan increased from 42.50 to 58.12, or at an average annual rate of 2.9% (see *Statistical Yearbook of the Republic of China 1980*, pp. 450–451). From 1977 to 1987, the general retail price index in the Mainland increased from 135.0 to 198.0, or at an average annual rate of 3.9% (see *Statistical Yearbook of China 1991*, p. 230). Some inflation took place in Taiwan in 1973 because of the world oil price shock. Two-digit inflation in the Mainland took place in 1988 because of the failure of the government to control the supply of money and credits, but price stability was restored by early 1990 mainly by contractionary monetary policy.

The fifth common element is the gradual decontrol of restrictions on imports and the setting of an official exchange rate close to the free market level. The official overvaluation of the Taiwan NT relative to the American dollar was gradually eliminated by increasing the effective exchange rate of NT$15.55 to one US dollar to somewhere between NT$18.60 and NT$20.43 in 1955, to NT$24.58 buying and NT$24.78 selling in April 1958, and further to an effective rate of about NT$37 by the end of 1958 (see Tsiang, 1980, pp. 329–330). Gradual devaluation of the currency of Mainland China took place when the official exchange rate of RMB/US dollar changed from 1.9 in 1980 to 2.93 in 1985, 4.79 in 1990 and 5.40 in 1992. By 1992, the RMB is nearly convertible as the official exchange rate and the free market rate have almost converged, making it easy for people in the Mainland to exchange RMB for US and Hong Kong dollars.

Together with the rapid growth of the economy in the Mainland since 1977 was a transformation of the economy to a mostly private economy in the sense that by 1990 a large fraction of the national output was produced by profit-seeking individuals and enterprises whose incentives are similar to those prevailing in a market economy. In Chow (1988), treating profit-oriented producers as accounting for .97, .20, .51, .08 and .63 of the outputs of the five sectors of agriculture, industry, construction, transport, and communications and commerce respectively in 1986,

I estimated about 52.6% of the national income in the People's Republic of China to be produced by profit-seeking economic units. If we apply the profit-motivated percentages of .97, .40, .51, .08 and .63 respectively to the above five sectors which contributed 34.65, 45.81, 5.76, 4.89 and 8.95 percent respectively to the national income in 1990 (see *Statistical Yearbook of China 1991*, p. 35) we would find 60.9% of the national income being produced by these profit-seeking economic units. The .40 figure for industry is based on the fact that state enterprises accounted for only 54.6% of output of industry in 1990 (see *Statistical Yearbook of China 1991*, p. 391). Hence China is approximately 60% of a market economy.

2.4. Reform in Urban Housing

This section provides briefly some institutional and historical background for housing reform and a proposal once suggested by the author.

The importance of economic reform was signified by the establishment of the Commission for Restructuring the Economic System in the State Council in 1981. The State Council is the executive branch of the government headed by the Prime Minister. It has over forty ministries, the large number due partly to the institution of Soviet-style central planning introduced in the 1950s, with each important product under the direction of a ministry. Above the ministries are several commissions to direct and coordinate important activities in the domain of several ministries. The Planning Commission and the Economic Commission are well-known examples. The Ministry of Education was transformed to the State Education Commission in July 1985 to emphasize the importance of education. The State Commission for Restructuring the Economic System was listed as the first among the commissions in official publications to emphasize its importance. It was headed by Premier Zhao Ziyang in the early 1980s, until Zhao became Secretary-General of the Communist Party in 1987.

The author began serving as a consultant to the Commission in the Fall of 1985 at the suggestion of Premier Zhao. A five-day meeting with several of its members, including its senior Vice Chairman An Ziwen and Vice Chairman of the People's Bank (Central Bank of China) Liu Hongru, took place in Hong Kong in January 1986 when all major issues of reform were discussed. In a letter dated 24 August 1985 to the author, the Premier suggested three important topics for discussion, namely (1) the establishment of a sound banking system, (2) financial markets and shares of enterprises, and (3) the supply and control of foreign exchange. During the meeting in Hong Kong, reform of state enterprises, reform of the price system and reform of urban housing were also discussed, among other topics. During that meeting, and a five-day meeting to follow in Beijing in June 1986 involving three other outside economists, John Fei of Yale, Anthony Koo of Michigan State and Lawrence Lau of Stanford, the author found the reform officials to be extremely open-minded. Any suggestions could be brought up for discussion. Important considerations are political feasibility and reaction of the population. Ideology becomes an issue only to the extent that Communist Party members and government officials with given ideological background needed to understand and be presuaded of the proposal if it is to be put into practice. Other than that I did not experience any more ideological constraints in our discussion and recommendations than in the discussions with economic officials in Taiwan in the 1960s to the 1980s when the same group of economists were advising them.

Concerning housing reform, it was recognized that housing should be "commercialized" in the terminology of the Chinese government. By the "commercialization" of housing, it meant making housing service a commodity subject to the law of demand and supply. One important consideration in housing reform is how to compensate the urban residents who, for several decades, have been accustomed to government subsidized housing. An obvious proposal is to increase urban wage to compensate for the increased cost of rent under a free market for housing. This creates the need to increase prices of products due to the increase in wage cost, which might be viewed by the population as a sign of inflation although some economists might argue that the effect would be a one-time increase in prices and not an inflationary process. The perception of the population concerning the inflationary process and the redistributional effects of increased rental with wage subsidies were important issues of discussion.

A proposal suggested by the author, in the form of a letter to Premier Zhao after the meetings of January and June 1986, is for the central government to allow all the local units (agencies) managing the housing supplies for the workers working in the units to sell the apartments to the tenants at prices mutually agreed upon. The prices may be quite low if the managing units desire to reduce its economic burden in maintaining the apartments with almost zero rental (equal to one to two US dollars per month). Some tenants might be willing to buy a unit for resale, possibly in order to move to a different neighborhood or to get rid of a second apartment occupied by families with two wage earners. If prices are allowed to be set by local conditions, a market for housing would be gradually developed, even if at the beginning only a small fraction of tenants would actually buy the apartments. At least the solution would be a Pareto improvement over existing institutions. After sending the above proposal to Premier Zhao the author did not receive any reply. Following proposals on economic reform and economic education in China sent directly to Premier and later Secretary-General Zhao, the author might or might not observe results immediately, but the proposals were always given due consideration as the author can conclude from knowledge of the way Zhao's office operated. When the author visited Guangzhou on July 10, 1993, Mr. Yi Zhenqiu, Director of the Guangdong Provincial Office for Restructuring the Economic System, told him that about 65 percent of the urban housing in Guangdong province had been sold to occupants at much-below-market prices along the lines suggested in the above proposal.

Prompted by the resolution of the Communist Party Congress in October 1992, one can expect that housing reform toward commercialization will make progress in the 1990s. It is interesting to observe how much and how rapid the progress will be.

References

Chow, G. C., 1985, *The Chinese Economy*, New York: Harper & Row; 2nd edn. 1987, Singapore: World Scientific.

―――, 1987, Development of a more market-oriented economy in China, *Science* **235:16**, 295–299. See chapter 1.

―――, 1988, Market socialism and economic development in China, Princeton University, Econometric Research Program, Research Memorandum no. 340. Presented before the International Seminar on Economic Reform in China, 1979–1988, Shenzhen, 7–13 November 1988. Also in Chinese in *Wen Wei Po* (Hong Kong, 11 November 1988), p. 13. See chapter 13.

―――, 1993, Capital formation and economic growth in China, *Quarterly Journal of Economics*, **108**, 809–842. See chapter 16.

Kuo, Shirley W. Y., 1983, *The Taiwan Economy in Transition*, Boulder: Westview Press.

Li, K. T., 1976, *The Experience of Dynamic Economic Growth in Taiwan*, New York: Mei Ya Publications, Inc.

Lin, Justin Yifu, 1988, Household responsibility system in China's agricultural reform: a theoretical and empirical study, *Economic Development and Cultural Change*, S199–S224.

Scott, Maurice, 1979, Foreign trade, in Walter Galenson, ed., *Economic Growth and Structural Change in Taiwan*, Ithaca, NY: Cornell University Press.

Statistical Yearbook of China, Beijing: State Statistical Bureau.

Statistical Yearbook of the Republic of China, Taipei: Directorate-General of Budget, Accounting & Statistics, Executive Yuan.

Survey of Current Business, Washington, D.C.: U.S. Department of Commerce, Bureau of Business Economics.

Tsiang, S. C., 1980, Exchange rate, interest rate, and economic development in L. R. Klein, M. Nerlove and S. C. Tsiang, eds., *Quantitative Economics and Development*, New York: Academic Press 309–346.

Vogel, Ezra, 1989, *One Step Ahead: Guangdong Under Reform*, Cambridge: Harvard University Press.

CHAPTER 3

HOW AND WHY CHINA SUCCEEDED
IN HER ECONOMIC REFORM

3.1. Introduction

In the late 1970s the world discovered an economic miracle in the rapid economic development of four economies of East Asia: Hong Kong, Singapore, Taiwan and South Korea, known in the annals of economic development as the four little dragons. In the early 1990s the world witnessed another economic miracle in the rapid development of Mainland China and its successful transformation from a planned economy to a market economy. This miracle was the more noticeable in view of the problems facing many formerly socialist countries in Eastern Europe and Northern Asia. Ever since economic reforms began in 1978 in China, rapid economic growth has followed, at the average rate of 9.5 percent per year in real national output in the first decade. During the first two years of economic reform, the former Soviet Union and several Eastern European economies experienced substantial declines in real output. This paper is an attempt to characterize the reform process in China since 1978 and draw some lessons from its success. It explains how and why economic reform in China has been successful. Section 2 describes the major institutions in the Chinese economy which needed to be transformed. Section 3 lists the major steps taken in the Chinese reform process. Section 4 summarizes several major characteristics of the reform process and draws some lessons from the Chinese experience.

3.2. What Economic Institutions to Reform

To describe briefly the economic institutions that needed to be reformed, let us start with the supply side of the market. By Chinese official statistics, which follow the statistical system of the former Soviet Union, national output is divided into the five sectors of agriculture, industry, construction, transportation and commerce. In 1978 when reform began, these five sectors accounted respectively for 32.8, 49.4, 4.2, 3.9 and 9.8 percent of national income [see *Statistical Yearbook of China (SYB) 1991*, p. 35]. Collective farming prevailed in agriculture under the Commune system

27

which had been introduced in 1958 during Chairman Mao's Great Leap Forward Movement. Of the total labor force of 401.5 million in 1978, 306.4 million or 76.3 percent were laborers in rural areas while 95.0 million were classified as staff and workers. Of the latter, 74.5 million or 78.4 percent worked in state enterprises and the remaining 20.5 million worked in collective enterprises in cities and towns (*SYB 1991*, p. 95). In 1978, 77.6 percent of the gross output value of industry was from state enterprises (*SYB 1991*, p. 396). Thus most of industry and other nonagricultural sectors consisted of state enterprises which were not operated for profit and were under the control of central planning, although the degree of control was not necessarily complete. In sum, in 1978 most of the China's productive units in agriculture, industry and the other sectors were not operating for profit as in a market economy.

Turning to the demand side, consumer demand in urban areas was controlled by the government in three essential aspects. First, housing of staff and workers was assigned by the unit in which they worked, with negligible rent (averaging about three to four yuan RMB per month, the official exchange rate being 1.9 yuan to $1). There was no market for urban housing. Second, important food items including grain, meat and oil were rationed at below market prices. Third, the purchasing power of the urban consumer was controlled by controlling wage rates. Demand for materials by production units was controlled by the State Bureau of Supplies in the State Council, which allocated inputs in production as part of central planning.

With the controlled allocation of many consumer and produced goods, prices of these goods were also controlled by the government. Agricultural products were purchased by government procurement units at regulated procurement prices. These products were distributed to urban consumers at below market prices under a rationing system. Prices of inputs including electric energy, raw materials, mineral products and transportation services were in many instances set below market prices as a form of subsidy to producers. That these were below market prices was evidenced by their rapid increase during the 1980s after the beginning of price reform [see *Price Statistics Yearbook of China 1989* (in Chinese), p. 29]. Thus the price system in 1978 failed to perform its function to regulate supply and demand as in a market economy. Note, however, that in spite of the government's attempt to control prices through the Administration Bureau for Commodity Prices in the State Council, market forces did work to a significant extent to influence the relative prices of industrial and agricultural products. As the output of industrial products increased relative to agricultural products between 1952 and 1978, the relative price of industrial products declined. Output indices in 1978 (with 1952 = 100) were 1679.1 for industry and 161.2 for agriculture. Price indices in 1978 (with 1952 = 100) obtained by taking the ratios of outputs in current prices to outputs in constant prices (*SYB 1991*, pp. 32–33) are 77.0 for industry and 179.9 for agriculture, reflecting the changes in relative supply and demand. For relative change in demand, see Sec. 16.5.3.

Besides the supply and demand of current output, capital formation in 1978 was heavily controlled by the government. Net capital formation is measured by accumulation in official statistics, which amounted to 108.7 billion RMB, as compared with 188.8 billion for consumption in 1978 (*SYB 1991*, p. 40). Of the 108.7 billion, 84.7 billion was accounted for by state enterprises, 3.6 billion by urban collectives, 16.9 billion by rural collectives (mainly agricultural communes at the time) and 3.5 billion by individuals (see Chapter 16, Table IV). These statistics show the importance of capital formation in nonagricultural state enterprises where investment projects required the approval of the State Planning Commission and the provincial and local units under its control. The banking system did not perform the functions prevailing under a market economy. The People's Bank controlled the supply of currency. However, the total supply of credits to state enterprises was regulated by the State Planning Commission through the approval of their budgets. The banking system played a passive role in providing whatever funds to the enterprises as they were approved. Commercial banking did not exist and played no active role in providing funds for investment. The People's Bank accordingly did not function to regulate the supply of such funds. State enterprises did not seek outside funding through the financial market for stocks and bonds. Foreign investment was practically nil in 1978 (see *SYB 1991*, p. 629).

Foreign trade was directed by central planning in 1978. When construction projects were included in a five-year plan, some required imports of foreign capital goods and materials. Certain consumption goods in the plan had to be imported, including food grain, when domestic supply was insufficient. All these projected imports required the use of foreign exchange, which has to be earned by the planned exports of domestic goods. Exports, imports and the demand for and supply of foreign exchanges were incorporated in a foreign trade plan which was part of China's economic plan. In the State Council, the Ministry of Foreign Trade directed the affairs of foreign trade, supervising the Bureau of Import–Export Control and the General Administration of Customs, assisted by the State Administration of Exchange Control. The official exchange rate was set below market rates; at the official rate of 1.9 RMB per U.S. dollar, the Chinese people could not obtain U.S. dollars without the approval of the government. Imports were restricted and exports managed by the government. In 1978 foreign trade totalled 27.25 billion RMB, with 13.97 billion exports and 13.28 billion imports, and accounted for 10.3 percent of national income of 164.4 billion (*SYB 1991*, p. 615).

If the non-market economic institutions described above had to be changed, the government economic planning apparatus had to be changed also. It included not only the Economic Planning Commission, but also the various industrial ministries in the State Council, each directing the state enterprises of the corresponding industry, the banking system and the ministries and bureaus related to price control and foreign trade. The nature of government planning had to be changed from directing the economic activities of Communes and state enterprises to regulating their activities through a system of economic incentives.

3.3. How Economic Reform was Achieved

Before describing the steps taken since 1978 to change the economic institutions, it is useful to characterize the political environment surrounding reform. Two characteristics of the political environment deserve to be noted: The stability of political institutions and the large amount of popular support for economic reform. The political institutions in China since the death of Mao Zedong in September 1976 have been quite stable. In spite of some political struggles at the top after Mao's death, which led to the downfall of four top leaders known as the Gang of Four and the rise of Deng Xiaoping at the expense of Hua Guofeng, the heir designate of Mao, the political system did not change. After Deng gained power in 1978, the country had learned the bitter lessons from the political upheavals of the Cultural Revolution of 1965–1975. Party leaders, government officials at all levels and the Chinese population were eager to have political order and economic reform as they had learned the shortcomings of the planning system. In 1978, the "Four Modernizations" in science, agriculture, industry and defense originally suggested by Zhou Enlai in 1964 were put forth as a program for the modernization of China.

Historians would attribute much of the credit for the successful economic reform in China to the able leadership of Deng Xiaoping and Zhao Ziyang, with the former providing overall leadership and the latter implementing concrete reforms. Although Deng, Zhao and other leaders were confident of the general direction of reform towards a more market-oriented economy, in the sense of reducing central control and providing economic reward to individuals and economic units willing to produce more, they were not sure of exactly what economic institutions to establish. The procedure followed was one of experimentation. A favorite saying was "touching the rocks as you cross the river," deciding on the next step only after you have completed the previous step.

Economic reform officially began with the decision of the Third Plenary Session of the Central Committee of the 11th Congress of the Chinese Communist Party in December 1978. (In January 1979, official diplomatic relations with the United States were established.) For excellent surveys of China's economic reform, see Perkins (1988) and Vogel (1989, Chapter 3). The first important step was the adoption of the responsibility system in agriculture. Collective farming under the Commune system was generally recognized to be inefficient in 1978. Reform of the Commune system occurred initially in 1978 when commune leaders in some regions recognized that they could fulfill their assigned output quotas for delivery to the government procurement departments by reorganizing the commune internally, following and improving upon the practices of private farming in the 1950s. In essence, under the responsibility system, each farm household was assigned a piece of land and was held responsible for delivering a given quantity of output to the commune to satisfy the latter's output quota. After fulfilling its output quota, the farm household could keep the remaining output for its own consumption or for sale at the market at market prices. The institution amounted to private farming with the farm household paying a fixed amount of rent for use of the land in the form of an output quota. Observing the success of the locally initiated experiments, the Fourth Plenary Session of the Central Committee of the Eleventh Communist Party Congress officially adopted the responsibility system as national policy in September 1979.

A second step was to allow private markets and small private enterprises to flourish. Rural markets used to exist in China in the 1950s. Once the farmers were allowed to dispose of their above-quota output, rural markets grew rapidly after 1978. Farmers also extended their productive activities to more profitable products such as ducks and cash crops, using privately owned trucks for transportation. In the meantime private restaurants, repair shops, peddlers, stores and street markets developed in urban areas. In two to three years one witnessed the growth of light industries in both rural and urban areas in the form of small collectives owned by several persons. Traditional handicraft manufacturing in rural areas and small clothing factories in urban areas were examples. The rural collectives later turned out to be an important part of Chinese industry.

The third step consisted of reform of state enterprises which progressed in several stages. For small enterprises, the principle of the responsibility system in agriculture was quickly put into practice. The idea was to allow the manager, like the farm household, to reap all the profits after paying a fixed rent to the government. State-owned stores, restaurants, small factories and later hotels were in fact privatized by the responsibility system, where the managers were often selected by auction. The right to operate a business for profit was leased to a manager who was willing to pay the highest. A nominally state-owned enterprise was being operated for profit like a private enterprise. Gradually in the 1980s some managers became entrepreneurs who used their own and borrowed funds to purchase assets to establish their own private enterprises. (*The New York Times* of Sunday, February 14 1993, p. 1, carried a story about an entrepreneur who founded and managed a domestic airline.)

While it was easy to adopt the responsibility system in small state enterprises, the system was not easy, and in the early stage of reform not intended, for large enterprises. Only after years of experience of reform did the government attempt to apply the responsibility system to large state enterprises. Reform of state enterprises began in late 1978 when six pilot enterprises in Sichuan Province were given some autonomy and allowed to retain a part of the profits. By the end of June 1980, 6600 industrial enterprises, which produced 45 percent of the output value of all state-owned enterprises, were allowed to make certain output, marketing and investment decisions and to retain a part of their profits. By the end of 1981, some 80 percent of state industrial enterprises were affected by the reform. The main elements of early industrial reform included: (i) A certain autonomy regarding the use of retained profits, production planning, sales of output, experimentation with new products, and capital expansion; (ii) adoption of features of an "economic responsibility system" by assignment of identifiable tasks to lower level units and payment to them according to productivity; (iii) increase in the role of markets; (iv) the streamlining of the administrative system at local levels for enterprises under local control; and, (v) the encouragement of the establishment of collectively owned enterprises (Chow 1985, pp. 148–151).

Reform in the industrial sector turned out to be more difficult than in the agricultural sector. It was much easier to make small farm households behave like private enterprises in a market economy than to make large state enterprises so behave, for four types of reasons. First, ideologically, members of the Communist Party of China believed in the ownership and the control of the means of production by the state. They were unwilling to surrender control of large state enterprises to nongovernment individuals and allow them to keep substantial profits for themselves, as in the case of small farms. Second, politically, government bureaucrats were unwilling to give up their power and vested interests by allowing the state enterprises to operate independently. Economic ministries tended to hold on to their control over the operations of the state enterprises. The bureau of material supplies tended to retain its control over the distribution of major material inputs. Third, economically, large industrial enterprises were more dependent on factors outside their control than were small household farms. Given a piece of land, a farm household could produce as it pleased, subject to climatic conditions. A large industrial enterprise needed the supplies of equipment and of material inputs produced by other enterprises. The entire system of pricing and distribution of industrial products and material input had to be changed to provide more autonomy to state enterprises. Fourth, administratively, the efficient operation of a large industrial enterprise was much more difficult than operations of a small farm. Chinese managers often did not have sufficient knowledge and experience to run a modern enterprise as an independent entity. Even with additional training, managers and administrators of state enterprises were reluctant to give up their old habits of dependence on the economic ministries. The mode of operation of a large economic organization was difficult to change. This is true for a large American corporation and for a large Chinese state enterprise.

To carry out further economic reform, a Commission of Restructuring the Economic System was established at the State Council in 1982, headed by Premier Zhao Ziyang, and listed in the organization of the State Council as the first Commission, above the Planning Commission, to signify its importance. This Commission had the responsibility to draft reform proposals and carry out the approved proposals through the Planning Commission and the relevant ministries. By 1983, however, reform of state enterprises did not appear to have increased the efficiency of state enterprises significantly. I estimated a Cobb–Douglas production function for Chinese state industrial enterprises using data up to 1981 (Chow 1985, pp. 123–126) and later found the same production function to fit the post-sample data for 1982, 1983 and 1984 very well (Chow 1988). I also estimated production functions for all of Chinese industry using data from 1952 to 1980, and found total productivities for the post-sample years of 1981 to 1985 to change by −0.006, 0.001,

0.042, 0.104, and 0.202 (Chapter 16, Table XIII). Total productivities for agriculture increased by 0.077, 0.181, 0.269, 0.422 and 0.436 in 1981 to 1985 as reported in Chapter 16, Table XI, and by 0.105, 0.203, 0.270 and 0.406 in 1981 to 1984 as estimated by McMillan, Whalley and Zhu (1989, p. 794).

Perhaps through observing the limited progress in the reform of state enterprises and stimulated by further success in the agricultural sector, the 12th Central Committee of the Chinese Communist Party at its Third Plenary Session on 20 October 1984 adopted a major proposal to achieve overall reform of the economic structure. Economic reforms in China in the late 1980s were based on this major decision. Implementation was to be formulated and carried out to a significant extent during the Seventh Five-Year Plan of 1986 to 1990. Seven key elements of the Decision of 20 October 1984 concerning reform of the economic system were to: (i) Give individual state enterprises autonomy in decisions regarding production, supply, marketing, pricing, investment, and personnel as independent profit-seeking economic units; (ii) reduce the scope of central planning and, except for certain major products, change the method from mandatory planning to guidance planning; (iii) allow prices of more products to be determined by the forces of demand and supply rather than by central control; (iv) develop macroeconomic control mechanisms through the use of taxes, interest rates, and monetary policy under an improved financial and banking system; (v) establish various forms of economic responsibility systems within individual enterprises to promote efficiency and encourage differential wage rates to compensate for different kinds of work and levels of productivity; (vi) foster the development of individual and collective enterprises as supplements to state enterprises; and (vii) expand foreign trade and investment as well as technological exchanges. An often-quoted slogan to capture the essential characteristics of the reform was, "Invigorate the microeconomic units. Control by macroeconomic means."

Under the Decision of October 1984, the responsibility system in agriculture was to be introduced into the management of the state enterprise by allowing subunits of each enterprises to act independently through contracts with the enterprise. This provision should be distinguished from the policy of allowing the enterprise itself to have financial independence after paying a fixed rental to the state, as in the case of individual farms. The distinction was made partly because the state enterprises are much larger than the individual farms, and the management of these enterprises could not be permitted to use the possibly very large profits as freely as the individual farm households could. It was not until 1986 that a major attempt was made to introduce the responsibility system to the level of the state enterprises themselves rather than their subunits. By 1986, some small state-owned commercial and industrial enterprises were leased to the managers who were given almost complete control of the profits after paying rent to the government. A number of successful cases with tremendous increases in outputs and profits were well publicized in the news media. The "contract responsibility system" was then introduced in 1987. The main feature of this system was to let the management and workers sign a contract with the state or provincial government to lease the enterprise, paying fixed amounts of taxes in the forthcoming years (often five) of the contract, and keeping the remaining profits for distribution among the management and workers in a way agreed upon by their mutual consent. Custom and workers' consent limited the amount a manager could draw as salary. However, profits could be used for distribution to management and workers, often in the form of durable consumer goods. Even though this system might look attractive on paper, in practice the results were not entirely satisfactory. The management and workers often complained that the fixed taxes imposed by the state or local government were too large, leaving too little profit for them; they would prefer to pay a fixed percentage from their profits, thus avoiding the risk of paying taxes if the enterprise operated at a loss. Also, limited compensation to management who attempted to increase profits might affect their incentives. See Byrd (1991) for a study of market reform for state industrial enterprises in the 1980s.

A fourth step in economic reform was to allow more prices to be determined by the market forces of supply and demand. This was also accomplished in stages, sometimes by the government setting prices closer to market prices, and sometimes by letting prices be determined freely in the market. An example of the former was the increase in procurement prices for agricultural products from an index of 217.4 in 1978 to 265.5 in 1979 and 301.2 in 1981 (*SYB 1991*, p. 230). An example of the latter was the policy to allow farm products in rural markets to be determined freely. Controlling the prices of certain government-distributed products while allowing them to be set in free markets led to a two-tier price system. The welfare effect of such a system was debated by economists. While admitting the virtue of free market prices, some criticized the simultaneously existing controlled prices. When the government was the purchaser of certain products at below market prices, the seller essentially paid a tax to the government. If the quantity of government purchases was fixed, it amounted to a lump sum tax which does not have adverse incentive effects. When the government was the seller of certain products at below market prices, as in the case of material inputs to state enterprises, the purchaser received a subsidy. If the quantity for sale was fixed, it might not have an adverse incentive effect. If the quantity can be increased by negotiation, the purchaser would have an incentive to resell the extra quantities in the free market to make a profit. State enterprises receiving supplies from the government at below market prices did resell some of them in markets; they also had a competitive edge over other enterprises not receiving the subsidy. Overall, it appeared that the ill-effects from subsidies might be outweighed by the positive effects of making the products available in free markets to benefit the consumers or producers. The October 1984 Decision of the Central Committee of the Communist Party singled out price reform as one of its important components. The decontrol and resetting of prices have continued until today.

A fifth step of reform was the decontrol of the supply of consumer goods. As the supply of agricultural products increased rapidly since 1978 and became available in free markets, rationing of food items for urban consumers and rationing of cloth became unnecessary in the mid-1980s. Supplies of durable consumer goods such as watches, bicycles, electric fans, sewing machines, refrigerators, and television sets also increased rapidly in the early 1980s, making government control of their distribution unnecessary. Government supply of housing to the urban population has taken much longer to decontrol, because the total supply of housing could not be increased as rapidly as other consumer durables and because the government was unwilling to abandon the virtually free housing provided for the urban population. The commercialization of housing still goes on as of 1993, with more and more urban families buying their apartments by installments from their working units at below market prices, and some rich families buying their apartments at market prices.

As the sixth step in the reform process, China expanded foreign trade and encouraged foreign investment in an open-door policy. An excellent analysis of foreign trade reform can be found in Lardy (1992). Exports were decentralized as provincial and local government units, as well as collective and private enterprises, were given authority to promote exports. Restrictions on imports were also reduced. The official exchange rate for the Chinese currency was lowered several times from $1.9 in 1980 to $5.6 in 1993, to approximate the market rate more closely. As a result, the ratio of foreign trade to national income increased from 10.3 percent in 1977 to 38.5 percent in 1990 (*SYB 1991*, pp. 32 and 615). Foreign investment also increased rapidly, from a negligible amount in 1978 to $10.3 billion of foreign funds utilized in 1990 (*SYB 1991*, p. 629). Special economic zones were established to encourage foreign investment, as foreign investors were given favorable tax concessions and a suitable infrastructure to establish their enterprises. Foreign trade and investments have performed three significant functions in China's economic development. First, foreign investment augments domestic investment in the process of capital accumulation while foreign trade expands China's production possibility frontier inclusive of trade. Second, foreign investment and trade are channels through which updated technology and management practices are introduced into China in the process of learning by doing. Third, and not the least, joint ventures, foreign enterprises, and foreign trade provide competition to Chinese state and collective enterprises, forcing them to be more efficient and at the same time putting pressure on the Chinese price system to reflect the forces of demand and supply.

The seventh step of the reform process was to change the government planning process to suit the more market-oriented economy. Central planning through providing output targets and approving investment budgets of state enterprises was being shifted to the regulation of more autonomous and financially independent enterprises through taxation and the control of credits. The People's Bank was to play a more important role as a central bank in regulating the supply of money and credit, after being officially declared a central bank in 1982. Commercial banking was to be developed. Banking reform was progressing only slowly as the existing specialized banks under the control of the People's Bank did not change to modern commercial banks rapidly. The staff of these banks had neither the knowledge and experience nor incentive to function as commercial banks in a modern market economy. Once given autonomy, local banks tended to extend loans and credits to local collective enterprises as personal favors or to promote economic growth of their own region. When inflation became more serious in 1985, and especially in 1988, as a result of overexpansion of money and credit, the People's Bank's only recourse was to rely on administrative directives to assign credit quotas to the branch banks in different regions. In both instances, the administrative directives of the People's Bank succeeded in controlling inflation within one year. Modern commercial banking regulated by a central bank is still in the process of being developed in 1993, as are stock markets in Shenzhen (the economic zone bordering Hong Kong) and Shanghai.

In October 1992, some fourteen years after the official beginning of economic reform introduced by the Third Plenary Session of the Eleventh Central Committee of the Communist Party in 1978, the Congress of the Communist Party was able to adopt a resolution moved by Deng Xiaoping to declare that China's economy is a socialist market economy. By that time, over 65 percent of China's national output was produced by profit-seeking economic units. In 1992, real national income increased by 12 percent by official statistics, with most observers projecting a 10-year growth rate averaging 7 to 9 percent. Private enterprises were flourishing. China had already become essentially a market economy.

3.4. Characteristics of the Reform Process

Having summarized the seven steps taken to achieve reform toward a market economy, I would like to discuss the main characteristics of the reform process.

First to be noted is the strong support of the country for the reform. The strong support from political leaders, government officials at different levels and the population at the initial stage of the reform has already been mentioned. After the success of the responsibility system in agriculture, the vast majority of the farmers who made up nearly 80 percent of China's population became strong supporters of the reform, thus assuring no return to collective farming under the Commune system. Urban industrial reforms, though less successful, made the urban population much better off than before in terms of the rise in income through increases in wages and bonuses distributed from increased profits, the availability of consumer goods, the freedom to travel and the opportunity to engage in private enterprise. The major discontent of part of the urban population occurred in the Fall of 1988 when inflation was at an annual rate of about 18 percent by official statistics and when government corruption became a major issue, contributing to demonstrations led by university students in Beijing and other cities in the Spring of 1989. Soon after the demonstrations were suppressed by force on June 4th, causing much criticism of the political leaders from around the world, the Chinese people continued to support economic reform. They cheered when Deng made a speech in Shenzhen in January 1992 urging the speeding-up of the reform process. They cheered when the Party Congress adopted the resolution to declare China a market economy in October 1992.

Second, the reformers only knew the general direction of reform but did not have a detailed blueprint. They admitted that they did not know the answers as to what the final system ought to be. They learned as they experimented and observed, touching the rocks as they walked across the river. As a result, China has developed a market economy with its own characteristics, as alleged by a slogan of the Communist Party. A notable feature is the flexible form of state and collective enterprises whose managers seek profits as in private enterprises. Another is the limited formalization of legal institutions under which economic transactions take place, although the legal system is being transformed.

Third, closely related to the second, is the extensive use of experimentation and practical experience. The official adoption of the responsibility system in agriculture by the Party Central Committee in 1979 was based on successful experiences in the communes of several provinces. Further success led to the adoption of the responsibility system for small enterprises. Reform in granting autonomy to state industrial enterprises started by experiment with six pilot enterprises in Sichuan in 1978 and some 6600 enterprises by June 1980. Expansion of rural and urban markets, of private and collective enterprises, of private housing, of foreign trade and investment and of special economic zones all proceeded in stages after successful experimentation. Successful experimentation helped the reformers not only in deciding what to adopt, but also in unifying skeptics in the Party and the government to support the reform.

Fourth, related to the third, is the pragmatic attitude of the reformers who are free from ideological restraints. This attitude was probably influenced by the attitude of Deng and Zhao. By pragmatism is meant the willingness to adopt whatever works with little ideological constraint. While conducting a workshop for officials of the Commission for Restructuring the Economic System in 1987, I was much impressed by a remark made by a member of the workshop: "Nothing prevents us from adopting in our socialist system anything that works well under a capitalist system." He probably would not have used the word "capitalist" in 1982. As Deng was quoted often since the late 1970s, "We don't care whether a cat is black or white as long as it catches mice." Of course the ideology of Communist Party members has changed greatly in the fifteen years of reform since 1978 as Chinese practice changed, but it was practice that led the ideology and not the other way around, following the principle of "seeking truth from facts" advocated by Deng.

The fifth characteristic is the absence of any drastic changes in the political system. The Communist Party continued to rule China, although political authorities have become more decentralized, with provincial and local governments now exercising more power, and a richer population outside the Communist Party exercising more economic power and enjoying more economic and political freedom. For evidence of increase in economic and political freedom, compare the amount of domestic and foreign travel and the content of writing by Chinese intellectuals between 1978 and 1993.

The above five characteristics are on the side of gradualism in economic reform as opposed to shock treatment. Gradualism was needed to secure the support of Party and government officials and of the population for the reforms, to help the reformers decide what reforms to adopt, to change the existing institutions such as state enterprises and banks to modern institutions, to allow consumers and producers receiving subsidies or entitlements to adjust to the competitive force of the markets, and to enable new enterprises and new entrepreneurs to develop as they were developed in other market economies all through history. Economic institutions require time to change and people who operate modern enterprises and financial institutions require time to acquire the necessary human capital. By the government simply announcing a new set of rules, small private enterprises might be established fairly rapidly as in China, but large state enterprises and state banks cannot change rapidly to an entirely new pattern of behavior as a result of institutional inertia and the lack of the required human capital. Rapid price changes often amount to the government taking away economic entitlements from its people, which is difficult to accomplish in Western market economies including the United States.

The Chinese economic reformers have taken a course of gradualism because of these difficult problems associated with rapid changes. Some of these problems may also exist in other countries attempting to reform their economies.

References

Byrd, W. A., *The Market Mechanism and Economic Reforms in China*, Armonk, New York: M. E. Sharpe.

Chow, G. C., 1985, *The Chinese Economy*, New York: Harper & Row; 2nd edn. 1987, Singapore: World Scientific.

———, 1987, Development of a more market-oriented economy in China, *Science* **235**, 295–299.

———, 1988, Economic analysis of the People's Republic of China, *J. Econ. Educ.* **1**, 53–64.

———, 1993, Capital formation and economic growth in China, *Quarterly J. of Econ.*

Lardy, N. R., 1992, *Foreign Trade and Economic Reform in China 1978–1990*, New York: Cambridge University Press.

McMillan, J., Whalley, J. and Zhu, L., 1989, The impact of China's economic reform on agricultural productivity growth, *J. Pol. Econ.* **97**, 781–807.

Perkins, D., 1988, Reforming China's economic system, *J. Econ. Lit.* **26**, 601–645.

Price Statistical Yearbook of China 1989, Beijing: State Statistics Bureau.

Statistics Yearbook of China 1991, Beijing: State Statistics Bureau.

Vogel, E., *One Step Ahead in China*, Cambridge, MA: Harvard University Press.

CHAPTER 4

ECONOMICS EDUCATION IN CHINA AND ECONOMICS EXCHANGES WITH THE UNITED STATES[*][†]

What kind of economic institutions China will have in the twenty-first century depends partly on the nature of economics education in Chinese universities today. Economics education affects the way future Chinese leaders think about economic issues and hence the design of the Chinese economic system in the future. This paper is concerned with economics education in China and economic exchanges with the United States.

4.1. Economics Education

Before 1949, the education system of China had incorporated many features existing in Western countries. Primary school took six years and middle school another six. University education took four years as in most Western countries. English was the most popular second language, followed by French and German. Private and public educational institutions coexisted. American and European style education had influenced the structure of both public and private universities.

In the 1950s, the government of the People's Republic of China abolished all private universities, took control of higher education, and adopted a new university system under Soviet influence. Technical education was emphasized at the expense of liberal education. Departments of engineering and natural sciences were separated from departments of humanities and social sciences by the reorganization of existing universities and by the establishment of separate institutes of science and technology. Modern social sciences were not taken seriously. Sociology and psychology disappeared from the curriculum. Economics was concerned mainly with Marxian teaching and not with analytical and empirical studies of the actual economies of various countries including China. When I visited China in the summer

[*]Originally published as "Economics Education and Economic Reform in China" (read on 13 November 1986, at the *Symposium on China — The Promise and the Problems*) in *Proceedings of the American Philosophical Society*, vol. 133, no. 1, pp. 64–74, 1989. Section on Economics Exchanges with the United States contains reports of the American Economic Association's Committee on U.S.–China Exchanges originally published in the May issues of *The American Economic Review*, 1982–1994.

[†]The author would like to acknowledge financial support from The Garfield Foundation and The National Science Foundation in the preparation of this paper.

of 1980 to teach econometrics at the Chinese Academy of Social Science in Beijing, I could not find any published studies on any aspect of the Chinese economy.

In 1982, I visited six universities in China, including Zhongshan University in Guangzhou, the Huazhong Institute of Technology and Wuhan University in Wuhan, Peking University and the People's University in Beijing and Nankai University in Tianjin. It was apparent that China's government had recognized the need to modernize economics education, but had not decided on how to proceed and what the content ought to be. Sensing this need, I wrote a textbook in 1983 to explain modern economics using China for its institutional setting (*The Chinese Economy* [Harper & Row, 1985; 2nd edn., World Scientific, 1987]). In October 1983, Wang Fusun, Chief of the Division of International Co-Operation, and Wang Zenong, Chief of the Division of Economics and Law in the First Department of Higher Education, both of the Chinese Ministry of Education, visited Princeton. We discussed possible ways to modernize economics education in China. During the discussion, I proposed and agreed to organize three summer workshops from 1984 to 1986 on microeconomics, macroeconomics and econometrics respectively to be sponsored by the Chinese Ministry of Education.

After the establishment of diplomatic relations with the United States in January 1979, China began to open its doors to American scholars and other visitors. Economists were invited to visit China to give lectures at various institutions, including universities, the Chinese Academy of Social Sciences and its regional affiliates, and educational and research units under various ministries of the Chinese State Council. The microeconomics workshop in the summer of 1984, however, marked the first time that the Chinese Ministry of Education (MOE) officially sponsored a course in post-Marxian modern economics. In my initial discussion with the officials of MOE, the Ministry was to provide the entire funding for the 1984 workshop, possibly using grants from private foundations or international organizations. As it developed, I was fortunate to receive financial support from Princeton University and the Alfred P. Sloan Foundation to pay for that part of the workshop expenses which had to be paid in American dollars, while MOE paid for the local expenses.

The microeconomic workshop took place from 11 June to 22 July 1984, at Peking University, with Sherwin Rosen, Marc Nerlove, Edwin Mills and myself as lecturers. The level of instruction was close to the first-year graduate level at a good American university. Approximately 60 graduate students, young teachers, and researchers were selected nationally by the Ministry of Education to attend. The lectures were given in English without interpretation. Some members of the workshop had difficulty in comprehension, but the results of a final examination taken by twenty-three students indicated that at least a third of them understood the material well. Some students of the 1984 workshop offered instructions in microeconomics during the academic year 1984–1985. For example, a participant from Peking University offered a course in Public Finance to some sixty students in the Spring of 1985 using Richard Musgrave's *A Theory of Public Finance* (McGraw-Hill, 1959).

On 5 July 1984, Premier Zhao Ziyang invited me to discuss with him problems of economic reform and economics education in China. The discussion took place at the Purple Light Pavilion and lasted for about one hour and thirty minutes. Our meeting was televised on the national news that evening and was reported on the front page of the *People's Daily* on 6 July. The publicity signified the official endorsement of modern economics in China and the recognition of the possible relevance of modern economics to Chinese economic reforms. During our meeting, Premier Zhao endorsed the publication of a Chinese edition of my book *The Chinese Economy* which later was published by Nankai University Press in 1985.

Before leaving China in 1984, I suggested to the Chinese Ministry of Education that graduate students be selected nationally to study economics in the United States and Canada. Universities and research institutions would nominate students to take national examinations in economics and mathematics given by the MOE; I was to provide the questions for the economics examination, based on my book *The Chinese Economy*. MOE agreed to this suggestion. The first examinations were given in the Fall of 1984 and eighty-two students received passing grades (60 percent) in both economics and mathematics. In September 1984, a committee consisting of Edwin Mills, Sherwin Rosen and myself recommended these students to some sixty Canadian and American universities. Sixty-three students were accepted for entrance in the fall of 1985, with most receiving financial support from the hosting universities, seventeen receiving partial support from the Chinese government, and thirteen receiving partial support from The Ford Foundation. This program has continued, and similar examinations were given in 1985 and 1986. Reports from various universities indicated that most of the students who entered in the fall of 1985 and 1986 have done well, in spite of initial difficulties with a foreign language and a strange environment during the first few months.

The 1985 and 1986 summer workshops in macroeconomics and in econometrics were organized at the People's University in Beijing. John Taylor, William Branson, Dwight Jaffee, Richard Portes and I lectured in the macro workshop, while Richard Quandt, Angus Deaton, Robert Engle and I lectured in the econometrics workshop. The quality of the students, both in analytical ability and in English comprehension, improved significantly from 1984 to 1985, and to a lesser extent from 1985 to 1986. During the last few years, proficiency in English has improved among Chinese youth in general. The selection process for students attending our workshops improved greatly between 1984 and 1985. Furthermore, instruction in modern economics in China has improved. Both workshops were attended by about one hundred graduate students and researchers in government units.

In January 1985, The Ford Foundation decided to increase its support for economics education and research in China. It provided partial funding for the summer workshops of 1985 and 1986. It is currently supporting some of the students selected through the MOE national examinations for graduate economic study in the United States and Canada. It also supports a year-round graduate program in economics at the People's University which began in the Fall of 1985, and will support a second graduate program in economics at Fudan University in Shanghai in 1987. Several distinguished American economists have taught or are teaching in the program at the People's University. The program covers microeconomics, macroeconomics, econometrics and some applied subjects. The visiting faculty members have found the students to be bright, well motivated and hardworking.

Today modern economics education has become official and is expanding in China. Many universities are eager to strengthen their economics curriculum with additional faculty, but the country is large and the need for economics teachers is great. This need will be gradually filled by indigenous instruction and by students returning from abroad. While the modernization of economics education has a good start and is heading in the right direction, future progress may be slow partly because supply of the required personnel is limited and partly because existing institutions and personnel have to adjust to the new ideas and new ways of doing things. These limitations apply to economic reform as well.

4.2. Economics Exchanges with the United States

Changes in economics education in China between 1981 and 1994 are partly reflected in exchange activities with the United States which are reported annually in the May issues of the *American Economic Review*. The reader will find the following reports of the American Economic Association's Committee on U.S.–China Exchanges informative.

Report of the Committee on U.S.–China Exchanges*

Since exchange activities in economics between the United States and the People's Republic of China (PRC) are fairly free and informal, as compared with similar exchanges with the Soviet Union, many such activities have taken place in the last year. This report is confined only to several activities.

(1) Through the Joint Committee with SSRC, we organized a workshop on economic development with the Institute of Economics of the Chinese Academy of Social Sciences from July 27 to August 29, 1981. The nine participants were D. Gale Johnson (group leader), Irma Adelman, Gary Becker, Anthony Koo, Ann Krueger, Gustav Ranis, Joseph Stiglitz, Anthony Tang, and Larry Westphal. The initial discussion for this workshop took place in Washington, D.C., on December 8, 1980, when the head of the Institute of Economics, Xu Dixin, led a group of ten economists to visit the United States. This group visited many campuses in the San Francisco, Chicago, Boston, New York, Princeton, Philadelphia, and Washington areas. They also attended a conference on economic development in Racine, Wisconsin, organized by Irma Adelman.

---

*May 1982

(2) Concerning the education of Chinese economists, many universities have accepted students or are receiving applicants from PRC. In the meantime the Chinese government has urged the universities in China to modernize their economics curricula. There is a need to train more economists in China. The Ford Foundation is reviewing a proposal to provide fellowships to applicants from China for graduate studies in economics, and possible programs to train Chinese economists at the middle management level.

(3) *Science & Technology Review*, a journal in Chinese, is being edited by a group of scholars in this country to be widely circulated in the People's Republic. The *Review* covers the fields of economics, management, science, engineering and education. Many colleagues from the AEA have contributed articles or interviews, including Kenneth Arrow, Ansley Coale, Milton Friedman, Lawrence Klein, Arthur Lewis, Theodore Schultz, and S. C. Tsiang among others.

The journal *Economic Research* of the Chinese Academy of Social Sciences has published articles by several American economists.

(4) The next item is probably fairly well known by this time. A number of American universities have established relations with Chinese universities. The latter include Peking University, Nanking University, Fudan University, and Zhongshan University, among others. Scholars from both sides of the Pacific have exchanged visits to and from these universities, including lectures in economics given by American visitors to China. A number of American universities are now hosting visiting scholars or students from the People's Republic, totaling more than 6,000 by the end of 1981. Only a small percentage are in economics, but it is a recently announced policy of the PRC government to increase the number of students and visiting scholars in economics.

Members of the AEA Committee (Kenneth Arrow, Gregory Chow, Lawrence Klein, and Theodore Schultz) would welcome suggestions and comments concerning economics exchange activities with PRC.

GREGORY C. CHOW, *Chair*

Report of the Committee on U.S.–China Exchanges*

Much has happened in exchanges in economics between the United States and the People's Republic of China since my report a year ago (see this *Review*, May 1982, p. 429). The news is essentially good.

Some bad news first. Under the sponsorship of the Committee on Scholarly Communication with the People's Republic of China, a team of U.S. economists, to be headed by Randy Barker and Robert Dernberger, was to visit China to study the recent changes in agricultural economic policy in China. The host of this team's visit was to be the Chinese Academy of Social Sciences. Because the Chinese Academy

---

*May 1983

could not agree to some of the requests from the team concerning their itinerary, the members of the team, after serious deliberations, decided to postpone the visit, leading to its eventual cancellation. In the meantime, however, other groups of economists have visited China, including a group from the National Bureau of Economic Research in May/June 1982 and a group from The Brookings Institution in June 1982.

Secondly, a volume entitled *Essays on the Economies of China and other Developing Countries by Foreign Economists* (in Chinese) was published in early 1982 by the Editorial Board of *Economic Research*, a journal of the Institute of Economics of the Chinese Academy of Social Sciences. This volume consists of essays by American economists, including Irma Adelman, Kenneth Arrow, Gregory Chow, Robert Dorfman, Ronald Duncan and Helen Hughes, Dwight Perkins, Joseph Stiglitz, Paul Streeten, and Laura D'Andrea Tyson.

Thirdly, and related to the second, is the proliferation of economics journals in China, published mostly by Chinese universities. A glance through these journals reveals that more and more articles deal with the tools of Western economic analysis. From these journals, a university student in China can get a fair exposure to Western economic concepts, though not a systematic treatment.

Fourthly, from my own visit to China in June/July 1982 for the purpose of lecturing and exchanging ideas with economists in five major universities located from Canton to Peking, I have found that many Chinese universities are expanding their teaching and research in economics. Major economics departments have introduced courses in micro- and macroeconomic theory and econometrics, while some are planning to have Western economics and econometrics as fields of concentration. Chinese scholars are learning these subjects rapidly and the rate of growth is impressive. A Society of Quantitative Economics and Econometrics was founded at a meeting of some 200 economists which took place in Xian in March 1982. Other organized activities, some affiliated with associations in industrial engineering and systems science, are being contemplated to promote research and communication in quantitative economics.

Fifthly, during the past year many more graduate students and visiting scholars in economics have come to the United States from the People's Republic of China than in past years, while American economists have continued to go to China to lecture and to visit Chinese economics institutions. Visits by American economists and scholars in general have been facilitated by the increase in housing for foreign visiting scholars in China. For example, Peking University completed a residential hall with some 250 rooms to accommodate foreign visitors. A distinguished American economist traveling to the Far East can arrange a side visit to China fairly conveniently through a Chinese university.

In summary, economics exchanges between the United States and the People's Republic of China have expanded and will continue to do so, mainly through the decentralized initiatives of economists and academic institutions in both countries wishing to promote them.

GREGORY C. CHOW, *Chair*

Report of the Committee on U.S.–China Exchanges*

In 1983, while official exchanges in economics through the Committee on Scholarly Communication with the People's Republic of China (CSCPRC) were slow moving, many other channels of exchanges continued to be active.

Herbert Simon, Chairman of CSCPRC in charge of exchanges in social sciences and humanities, during his visit to China in the spring of 1983 to lecture and to conduct joint experimental research with Chinese psychologists, had discussions with officials of the Chinese Academy of Social Sciences (CASS) concerning exchanges in social sciences with CASS. In economics, in spite of the cancellation of the intended trip of a team of U.S. economists to study Chinese agricultural economic policy in 1982, CSCPRC expressed to the Chinese officials in CASS that we would welcome a delegation of Chinese economists to visit the United States to study the formulation of economic policy here. Under discussion was a delegation from CASS to pay a return visit to the United States following the visit of a group of economists from the National Bureau of Economic Research (NBER) in 1982, whom CASS had received as an official delegation from the United States. This Chinese delegation, to be hosted by NBER and CSCPRC, did not arrive in 1983, but is scheduled for September 1984.

One problem facing the discussions between CSCPRC and CASS is the difference in the interests of these two organizations. CSCPRC insists on exchanges which will yield mutual benefits including the promotion of the research interests of American scholars working on China. CASS is more interested in cosponsoring lectures by American economists or workshops for the Chinese economists to learn modern economics, and is less interested in cooperative research. Besides this basic problem, cultural exchanges were terminated by PRC in April 1983 because of political and diplomatic events such as the granting of political asylum to the Chinese tennis player Hu Na.

A strong force promoting further exchanges in economics is the firm policy of the Chinese government to expand foreign trade and investment and to modernize the economy. In his report to the Twelfth National Congress of the Communist Party of China on September 1, 1982, the Party Secretary-General Hu Yaobang stated, "We must improve our study and application of economics and scientific business management and continuously raise the level of economic planning and

---

*May 1984

administration and the operation and management of enterprises and institutions."
A manifestation of this policy is the series of short courses on project evaluation
sponsored by the World Bank. In the Spring of 1983, Arnold C. Harberger and
James Henderson participated in such a course in China.

Other examples include two series of workshops on agricultural economics
sponsored by the Agricultural Development Council with financial support from
the Ford Foundation. One series was jointly sponsored by the Chinese Association
of Agricultural Sciences Societies. D. Gale Johnson conducted the workshop in the
summer of 1983. The second series was cosponsored by the Chinese Academy of
Agricultural Science. Besides these workshops, the Agricultural Development Council also sponsors visits by Chinese and American scholars, and provides fellowships
to Chinese students to study agricultural economics.

The Chinese Ministry of Education has been supporting a small number of
students to study economics abroad. In 1983 a number of American universities
had graduate students from China studying economics, including Chicago, Cornell,
Illinois, Minnesota, Rochester, Princeton, and Yale, among others. About half of
these students were sponsored by the Chinese Ministry of Education. Many Chinese
economics professors were visiting American universities, some being supported
by the Luce Foundation. The Chinese Ministry of Education is committed to
promoting the education of modern economics in China.

The communication of economic ideas between both sides of the Pacific
continued in 1983. To facilitate this communication I completed a textbook, *The
Chinese Economy*, in 1983, to be published by Harper & Row in the summer of 1984.
This book is an attempt to apply the tools of economic analysis to study the Chinese
economy. It may help American students to understand the Chinese economy and
Chinese students to understand modern economics through its application to China.

By the end of 1983 it became very clear that further communications between
American and Chinese students and scholars in economics would continue in the
future.

GREGORY C. CHOW, Chair

Report of the Committee on U.S.–China Exchanges*

As the reports of our Committee in the last three years reveal, there have been
continued and expanding exchange activities between American and Chinese
economists. In 1984, a great step was taken by the Chinese government to make
post-Marxian modern economics official, in the sense of introducting it to the
Chinese university curriculum, side by side with Marxian economics, as being
important for China's economic development. Previously, modern economics was
taught as an elective for the understanding of capitalist economies only.

---

*May 1985

To illustrate the change in viewpoint, the Chinese Ministry of Education sponsored a workshop in microeconomics for university teachers, graduate students, and government officials. The workshop was held at Peking University from June 11 to July 21. The lecturers were Sherwin Rosen (micro theory, human capital and labor), Marc Nerlove (micro theory, agricultural supply, and empirical studies), Edwin Mills (development, urban, and environmental economics), and Gregory Chow (applications to China). Microeconomics was to become an important part of economics education in China. Workshops in macroeconomics and econometrics are planned for the summers of 1985 and 1986, respectively.

The Ministry of Education decided to send students abroad to study economics. On November 17–20, TOEFL, mathematics, and economics examinations (given in English, with economics questions provided by Mills, Rosen, and Chow) were administered by the Ministry to 151 candidates who had been carefully selected from twenty-seven major Chinese universities and economics and finance colleges, using scholastic records and preliminary tests. Eighty-one candidates, who received a total grade of 120 or higher in mathematics and economics, have been recommended for graduate work to sixty-one American and Canadian universities, including all major economics departments.

Both the Ministry of Education and the Chinese Academy of Social Sciences (CASS) are seeking financial support to strengthen economics teaching and research at the universities and economic research institutes. The Ford Foundation, together with other interested Foundations and Corporations, has formed a committee to consider such support. Activities to be supported might include workshops, Boulder-like institutes, and research programs in China, fellowships for students and visiting scholars from and to China, joint research projects, and library and computer facilities.

In 1984, many American economists lectured in China. Many Chinese economists visited the United States, including a delegation from CASS in September, mentioned in our report last year. From 1984 on, many teaching and research opportunities in China are becoming available to American economists. To find a suitable hosting institution, a potential visitor can consult published material such as bulletins of universities and research institutes, and Chinese economics journals reporting on research conducted at various institutions. Helpful information can be found in Teh-wei Hu's research report, "The State of American Economic Studies in the People's Republic of China" (U.S. Information Agency: April 1984) and in Gregory Chow's report, "Economic Research in China" (Princeton University, 1984). Personal contacts will also be useful to generate a suitable visiting arrangement, as in the case of searching for a visiting position in the United States.

GREGORY C. CHOW, *Chair*

Report of the Committee on U.S.–China Exchanges*

As mentioned in the Report of our Committee last year, 1984 could be considered as the year when modern economics became official in China. In 1985, the Chinese State Commission on Education (formerly the Ministry of Education) continued actively to strengthen economics education in China. Several important activities can be reported.

First, a Macroeconomics Workshop, sponsored by the State Commission on Education with partial financial support from the Ford Foundation, took place at the People's University in Peking from June 10 to July 20. Ninety-four persons from various universities and government research and planning organizations attended, with approximately 50 regular attendants and the remaining auditors. The instructors were John Taylor of Stanford, William Branson and Dwight Jaffee of Princeton, Richard Portes of the University of London, and Gregory Chow of Princeton, who also served as organizer and coordinator. The topics covered included macroeconomic theory and modeling by Taylor, open-economies macroeconomics by Branson, money and banking by Jaffee, macroeconomics of centrally planned economies by Portes, and applications to China by Chow. The quality of the students was on average better than those who attended the Microeconomics Workshop in 1984. The impact of the workshop is to enable the regular attendants coming from various universities to teach macroeconomics after their return to their respective schools. Also the attendants from government research and planning organizations will be able to use macroeconomics in their work. Represented were the Planning Commission, the combined Economic Research Centers of the State Council, the Economic Reform Committee of the State Council and the People's Bank.

Secondly, a year-round training program towards a master's degree in economics began in September 1985 at the People's University, also with financial support from the Ford Foundation. Forty-nine students enrolled in this program, having been selected mainly from seven major Chinese universities including Peking, People's, Nankai, Wuhan, Jilin, Fudan, and Xiamen. Daniel Suits from Michigan State and Kenneth Chan from McMaster taught micro and macro, respectively, in the fall semester of 1985. Leonid Hurwicz of Minnesota and Elizabeth Li of Temple will teach micro and macro, respectively, in the spring of 1986.

Sixty-two students from China who had been recruited by the Ministry of Education in the fall of 1984 entered fifty-odd graduate programs in economics in the United States and Canada in September 1985. These students are financially supported mainly by the universities accepting them, but some are supported by the Chinese government and the Ford Foundation. Again, in October 1985, examinations in mathematics and economics were given by the Chinese State Commission on Education to recruit students with the cooperation of a committee consisting of Edwin Mills, Sherwin Rosen, John Taylor, and Gregory Chow.

---

*May 1986

These students are being recommended by the Committee to sixty-odd U.S. and Canadian universities for admission in 1986.

It may be of interest to note that in July 1985, Premier Zhao Ziyang asked me to invite foreign scholars to study problems of the Chinese economy. My first response was a suggestion to establish an economic data center at the People's University, a suggestion which the Premier promptly accepted. This center is now under preparation. I hope that in the future American scholars interested in studying the Chinese economy will take advantage of the material available in the center.

GREGORY C. CHOW, Chair

Report of the Committee on U.S.–China Exchanges in Economics*

Exchanges in economic ideas and cooperation in economics education between the United States and the People's Republic of China entered a mature stage during 1986, as witnessed by the following events.

Responding to a request of Chinese Premier Zhao Ziyang, I invited several AEA members including John Fei, Anthony Koo, and Lawrence Lau to work with leading officials of the State Commission on Restructuring the Economic System and the People's Bank on current issues of economic reform in China. We had a three-day meeting in Hong Kong in January 1986, and a five-day meeting in Peking in June 1986. Some of the issues discussed include price reform, reform of the administrative organization of state enterprises, reform of the banking system, macroeconomic control mechanisms, and problems of foreign trade and foreign investment. After the June meeting, I agreed with the Economic Restructuring Commission to organize two workshops a year to teach economics to national and provincial officials working on economic reform.

For the graduate economics program established at the People's University in Peking, I invited Leo Hurwicz and Elizabeth Li to teach in the spring semester, and Roger Gordon and Michelle White to teach in the fall semester of 1986. Some 48 students completed a one-year training program by July 1986.

A summer workshop on econometrics sponsored by the Chinese State Commission on Education took place from June 9 to July 19, 1986, serving the graduate students of the year-round program mentioned above and about 50 other graduate students and research economists from the People's Bank, the State Council's economic research institutes, the State Planning Commission, the State Statistics Bureau, and the Chinese Academy of Social Sciences. This was the third of a series of summer workshops to modernize economics education, following the micro- and macroeconomics workshops in 1984 and 1985, which I organized in cooperation with

---

*May 1987

the Chinese Ministry of Education. Richard Quandt, Angus Deaton, Robert Engle, and myself served as lecturers. This workshop and the graduate training program at the People's University received financial support from the Ford Foundation.

A group of eleven economists from the Research Institute on Economic Reform visited the United States. Eight of them joined a group of approximately twelve American and European economists in a conference on Chinese economic reform held in October in Harriman, New York, organized by Bruce Reynolds and sponsored by the *Journal of Comparative Economics* and Union College. Sixteen papers were presented and discussed.

In the fall of 1985, I helped place 63 students sponsored by the Chinese Ministry (now State Commission) of Education to some 50 American and Canadian Universities for graduate studies in economics. In the fall of 1986 about 50 more students were so placed. The students by and large have performed very well. Most of them are receiving financial support from the host universities, while a minority receive support from the Chinese government or the Ford Foundation.

Many economists and graduate students from China and the United States visited each other's countries in 1986. The study of modern economics is flourishing in China.

GREGORY C. CHOW, *Chair*

Report of the Committee on U.S.–China Exchanges in Economics*

Exchanges in economics with the People's Republic of China continued to expand in 1987. Besides the numerous individual arrangements made by scholars and graduate students from each country to visit the other, important official exchanges took place.

The U.S. Committee on Economics Education and Research in China, in cooperation with the Chinese Committee on Economic Exchanges with the United States and with financial support from the Ford Foundation, has been responsible for the following activities.

First, a year-round graduate economics training program at the People's University continued its operations for the third year, with T. Dudley Wallace, Duke University, and Donald D. Hester, University of Wisconsin, teaching in the fall of 1987, and Luis Guasch, University of California at San Diego, and Nicholas H. Stern, London School of Economics, teaching in the spring of 1988. A new graduate training program was established at Fudan University with Daniel Suits, Michigan State University, and Kar-yiu Wong, University of Washington at Seattle, teaching in the fall of 1987, and Andrew Feltenstein and Anne Sibert, both of the University of Kansas, teaching in the spring of 1988. Anyone interested in teaching in one of

---

*May 1988

these two graduate programs should write to Dr. Todd Johnson, Executive Director of the Committee, CSCPRC, National Academy of Sciences, 2101 Constitution Avenue, N.W., Washington, D.C. 20418.

Secondly, graduate students, sponsored by the Chinese State Education Commision, continued to come to the United States and Canada, with twenty-seven arriving in the fall of 1987 and twenty-one having been selected in late fall 1987 to apply for admission in September 1988.

Thirdly, a summer workshop on Information and Coordination in Enterprise and the Economy, organized by Lawrence J. Lau of Stanford University, took place at the People's University in June–July 1987, serving the students of the year-round graduate economics training program and research economists from the government. Other lecturers of the workshop include Michael Riordan, Hoover Institute at Stanford; Peter Hammond and B. Douglas Bernheim, Stanford University; and Debraj Ray, Indian Statistical Institute in New Delhi.

In September, the Chinese Committee on Economic Exchanges with the United States visited the United States and held a joint meeting with the U.S. Committee on Economics Education and Research in China. The former committee, headed by Vice President Huang Da of the People's University, consists of officials of the Chinese State Commission of Education responsible for economics education as well as representatives of seven major universities, including Beijing University, Fudan University, Jilin University, Nankai University, the People's University of China, Wuhan University, and Xiamen University. The two committees decided to continue the above three activities for another three years, until 1990. The Chinese Economics Committee plans to select candidates to be visiting scholars in the United States for a period of up to one year. The U.S. Committee is also exploring possible joint research by European and American scholars with the staff of the Chinese Academy of Social Sciences and the Institute of Economic System Reform of the Chinese State Council.

A Conference on PRC–U.S. Economic Cooperation was held from June 28 to July 2 in Wuhan. It was sponsored by the American Committee on Asian Economic Studies and was organized by Pei-kang Chang and Shao-kung Lin, Huazhong University of Science and Technology, and M. Jan Dutta, Rutgers University. Numerous papers were presented by American and Chinese scholars.

A delegation of economists representing the World Bank and including AEA members Carl Christ, Peter Diamond, Gustav Ranis, and Jacob Siegel visited Shanghai in August to give lectures and to exchange views with the Chinese Review Committee, appointed by the Chinese State Education Commission and headed by President Xie Xide of Fudan University, on economics curriculum reform at Chinese universities. They recommended the inclusion of microeconomics, macroeconomics, public finance, monetary economics, and accounting as subjects for the curriculum, which, until now, has consisted mainly of Marxian economics.

Ma Hong, Head of the Research Center of Economic, Technological, and Social Development of the State Council, led a delegation to visit the United States in November to widen contact with American institutions engaged in economic research relevant for policy analysis.

GREGORY C. CHOW, *Chair*

Report of the Committee on U.S.–China Exchanges in Economics[*]

Along with the open-door policy, economic and other activities in China have become more decentralized in recent years. Provincial and local governments have been active in the development of China's economy to supplement the activities of Beijing. Economic exchanges with other countries, including the United States, are also decentralized. Therefore, it is not possible to report all the major events associated with economic exchanges between the United States and the People's Republic of China.

For illustrative purpose, I mention three events which have come to my attention. First, the Society on Economic and Financial Management in China (the word "financial" being dropped in December) has encouraged its members to take part in various activities relevant for the development of economics and management in China. Interested readers may write to Richard H. Holton at the Center for Chinese Studies, University of California–Berkeley, to obtain newsletters of the Society. Secondly, the American Committee on Asian Economic Studies in cooperation with a Chinese committee of economists sponsored a Second International Conference on P.R.C.–U.S. Economic Cooperation on September 4–8, 1988, which took place at the Shanghai Academy of Social Sciences in Shanghai. A number of papers were presented by American Chinese participants. Thirdly, Milton Friedman spoke in Shanghai on "Using the Market for Social Development" in September, and had a meeting with Secretary-General Zhao Ziyang in Beijing on current issues of Chinese economic policies and economic reform, which received wide publicity in China.

An important event in Chinese economics education and in Chinese higher education in general occurred on Sunday, March 27, 1988, on the occasion of the 100th Anniversary of the Establishment of Lingnan University in Guangzhou. On this occasion, President Li Yueshen of Zhongshan University announced that a Lingnan (University) College would be established with the approval of the Chinese State Education Commission. The college was initially formed by the Departments of Economics and Computer Science of Zhongshan University and has about 1600 students. Lingnan was a private university originally founded by American educators; it became an entirely Chinese institution in 1927. It was absorbed by Zhongshan University in 1954 when all private universities in China ceased to exist. The reestablishment of Lingnan University College marked the first time that a former private university was at least partly reestablished in China. It has a Board

---

[*]May 1989

of Trustees consisting of two-thirds of its members from overseas and one-third from the Chinese Mainland. In the spring semester of 1989, Eytan Sheshinski, Hebrew University and Harvard University, and Athar Hussain, London School of Economics, will be lecturing at Lingnan (University) College. The college encourages American economists and computer scientists to lecture and visit, and it provides flexible conditions and arrangements. Anyone interested should write to President Li Yueshen of Zhongshan or to me.

The U.S. Committee on Economics Education and Research in China had a meeting in New York City during the annual ASSA meetings. It has decided to continue cooperation with a corresponding Chinese committee sponsored by the State Education Commission (1) supporting the two graduate economics training centers at the People's Univesity in Beijing and Fudan University in Shanghai, (2) assisting graduate students sponsored by the State Education Commission to come to the United States and Canada for graduate studies, (3) sponsoring visiting scholars from China, and (4) joint research projects with Chinese universities, the Chinese Academy of Social Sciences, the Institute for Economic Reform, the Research Center for Technical and Economic Development at the State Council, and other Chinese organizations.

Any member of the AEA who has news concerning important exchanges in economics between the United States and the People's Republic of China is welcome to communicate with members of this Committee.

GREGORY C. CHOW, *Chair*

Report of the Committee on U.S.-China Exchanges in Economics*

In spite of the unfortunate political events in June, China's economics education and economics exchanges with foreign countries have remained essentially unchanged.

On June 19, Chinese participants in the Fourth Biannual Conference of United States–Asia Economic Relations, sponsored by The American Committee on Asian Economic Studies in cooperation with The Pacific Basin Study Program of Columbia University, arrived in New York to deliver their papers as scheduled. In September, nearly all Chinese students planning to come to the United States to pursue their studies in economics and other subjects arrived as planned.

On August 23-24, members of the U.S. Committee on Economics Education and Research in China, including Gregory Chow, Robert Dernberger, D. Gale Johnson, Lawrence Lau, and Dwight Perkins, went to Beijing to meet with the Chinese Committee on Economics Education Exchanges with the United States and colleagues of the State Education Commission to discuss cooperative activities as originally scheduled. At the meeting, it was decided that the main cooperative programs that were to expire in August 1990, including the two economics training

---

*May 1990

centers at the People's University and Fudan University, would continue until August 1992, and that the U.S. committee would help strengthen Ph.D. training at selected Chinese universities by using the above training centers and sponsoring one-year visits of Ph.D. candidates to the United States. Four American faculty members arrived at the two training centers to assume their teaching duties in the fall semester as they had agreed, Moshe Justman and Wing Thye Woo at the People's University, and Charles Hultman and John Huttman at Fudan University. Anyone interested in teaching at these two training centers may contact Dr. Todd Johnson, Executive Director, Committee on Economics Education and Research in China, National Academy of Sciences, 2101 Constitution Avenue, Washington, D.C. 20418.

On November 1–3, eight American economists went to Shanghai to participate in a conference with Chinese colleagues to discuss drafts of new economics texts being written for use in Chinese colleges and universities. In 1987, the Chinese State Education Commission had accepted the recommendation of an international panel of consultants of the World Bank to include as core courses for economics majors the subjects of micro- and macroeconomics, development, comparative economic systems, statistics, computer applications, public finance, money and banking, international trade and finance, and accounting along with Marxian economics. Committees of Chinese economists were appointed to prepare texts for these courses. Texts for the first four subjects listed above were discussed in the November 1–3 conference that had originally been scheduled in July. The American participants were impressed by the quality of the texts prepared and by the openmindedness of their Chinese colleagues in the discussion. This is an activity of the Chinese University Development Project II sponsored by the World Bank. Programs to train teachers for the core subjects were being planned by officials of the State Education Commission. It will take some years before the core courses can be successfully implemented at the large number of Chinese colleges and universities.

On August 27, three American members attended a meeting of the Board of Trustees of Lingnan (University) College of Zhongshan University in Canton. At the meeting, the introduction of micro- and macroeconomics, economic development, and international trade into the economics curriculum was being planned. Visiting professors from the United States, Great Britain, and Hong Kong were to be invited to teach these subjects in the 1989–90 academic year.

It is difficult to forecast the ultimate impact of the political events of June. However, continued modernization of economics education and continued economics exchanges with the United States and the outside world appear to have survived and may even assert some influence in the future development of China.

GREGORY C. CHOW, *Chair*

Report of the Committee on U.S.–China Exchanges in Economics*

Modern economic education and research continued to develop in China in 1990 as evidenced by the following events.

1) American economists continued to teach in China, including the two graduate economics training centers at the People's University in Beijing (Harold Watts of Columbia University and Kajal Lahiri of the State University of New York at Albany in Spring 1990; Mark Machina of the University of California–San Diego and Belton Fleisher of Ohio State University in Fall 1990) and at Fudan University in Shanghai (Alastair MacBean of Lancaster University and Summer LaCroix of the University of Hawaii in Spring 1990; Dudley Wallace of Duke University and Albert Schweinberger of Australian National University in Fall 1990), and Lingnan (University) College at Zhongshan University in Guangzhou (Anthony Koo of Michigan State University).

2) A delegation of deans and chairmen of colleges and departments of economics headed by the Dean of Economics at the People's University, Yu Xueben, visited the United States on October 27 to November 18 to study economic education in the United States. The seven major universities represented were Fudan, Jilin, Nankai, Peking, the People's, Wuhan, and Xiamen Universities. Besides visiting Columbia, Harvard, Washington, D.C., and Stanford, the delegation spent ten days at the University of Michigan, hosted by Michael Oxenburg of the Center for Oriental Studies and Robert Dernberger of the Department of Economics, and participated in intensive discussions on the administrative and academic aspects of American economic education. Other visitors from China included visiting fellows supported by The Ford Foundation. Dr. Justin Lin of the Rural Development Department, Development Research Center of the Chinese State Council and Beijing University, served as Visiting Associate Professor at the University of California–Los Angeles, in the fall quarter 1990.

3) An International Conference on Quantitative Economics and Its Applications to Chinese Economic Development and Reform in the 1990s, sponsored by the Chinese Academy of Social Sciences and the United Nations Development Programme in China, took place in Beijing, June 24–28. Sixteen foreign economists participated, mostly American, but including French, Hungarian, and Taiwanese economists. The conference was to celebrate the tenth anniversary of the Econometrics Workshop organized by Lawrence R. Klein of the University of Pennsylvania and Xu Dixin of the Chinese Academy of Social Sciences in Beijing in the summer of 1980. The instructors of the 1980 workshop, including Albert Ando, Gregory Chow, Cheng Hsiao, Lawrence Klein, Lawrence Lau, and Vincent Su, returned to Beijing to present papers and to visit the site of the 1980 workshop. A number of papers were presented by Chinese scholars, including those of the Chinese Academy of Social Sciences doing cooperative research with their American colleagues.

---

*May 1991

4) The Chinese State Education Commission continued to develop modern economic education by introducing the core courses of micro, macro, statistics, accounting, international trade, economic development, and money and banking, which were adopted in 1988. In the summer, a number of workshops were organized to train the university teachers to teach some of these core courses. Winston Chang of the State University of New York at Buffalo and Frank Hsiao of the University of Colorado were among the visiting professors teaching the workshops.

GREGORY C. CHOW, *Chair*

Report of the Committee on U.S.–China Exchanges in Economics*

Before summarizing the events in 1991, it is useful to review the U.S.–China exchange activities beginning in 1981. The committee report for 1981, published in the May 1982 *American Economic Review* (*Papers and Proceedings*) mentioned three activities: (1) an economics workshop in Beijing was conducted by American economists and hosted by the Chinese Academy of Social Sciences; (2) Chinese students in economics began to appear on American campuses; and (3) exchanges were initiated between American and Chinese universities.

In the interim, the committee report for 1985, which appeared in the May 1986 *American Economic Review* (*Papers and Proceedings*), mentioned three activities. (1) A macroeconomics workshop, sponsored by the State Education Commission (SEC) with partial support from the Ford Foundation, took place at the People's University in Beijing. (2) Sixty-two students officially sponsored by the SEC arrived in September 1985 to enter some 50 graduate programs in economics in the United States and Canada. (3) A year-round training center began operating in September 1985 at the People's University under the sponsorship of SEC and with financial support from the Ford Foundation.

In 1991 the Economic Training Center at the People's University and a second Training Center at Fudan University continued operating. The faculty at the former includes Saquib Jaffrey of the State University of New York at Buffalo and De-min Wu of the University of Kansas in Spring 1991, and Moshe Justman of the Ben Gurion University of the Negev and Mark Machina of the University of California–San Diego in Fall 1991. The faculty members of the latter include Henry Wan of Cornell University and Hans Wijkander of the Stockholm School of Economics in Spring 1991, and Richard Pomfret of Johns Hopkins University and Dudley Wallace of Duke University in Fall 1991.

Secondly, while no new students sponsored by the SEC arrived in 1991, many students from China continue to come to study economics as private citizens. In the meantime, Ph.D. candidates on the job market in 1991 originally coming from the People's Republic of China can be found in many American universities. The

---

*May 1992

Chinese Economists Society, which was formed in 1985 under the name Chinese Young Economists Society by a group of students from China, now has a membership of approximately 300 and is applying for sub-associate membership in the Allied Social Science Associations.

Economic exchanges with the People's Republic of China continue. The most effective means to cooperate with China in modernizing its economics education and research are being reexamined. The Committee on Economics Education and Research in China, which cooperates with the State Education Commission and is supported financially by the Ford Foundation, is reviewing its activities. With reduction of support from the Ford Foundation, it is envisaged that at least one of the two training centers will continue. Perhaps the target participants may be changed to include more existing teachers to ensure that they will remain in China to teach economics. Joint sponsorship of students by SEC and the above Committee to study in the United States has ceased since 1989, partly because the percentage of students returning to China is very small. To upgrade the teaching of economics in China in the near future, one means is to utilize the economic training center described above. A second is to offer some summer workshops with potential participants to be drawn from former students of the two Economic Training Centers and those who have studied abroad for short periods. Third, the program to sponsor visiting scholars from China is expected to continue. The Chair is in frequent contact with colleagues at the SEC to discuss these and other topics related to economic exchanges. Any suggestions from members of AEA would be welcome and may be directed to members of this Committee, including Kenneth Arrow, Gregory Chow, Richard Holton, and Lawrence Klein.

GREGORY C. CHOW, *Chair*

Report of the Committee on U.S.–China Exchanges in Economics*

A major event in 1992 affecting future U.S.–China exchanges in economics is the adoption of economic reform policies toward a socialist market economy by the Communist Party's 14th Congress held in Beijing in October. For the first time, a market economy was officially recognized to be China's aim, and not a planned economy. Economists from the West will be asked to assist in the transition to a market economy. An example is the appointment in November of Lawrence Klein, a member of this Committee, as an economic advisor to the Chinese State Planning Commission. As of December, a Chief Technical Advisor was sought for a United Nations Development Programme funded project to assist the Chinese State Planning Commission to redefine its role and to train its staff through the use of foreign lecturers and consultants, group training abroad, study tour abroad, and collaborative research.

---

*May 1993

In 1992 ongoing exchange activities with China continued. The year-long Economic Training Center at the People's University in Beijing, under the sponsorship of the State Education Commission with financial support from the Ford Foundation, was staffed by Paul Trescott of Southern Illinois University for micro and Alasdair MacBean of the University of Lancaster for macro in the Spring semester, and by Rachel Connelly of Bowdoin College for micro and George Horwich of Purdue University for macro in the Fall semester. The Economic Training Center at Fudan University in Shanghai hosted Hans Wijkander of the Stockholm School of Economics for micro and Liang-shing Fan of Colorado State University for macro in the Spring semester. It was discontinued in the Fall as Ford Foundation funding was reduced.

Five members of the Chinese Committee on Economics Education Exchanges with the United States, headed by its chairman, President Huang Da of the People's University, held a joint meeting with the U.S. Committee on Economic Education and Research in China, cochaired by Gregory Chow and Dwight Perkins, in Washington, DC on September 12. The two Committees agreed to continue their cooperative activities for at least two more years, including the operation of the Economic Training Center at the People's University, summer workshops on applied economics (the 1993 workshop in international finance to take place at Nankai University), and a program for visiting economists from seven designated universities in China to study and do research in the United States. The U.S. Committee members Robert Dernberger, D. Gale Johnson, Lawrence Lau, and Herbert Simon attended the meeting. A topic discussed was finding ways to assist Chinese students who have completed their economics training to return to China to teach in short and long terms.

The Board of Trustees of the Lingnan Foundation of New York met in November to approve financial support for Lingnan (University) College of Zhongshan University, including the sending of American professors to teach economics and the financing of faculty members from Lingnan to study and do research in the United States. James McDonald of Brigham Young University will teach econometrics in Spring 1993. Former President Li Yuesheng of Zhongshan, a faculty member of Lingnan College, was visiting the United States in 1992.

The Chinese Economists Society, founded in 1985, has a membership of over 300 students and professionals from China. Many are teaching in universities in the United States and Canada. The Society joined the Allied Social Science Associations (ASSA) in 1992 and held its seventh annual conference in Austin, TX, where papers on economics in general and on China's economy in particular were presented. It will organize sessions in the January 1993 meetings of the ASSA in Anaheim, CA. It has received a grant from the Ford Foundation to sponsor a "Teaching Economics in China" project which supports teaching of its members in China for at least one full term. Under this grant six members had completed their teaching by the summer of 1992.

GREGORY C. CHOW, *Chair*

Report of the Committee on U.S.–China Exchanges in Economics*

By 1993 China's economy is essentially a market economy. By this it is meant that some two-third or more of the national output in China is produced by profit seeking economic units. Although Marxian economics remains in the curriculum of Chinese universities, modern economics including microeconomics, macroeconomics, international trade, economic development, accounting, statistics and money and banking is part of the economics curriculum of Chinese universities, which is officially approved by the State Education Commission (SEdC).

The U.S. Committee on Economics Education and Research in China (CEERC), with financial support from the Ford Foundation, and the Chinese Committee on Economics Exchange with the U.S. under the direction of SEdC jointly sponsored a group of chairmen or deans of Economics in the People's, Nanjing, Fudan, Peking, Wuhan, Jilin, Xiamen and Nankai universities to visit several major universities in the United States from January 18 to February 4, 1994. The purpose is to find out how teaching and research in economics are practiced in this country in order to assist them in designing economics curricula in their universities to suit the need of a market economy. During 1993, the two Committees mentioned above were placing professors from seven Chinese universities (listed above, except Nanjing) to be visiting scholars in the U.S. to do research in economics.

The Graduate Economics Training Center at the People's University sponsored by the two Committees continued operation in 1993. The faculty included Frank Shupp of the University of Illinois (teaching macro) and Yew-Kwang Ng of Monash University, Australia (teaching micro) in Spring 1993, Rachel Connelly of Bowdoin College (micro and labor) and Mark Machina of University of California–San Diego (macro and econometrics) in Fall, 1993. Over forty students selected from the above seven and other major universities attended.

Lingnan (University) College of Zhongshan University in Guangzhou hosted James McDonald of Brigham Young University who taught a course in econometrics in the spring May–June) and Jean Woelbroek of Free University of Brussels who taught international trade and finance in the fall of 1993. Lingnan (University) College receives financial support from the Lingnan Foundation of New York and from Lingnan Development Fund of Hong Kong which receives contributions from and is managed by alumni of the former Lingnan University in Guangzhou (before 1953).

---

*May 1994

A conference on economic reform in China was held in Hainan Province (an island formerly a part of Guangdong Province). It was sponsored jointly by the Chinese Economists Society in the U.S., a similar organization in the U.K. and the Chinese Economic Reform Commission of Hainan Province. Over 150 persons attended including about 35 foreign economists and about 15 American economists. Selected papers from this conference have appeared in the September 1993 issue of *China Economic Review*, a special issue devoted to China's economic reform.

GREGORY C. CHOW, *Chair*

References

Chow, G. C., 1985, *The Chinese Economy*, New York: Harper & Row; 2nd edn., 1987, Singapore: World Scientific.

———, 1987, Development of a more market-oriented economy in China, *Science* **235**, 295–299.

———, 1988, Economic analysis of the People's Republic of China, *J. Econ. Educ.* **1**, 53–64.

Musgrave, Richard A., 1959, *A Theory of Public Finance*, New York: McGraw-Hill.

Statistical Yearbook of China 1985, Hong Kong: Economic Information & Agency.

CHAPTER 5

TEACHING ECONOMICS AND
STUDYING ECONOMIC REFORM IN CHINA*

5.1. Introduction

Economic reform in China initiated by the Third Plenary Session of the 11th Central Committee of the Communist Party in December 1978 has just reached a ten-year mark. My participation in the teaching of economics and the studying of economic reform in China covered the second half of this period. I had served as a lecturer of an econometrics workshop in Beijing in the summer of 1980, hosted by Xu Dixin, then Vice President of the Chinese Academy of Social Sciences, and organized by Lawrence Klein of the University of Pennsylvania. I had lectured in Zhongshan, Wuhan, Huazhong, Peking and Nankai Universities in the summer of 1982. As Chairman of the American Economic Association's Committee of Exchanges with PRC, I had organized lectures by American economists in China and hosted delegations of economists from the Chinese Academy of Social Sciences. However, it was not until October 1983 that I became seriously involved in economics education in China. Perchance I met Wang Fusun and Wang Zenong, respectively Director of International Cooperation and Director of Law and Economics of the 1st Department of Higher Education of the Chinese Ministry of Education, while they were visiting Princeton on October 20–21, 1983. Learning of their interest in modernizing economics education in China, I offered to organize and teach three summer workshops in China in 1984–1986, to cover respectively microeconomics, macroeconomics, and econometrics. They were enthusiastic and accepted my proposal. I made it clear that the Chinese government had to provide all the funds required. Wang Fusun said he would take care of that, perhaps through applying for support from international organizations or American foundations.

In January 1984, a letter from Wang Fusun arrived to tell me that, regretfully, he was unable to obtain the required funding in U.S. dollars and that the micro-

*For moral and financial support respectively in the preparation of this paper the author is much indebted to Paula K. Chow and the National Science Foundation. This paper originally appeared in *China Economic Review* 1, 193–199 (1989). Copyright 1990 JAI Press.

economics workshop contemplated for the summer of 1984 had to be cancelled. I was ready to abandon the project, if not for a conversation with Leon Gordenker, Professor of Political Science at Princeton, during a dinner party at my home. When I mentioned this correspondence from Wang Fusun, Gordenker said that the 1984 summer workshop was too important to forgo and that I myself should try to obtain some funds for it. He convinced me. After some unsuccessful attempts negotiating with American foundations and with a potentially interested agency in Washington, D.C., I finally called the secretary of President William Bowen of Princeton at 9:30 a.m. on March 28, 1984, to make an appointment. I went to see Bowen at 11:15 for about fifteen minutes. Around 2:00 p.m., Vice President Robert Durkee called to tell me that Bowen had decided to provide funds for the lecturers' international travel. They later referred me to Albert Rees, President of the Sloan Foundation and a former colleague at the Economics Department of Princeton, for possible funding of the honoraria for the lecturers. I was impressed by the swift decisions and grateful to these Princeton colleagues for their contributions to the 1984 summer workshop.

5.2. Economics Education

The microeconomics workshop took place in Peking University for six weeks from June 11 to July 21, 1984. It was fortunate that distinguished economists Sherwin Rosen, Edwin Mills, and Marc Nerlove (in order of appearance) agreed to lecture for two weeks each. There were about 45 to 50 students selected by the Chinese Ministry of Education from various universities. The main textbooks used were Gould and Ferguson's *Microeconomic Theory* and Henderson and Quandt's *Microeconomic Theory: A Mathematical Approach*. The lectures were given in English without translation, such a decision having been made after consultation with Wang Fusun and Wang Zenong. Classes met six days a week for two to two-and-a-half hours in the morning. Following the lectures given by the above-mentioned economists, I lectured briefly, providing applications to China and commenting on the relevance of the lectures. At the end of the six weeks, a final examination was given. Twenty-four students took the examination, and some did very well. Considering the limited background of the students in both modern economics and in English, we were impressed by their performance.

At 5:00 p.m. on July 5, I met with Premier Zhao Ziyang. We discussed economics education, economic reform, and the future of Hong Kong for about one hour and a half. It was my first meeting with Premier Zhao. He met me at the door when I arrived at the Purple Light Pavilion. During our conversation, Premier Zhao impressed me by his very personable style, his intelligence and his firm grasp and intuitive understanding of economic issues. Forty-five minutes or so into our conversation, I commented that he was a very good economist. He said he was not an economist but a practitioner of politics. Our meeting was broadcast on national television the same evening and reported on the front page of the *People's Daily* the following day (showing a picture of the two of us). The publicity signalled that China officially endorsed modern economics. During our conversation,

I mentioned that I had written a textbook entitled *The Chinese Economy* which attempts to introduce modern economic tools to study the Chinese economy. The book was used as a supplementary text in the microeconomics workshop. The Premier commented immediately, "We should translate it." I said, "It is already translated into Chinese." "We should publish it," was his response. Without his comment, the book would not have been published in China at that time, as three university presses in China had rejected the manuscript before July 5. A Chinese edition of the book was finally published by Nankai University Press in July 1985.

After the completion of the microeconomics workshop, my wife, our daughter and I travelled South to Shanghai and from Shanghai to Hangzhou in order to go by car to visit Huang Shan. This summer and in the summers to follow I travelled as a guest of the Premier, meeting leaders of cities and provinces and discussing economics and world affairs with them. Most of them expressed great respect for Premier Zhao, telling stories about him and his leadership. My family and I have enjoyed and learned a great deal from these travels. Sometimes we encountered difficulties *en route* in spite of the special treatment given to us.

On the train ride from Shanghai to Hangzhou on July 21, 1984, I thought of the idea of asking the Ministry of Education to sponsor graduate students to come to the United States and Canada to study economics. I was willing to help place the students, provided that they passed a nationally administered examination in economics and mathematics, with the questions on economics given by me and based on *The Chinese Economy*. Students were to be selected nationally from those majoring in the natural sciences, mathematics, and engineering, besides economics. This would provide a larger pool for selecting students with analytical abilities. Since very few students had previous training in modern economics, they could read *The Chinese Economy* to acquire some knowledge before entering graduate schools in Canada and the United States. I wrote a short note describing this idea to Xia Ziqing, Deputy Director of the 1st Department of Higher Education as well as Wang Fusun and Wang Zenong, indicating that if they accepted the idea, they could send me a telegram in Guangzhou, within eight to ten days, before my return to the U.S. I thought that they could make the decision that soon. I did not hear from them in Guangzhou, but within two weeks after my return to the U.S. I received a communication from Wang Fusun saying that my recommendation concerning sending graduate students to the U.S. was accepted by the Ministry of Education.

The first examination was given in the fall of 1984. Over 160 students selected from about twenty universities took the examinations in mathematics and economics. They were first selected by their own universities. Each university was given a quota of candidates to take the examination — Peking, Fudan, and one or two other major universities had a quota of 10 students, whereas some lesser known universities had a quota of one or two. In January 1985, I received a list of 81 students who had passed the examinations, meaning they received a score of 60 percent in both economics and mathematics. Later, 63 of these students were placed in about 45 universities, most receiving financial support. Edwin Mills, Sherwin Rosen and I formed an *ad hoc* committee to sign letters of recommendation on behalf of the students describing the examinations and the method of selection. (John Taylor joined the Committee in the following two years.) The program of sending students abroad has continued. During the first three years of 1985, 1986 and 1987 I provided the economics examination questions based on *The Chinese Economy*. Afterwards, the students were asked to take GREs given by the Educational Testing Service in the same ways as other students wishing to apply to graduate schools in the United States.

In January 1985, at the initiative of Peter Geithner of the Ford Foundation, a U.S. Committee on Economics Education and Research in China was formed, with Dwight Perkins and me serving as co-chairs, and Robert Dernberger, D. Gale Johnson, Lawrence Klein, Lawrence Lau and Herbert Simon as the other members. This Committee cooperates with the Chinese Committee on Economics Exchanges with the U.S. formed by the Chinese Ministry of Education (or the State Education Commission since July 1985), consisting of representatives from seven universities, Peking, People's, Fudan, Nankai, Wuhan, Jilin, and Xiamen, and chaired by Vice President Huang Da of the People's University. One activity of the U.S. Committee is to support some of the students who did not receive financial support from the universities accepting them. Out of the 61 students accepted in the first year to enter in 1985, only 11 required support from the Committee. The funding of the Committee is mainly from the Ford Foundation. Other activities supported by the Committee include the summer workshops from 1985 to 1988, a year-round graduate economic training center (at the M.A. level) at Renda (The People's University) beginning in 1985, a second graduate economic training center with some emphasis on international economics at Fudan University beginning in 1987, visiting scholars from China to the United States, and joint research projects with the Chinese Academy of Social Sciences and other research, academic and government institutions. Peter Geithner is to be congratulated for the energy, resourcefulness and insight in guiding and supporting the activities of this Committee, not to mention the contributions from its distinguished members. The activities of the Committee are continuing.

The macroeconomic workshop took place in Beijing from June 10 to July 20, 1985. The People's University served as the host institution. Over 90 persons attended, including graduate students, young teachers as well as research staff members from government organizations such as the People's Bank, the State Statistics Bureau, research centers at the State Council, and the Chinese Academy of Social Sciences. It was again fortunate that such distinguished economists as William Branson, Dwight Jaffee, Richard Portes, and John Taylor served as lecturers. I played a similar role of interpreting their lectures, adding some of my own, and discussing relevance and applications to China. The average student's comprehension of English and basic economics definitely improved as compared with that of the participants of the microeconomics workshop in 1984. The lecturers were impressed by the quality of the students. A final examination was also given, and the results were good.

On June 28, 1985, Chen Yiji, Gong Jumin and two other persons working on economic reform and economic policy at The State Council came to the Xiyuan Hotel to visit me. I was told that Premier Zhao would be interested in an estimate of the rate of inflation resulting from the rapid increase of the supply of money (currency in circulation) in China by 50 percent during 1984. I estimated this with two or three econometric equations relating the rate of inflation to current and past money supply and real output increases and presented them in the macroeconomic workshop for illustrative purposes, emphasizing the possible pitfalls of these equations and econometric equations in general. (Revised versions of these equations can be found in my paper "Money and Price Level Determination in China," *Journal of Comparative Economics*, **11**, 1987.)

In the evening of Monday, July 15, 1985, Premier Zhao invited my wife, our son and daughter, and me for dinner. One of his first remarks was on my estimate of possibly 7 to 9 percent annual inflation in the coming year or two resulting from the recent increases in money supply, which had been reported to him. Attending the dinner, I was expecting an entirely social evening, having prepared nothing to say to our host. After drinking a few glasses of Moutai, I heard the Premier ask, "Would you help invite some overseas economists to study issues of economic reform in China?" This question took me by surprise, and I could not think of an appropriate direct response. Just to keep the conversation flowing, I said "How could we study economic reform without sufficient economic data?" That remark was partly to buy time before I could think about the Premier's question. I then mentioned that I had visited the State Statistics Bureau and could not find certain economic data. The Premier commented that the officials of the State Statistics Bureau might not have revealed everything they knew to me, which I could believe. The dinner went on. I forgot much of the conversation, but remember one comment of our host: "In spite of the great turmoil and suffering inflicted on the Chinese people, the Cultural Revolution has one positive effect. It frees us from certain ideological restrictions."

Waking up the next morning on July 16 I thought that, in view of the conversation concerning the availability of economic data in the previous evening, it would be useful to write to the Premier to suggest the establishment of an economic data center at the People's University, which was hosting our macroeconomic workshop. Around 7:30 a.m., I called Vice President Huang Da to obtain his opinion concerning the suggestion, and he was enthusiastic. I immediately wrote a short letter making the suggestion to Premier Zhao, and had the chauffeur deliver the letter on the same day. Two days later on July 18, I received a call early in the afternoon from the Premier's office informing me that the Premier had already approved my suggestion to establish an economic data center at the People's University. I was very happy and impressed. The Center is now in good working condition.

Soon after returning to the United States, I wrote to Premier Zhao on August 13, 1985, saying that I had been thinking about his suggestion to invite foreign economists to study issues of China's economic reform. I made several suggestions concerning economic reform and asked for guidance as to how to proceed. Soon afterwards I received a letter from the Premier dated August 24, 1985 suggesting three topics for deliberation: (1) the establishment of a sound banking system, (2) money markets and stocks and bonds of state enterprises, and (3) the supply and control of foreign exchange. The letter stated that these problems can be discussed by economists in and outside China. For further arrangements I was asked to contact An Zhiwen, Vice Chairman of the Commission for Restructuring the Economic System (Premier Zhao being Chairman of the Commission) and Liu Hongru, Vice Chairman of the People's Bank. This was the beginning of my working relationship with these and other colleagues in China concerned with economic reform.

Before discussing economic reform further, let me return to economic education. In May 1984 I attended a meeting of 11 students from China, including Yang Xiaokai and Yu Dahai, two students of Princeton, at the home of Liang Heng, co-author of *Son of the Revolution*. This meeting marked the beginning of the Chinese Young Economist Society, Inc., which was officially formed soon after the June 1985 meeting of over 50 Chinese students in economics, management, and related subjects in the Chinese Consulate General in New York. This organization now has over 300 members. It sponsors annual conferences, in which members and guests deliver papers on economics in general and on Chinese economic reform issues in particular. The quality of the papers presented at the annual conferences has improved a great deal in the last few years, as one can expect. The Society also sponsors a new journal, *China Economic Review*, beginning in 1989.

An important event in Chinese economic education and in Chinese higher education in general occurred on Sunday, March 27, 1988 on the occasion of the 100th Anniversary of the establishment of Lingnan University in Guangzhou. On this occasion President Li Yueshen of Zhongshan University announced that a Lingnan University College would be established with the approval of the Chinese State Education Commission. The College in the beginning is formed by the Departments of Economics and Computer Science of Zhongshan University, and has about 1600 students. Lingnan was a private university originally founded by American educators. It became an entirely Chinese institution in 1927. I was a student of Lingnan Primary School, Middle School and University for most of my school life beginning in the second grade in 1938 in Hong Kong through the completion of my freshman year at Lingnan University in Guangzhou in 1948, before coming to the United States to attend Cornell University as a sophomore. All private universities in China were absorbed by national universities in 1954. The reestablishment of Lingnan University College marked the first time that a former private university was at least partly reestablished in China. It has a Board of Trustees, two thirds of whose members are from overseas and one third from the

Chinese Mainland. I am fortunate to serve as its Honorary President as well as a member of its Board of Trustees.

In the Spring semester of 1989, Eytan Sheshinski of Hebrew and Harvard Universities and Athar Hussain of the London School of Economics will be lecturing at Lingnan University College. The academic programs of this College, unlike those of the graduate economics training centers at Renda and Fudan, are a part of a Chinese university. It is interesting to observe how modern economics is being integrated into the Chinese university curriculum. Many organizations and scholars, including the World Bank in particular, have helped promote modern economic education in China, by suggesting certain reforms in the curriculum. The Chinese State Education Commission is paying serious attention to their recommendations, now organizing several study groups to prepare teaching material on ten subjects suggested by a committee of the World Bank in the summer of 1987. How individual universities will integrate the new material into their curricula remains to be seen. Lingnan University College is one institution in which such an integration is taking place.

In the process of promoting modern economics education in China, I have been much impressed by the talented people in the Chinese government and among the Chinese students. To illustrate, the dedication of Wang Zenong to higher education in China deserves admiration. Besides developing higher education in economics, Wang Zenong is also responsible for education in law. Furthermore, when an opportunity became available, he seized it to promote education in statistics by working with George Tiao of the Graduate School of Business of the University of Chicago, initiating a program to send graduate students to the United States to study statistics. The efficiency of Wang Fusun compares well with that of any administrator that I have met. After the first summer workshop in 1984, I received a phone call from Edwin Kuh of the Sloan School of Management at M.I.T. expressing an interest in visiting China in connection with his trip to Japan. I sent an airmail letter to Wang Fusun recommending Kuh. About ten days later, which was the time it took for my letter to reach Beijing, Ed Kuh read to me over the phone a telegram from Wang Fusun inviting him to lecture in Beijing for a week in a format similar to the 1984 summer workshop, stating that by showing this telegram to the Chinese Consulate General in New York, Kuh and his wife could obtain their visas. Both Kuh and I were very impressed by Wang Fusun's efficiency.

Government officials and educators such as Wang Zenong, Wang Fusun, Huang Da and Li Yueshen make it worthwhile for me to work on the modernization of China's economic education. Huang Da, a noted economist trained in the Soviet Union and Vice President of The People's University, is able, energetic, and eager to introduce important economic ideas and knowledge from the West as well as from Eastern Europe to China. He chairs the China Committee on Exchanges with the U.S. effectively. I have a favourite story about President Li Yueshen of Zhongshan University. In 1985, after the macroeconomic workshop, I visited Zhongshan University to give a lecture. At 10 a.m. I arrived at the Zhongshan campus, half an hour before my lecture. I found President Li and several faculty members, including chairmen of the Economics, Computer Science and Mathematics departments waiting in the reception room. Li held an informal meeting with these faculty members in my presence, opening the meeting with the remark that in Zhongshan the development of modern economics should become an important task. He pointed out that faculty talents were limited and were scattered around several departments represented at the meeting. The interested faculty members from these departments should help organize an informal seminar on modern economics. Before my lecture at 10:30 a.m., such a seminar was already decided upon, with its coordinator appointed. Later I reported this event to friends at Princeton University, saying that people in Princeton could not have done it more efficiently.

Certainly there are many bureaucrats in China with whom one would not like to cooperate. However, there are enough talented and devoted colleagues in China to do much good, if we try to find them. There are more talented people in China for us to work with than we have time and energy to spare. Never mind the corrupt government officials.

Turning to the talents among Chinese students, I have often received very complimentary reports from faculty members of the universities which have accepted Chinese students in economics coming out through our program. From my own observations, among the students passing the national examination sponsored by the Ministry of Education in 1984, Zhao Lin from Fudan University is now completing his Ph.D. in Princeton, writing an outstanding thesis in mathematical economics. Before the program began, Yang Xiaokai and Yu Dahai had come to Princeton in 1983. Yang had had no formal college education and was much older than the average graduate student when entering Princeton, but he worked every hard and managed to catch up and complete a good thesis on the division of labor. He is now teaching at Monash University in Australia. Yu Dahai, receiving A+'s in both microeconomics and macroeconomics during his first year in Princeton, impressed me also by his leadership in forming the Chinese Young Economist Society, Inc. Instead of consulting a lawyer as I would have, Yu looked up the required law books in the library and had the Society incorporated himself, being one of its leaders. I am constantly being impressed by the students from China whom I meet in Princeton and elsewhere.

5.3. Economic Reform

My involvement in economic reform in China began at the meeting with Zhao Ziyang in June 1984 when we exchanged views on economics education, economic reform and the future of Hong Kong. One important issue discussed at the meeting was price reform, a subject which was soon to be a main component of the October 20, 1984 Decision of the Central Committee of the Communist Party on economic reform. In 1984, after the meeting with Premier Zhao, I wrote to him suggesting the abolition of the foreign exchange certificate, which is a second currency besides the RMB being circulated in China. The foreign exchange certificate is obtained by surrendering foreign currency. It is supposed to have the same value as the RMB, except that certain foreign goods can be purchased only with the certificate and not RMB. There are pros and cons concerning the use of the foreign exchange certificate in China, which I do not have space to go into. My view has been that China is better off in having only one currency which, in spite of the low per capita income of China, would command a set of equilibrium exchange rates with the hard currencies of the world. Whether the reader agrees with me or not, it was my suggestion to Premier Zhao in 1984 to abolish the exchange certificate. In 1986, I was delighted to read that the government was to abolish the exchange certificate as of July 1, but the date was later postponed to September 1, and later postponed indefinitely, for reasons it is beyond the scope of this paper to discuss.

My official participation in economic reform in China took place at a meeting in Hong Kong in January 1986 with An Zhiwen, Liu Hongru, and six other officials from Beijing. The meeting was the result of the suggestion of Premier Zhao Ziyang at the dinner on July 15, 1985 as mentioned above. An Zhiwen and I decided to hold the meeting in Hong Kong. He and Liu Hongru sent documents to me providing background on the relevant issues to be discussed. I invited John Fei of Yale University to join us. It was a private meeting. People in Hong Kong did not know about it. The meeting lasted for four days, from Wednesday, January 15 to Saturday the 18th. We discussed all relevant issues concerning economics reform at the time. A similar meeting occurred on June 26 to June 30 in Beijing when the participants from the Chinese government increased to about 18, and I invited John Fei, Anthony Koo and Lawrence Lau to join us. This five-day meeting covered all important aspects of economic reform as well as current economic policy including the possible devaluation of the RMB which had a rate of 3.2 per U.S. dollar. I did not know the timing and exact amount of the devaluation which, to my surprise, took place two days later.

At the end of our meeting on June 30, the four visiting economists and their wives were invited to dinner by Premier Zhao Ziyang. A picture of the five of us appeared on the front page of the *People's Daily* the following day. After leaving Beijing, all four of us went to Taiwan to attend a biannual meeting of Academia Sinica. We received some comments from our friends and colleagues in Taiwan concerning the picture in the *People's Daily*. Regarding Taiwan and Mainland China, in spite of some political differences among some government officials, the Chinese people are relatives and friends. There are some difficulties in communications, however. For example, the parting words from Premier Zhao to the four of us at the dinner party were, "Please convey my best to Vice President Lee Tenghui and Premier Yu Kuohua. I wish them economic prosperity and political stability." I believed that Premier Zhao meant exactly what he said. But when I met with Vice President Lee (now President Lee) and Premier Yu in Taiwan, privately and separately, I could not find an appropriate moment to convey the message.

In the summer of 1987, I invited Anthony Koo to join me in leading a workshop for members of the Association of Economic Reform. We benefitted from discussions with a group of some 40 persons working at the provincial and other levels of economic reform. At the time, a major issue was the introduction of the contract responsibility system to state enterprises. Several participants at the workshop were in favor of this system. In fact, the system was rapidly introduced into state enterprises, covering over 90 percent of them by the end of 1987. Later when I travelled to some cities including Xianmen, I talked to local officials and heads of state enterprises and discovered some problems with such a system. These problems are discussed in a paper entitled "Market Socialism and Economic Development in China," which I presented at the International Seminar on China's Economic Reform, 1979–1988, in Shenzhen on November 7, 1988.

From November 2 to 12, 1988, I was in China, spending the first two days in Beijing, two days in Shanghai, one day in Guangzhou, and five days in Shenzhen to attend the above International Seminar. I delivered a speech on "Economic and Political Reform in China and the Future of Hong Kong" before some one hundred and sixty participants (including about 35 foreign visitors). While in Beijing, I met with Secretary-General Zhao Ziyang for an hour and twenty minutes on Thursday, November 3, to discuss the topics of my speech. In Beijing, I did further work with officials responsible for economic reform, including the planning of a future meeting in 1989. Economic reform officials are open-minded and interested in listening to ideas from many foreign countries, including the West, Japan, and Taiwan as well as Eastern Europe, as a traditional Chinese in the process of assimilating foreign cultures would.

As during the process of working on economic education, I also discovered talented officials while working on China's economic reform. The able leadership and the remarkable economic sense of Zhao Ziyang have already been mentioned. Milton Friedman, who had a meeting with Secretary-General Zhao in October 1988, wrote in a letter to me: "With respect to the Secretary-General we were very much impressed with his sophistication about economic arrangements and organization, and with his own commitment to moving in the direction of greater reliance on markets."

I was impressed by the openmindedness and the political sense of Mr. An Zhiwen. He has a deep understanding of what kinds of reform proposals would be politically feasible, besides being a very personable individual to work with. Liu Hongru, having been educated in the Soviet Union, has received some poor publicity in some of the Chinese press published in Hong Kong and in the United States. I have been impressed by the intelligence and quick mind of Mr. Liu. The criticism of him by some writers, mainly because of his Soviet education, is unfounded. His education in the Soviet Union, where he completed a thesis on the central banking system of Eastern Europe, qualifies him to take responsibility in China's banking system. He understands the working of a market economy, being an interested reader of Milton Friedman. These and other colleagues make it very enjoyable to work on China's economic modernization.

5.4. Political Reform and Hong Kong

While meeting with Secretary-General Zhao on Thurday, November 3, 1988, I discussed the possibility of having more political freedom, including freedom of speech, of publication and of assembly, and the possibility of promoting the respect for law in China. The Secretary-General believes that China can make progress towards having more political freedom and respect for the law, but the process, as I see it, is probably going to be slow given China's historical and political background. After the meeting, it become clear to me that if Mainland China practiced political freedom and the respect for the law, which is being practiced in Hong Kong, the Hong Kong people would increase their confidence in the government of the People's Republic of China. In my speech before the International Seminar on Economic Reform in Shenzhen on November 7, I pointed out that the confidence of the people of Hong Kong in the Chinese government and political reform in China towards more freedom and respect for the law are interrelated. I expressed my hope that China would make progress towards such political reform, which is not only good for Mainland China, but would also increase the confidence of the people of Hong Kong.

Soon after the Shenzhen seminar, I discovered that Hong Kong could assert a positive influence on political reform in China. On December 5, 1988, concerned about the situation in Hong Kong after 1997, I wrote a letter to sixteen leaders of Hong Kong, suggesting the formation of a group to study Hong Kong's future. A Study Group on the Future of Hong Kong was formed on January 24, 1989. Several members of this group visited Secretary-General Zhao Ziyang in Beijing on March 18 to exchange views on problems associated with Hong Kong's future.

Part II
Prospects for Growth

CHAPTER 6

PROSPECTS FOR CHINA'S ECONOMIC GROWTH, FOREIGN ECONOMIC RELATIONS AND CULTURAL EXCHANGES WITH THE U.S.*

The student movement and the ensuing mass demonstrations split China's political leadership. One unfortunate outcome was the resignation of Party Secretary-General Zhao Ziyang. The economic policies of Premier Li Peng and Vice Premier Yao Yilin were not, and are not, very different from Zhao's. Although Zhao would rely on free markets to a larger extent, all three, together with nearly all other current economic administrators, had by 1979 given up Soviet-style central planning and accepted the usefulness of decentralization and markets. Supporting evidence (Chow 1988) can be found in Li Peng's pronouncements before June 1989 and Yao Yilin's policy statements (Chow 1985). Statements by Deng Xiaoping and Li Peng after June 4 emphasized the continuation of the open-door policy, economic reform and the maintenance of capitalism for Hong Kong after 1997.

The prospect for further economic reform (including the determination of prices by market forces to a larger extent, decentralization and proper incentive systems for state enterprises with shares possibly held by many central and local government units and individuals, the establishment of an effective macroeconomic control mechanism, change in labor policy, etc.) depends not only on the intent of the top leadership, but also on the political and economic reality of China. Bureaucracy, vested interests, inertia to change, persistence of old ideas and lack of education and training on the part of economic officials, enterprise staff and managers all contribute to slowing down economic reform. In addition, serious inflation of over 30% per year led to a policy, adopted by the Central Committee of the Chinese Communist Party in late September 1988, of reinstituting some administrative control over prices and a postponement of further price reform until the inflation problem is resolved. Hence the prospect of significant changes in basic economic institutions in the next few years was not good before June and remains so today.

---

*Written in August 1989.

What are the prospects for economic growth? The Chinese economic system is a mixed economy, which relies on market forces, bureaucratic administration at the enterprise and local levels, and central planning. Under such a system, corruption by government officials prevails. Such corruption often enables economic activities to take place, which otherwise would not. It may thus lead to an improvement in economic efficiency, although the distribution of income may be unfair. State enterprises are often inefficient and reap monopoly profits by having access to cheap material supplies under price control and administrative allocation. Many corrupt managers and staff make money by selling underpriced products or reselling underpriced materials in the market or to other enterprises. Small private enterprises and collective enterprises in urban and rural areas are mostly efficient. Agricultural production remains quite efficient under the responsibility system with individual households operating their own farms. Foreign investment leading to jointly- or foreign-owned enterprises and foreign trade add to the vitality and productivity of the Chinese economy. All these factors combined, together with the advantage of a recovery from a low level of economic activity to start with, contributed to an average annual rate of growth of real output of about 9% during the first ten years of economic reform (1978–1988).

If there were no political disturbance, the economic institutions described above would continue to operate, leading to an average annual rate of growth of perhaps about 8% in the next ten years. The recent political events would slow down economic growth mainly by reducing new foreign investment. There is much talk about the dramatic reduction in tourism, but the foreign exchange earnings from tourism are about 5% of the earnings from exports ($1.531 billion as compared with $30.94 billion in 1966, as reported in *Statistical Yearbook of China*, 1987, pp. 536 and 519). There is no reason for exports to be drastically affected. Even if new foreign investment is to be reduced substantially in the near future, the likely maintenance of economic activities generated by foreign capital already invested and the much larger domestic investment will help move the economy forward.

The effects on domestic economic activities are more limited than on foreign investment. Inflation was not caused by the political upheavals. In fact, it contributed to the public's discontent which led to mass support for the students' demonstrations — many workers and the public at large were probably not demonstrating for democracy, something they hardly understand. For reasons not entirely clear, but possibly including the administrative restrictions on aggregate demand, the rate of inflation seemed to have slowed down from April to July, as reported by some residents of Guangzhou and Beijing. Partly to limit the expansion of the money supply, the government has tried to pay farmers for the assigned quotas of output using IOUs. This might lead to some discontent among farmers, but should not affect their incentives to produce, since they continue to receive extra money for extra work by selling the output in excess of the procurement quota in the free market. It is also claimed that general discontent with the current political leadership affects people's incentives to work. There is not much justification for this claim as the incentive to work depends mainly on the individual's economic calculations.

Furthermore, many Chinese people, especially those living in the coastal provinces of Guangdong and Fujian are not politically-minded. They are interested in carrying on their economic and other personal activities as long as central government does not interfere with them. The central government has neither the intent, nor the ability, to prevent these people from making a good living and thus contributing to economic growth in China. This view is shared by Ezra Vogel of Harvard, as stated in an interview published in the June 1989 issue of *Common Wealth* (a magazine in Chinese published in Taipei), pp. 253–259, and by Nicholas Kristof in his article in the *New York Times*. These authors emphasize, for Guangdong and Fujian respectively, the prevailing attitude of money before politics, the continued economic freedoms and the prospect of substantial economic growth in the future. Summarizing the above considerations I would, because of the political disturbances, scale down my estimate of the average rate of annual growth of real output in the next ten years by about half a percentage point. This means a total reduction of approximately 5 percentage points distributed over ten years, with much of it occurring in the first year or two.

While China's economic growth depends largely on her own domestic economic institutions (given the existence of an open-door policy), the level of trade with and investment from the United States and other Western countries is more seriously affected by recent political events. Moral outrage has led some citizens of these countries to advocate the use of economic sanctions including the termination of trade and investment. Trade is beneficial to both trading partners. It takes a great deal of moral outrage and moral persuasion to stop businessmen from making money through trade. (Tourism is different because it does not cost a tourist much to cancel a trip to China.) Advocates of economic sanctions usually do not have much at stake. If economic sacrifices are substantial among many people in the country concerned, a trade embargo is unlikely to take place. New foreign investment has slowed down not because of morality, but because of risk calculation on the part of investors. As long as investors believe that investment in China is profitable and not very risky, they will continue to invest. Given the fact that, before June 4, many investors considered China a suitable place to invest, many of the perceived investment opportunities still remain as the above analysis of the Chinese economy suggests. Therefore, many investors will become active as soon as they are assured of sufficient political stability. Virginia Kamsky remarked in Adam Smith's *Money World* TV program on June 9 that, of her sixty-five clients doing business in China, none had informed her to withdraw and some had expressed determination to continue.

Concerning trade with and investment from Hong Kong and Taiwan, the same remarks apply with two additional considerations. On the side of reducing economic relations with China, the emotional reaction of the people is much stronger, especially in Hong Kong, which will be a part of China after 1997. On the side of maintaining economic relations, the degree of economic dependence, especially for Hong Kong, is stronger. Many Hong Kong residents earn their living by trading with China. Using the low-cost labor in China, Hong Kong and Taiwan manufacturers can compete effectively in the world market. Thus the economic incentives for setting up manufacturing enterprises in China are great. Hong Kong has about 800,000 local manufacturing workers but its enterprises use about two million workers in China. Therefore investment will resume as soon as political uncertainty affecting economic activities diminishes.

Turning to cultural and academic exchanges between China and the United States, some administrators of the National Academy of Science decided in June to suspend such exchanges. The opinions of academic colleagues concerning this decision differ. Supporters consider it a signal to the Chinese leadership that they do not approve of the handling of the crisis in June. Others believe that such exchanges are good for the American and Chinese people, and these people should not be penalized by actions taken by a few leaders on both sides. It is difficult to say which view is more popular. Most of my colleagues performing useful work in such exchanges have decided to continue. For example, all five members of the U.S. Committee on Economics Education and Research in China (with financial support from the Ford Foundation) who agreed in April to go to Beijing will be there in the week of August 21 to meet with our Chinese colleagues as planned. All four American professors who agreed to teach next fall at the two graduate economic training centers in China which are sponsored by this Committee will be going. All three American members of the Board of Trustees of Lingnan (University) College at Zhongshan University in Canton are joining their colleagues from Hong Kong to attend a meeting of the Board in Canton on August 27. Three economists, from Michigan State, the London School of Economics, and the Chinese University of Hong Kong (Princeton Class '71) will teach at Lingnan in the coming academic year. A meeting with Chinese colleagues to prepare economics text material for Chinese universities, jointly sponsored by the Chinese State Education Commission and the World Bank, has been rescheduled from early July to mid-November.

References

Chow, G. C., 1985, *The Chinese Economy*, New York: Harper & Row; 2nd edn., 1987, SIngapore: World Scientific.

———, 1988, Market socialism and economic development in China, Princeton University Econometric Research Program, Research Memorandum No. 340.

Kristof, N., 1989, *New York Times*, August 6, p. 12.

CHAPTER 7

CHINA'S ECONOMY: THE CASE FOR STRONG GROWTH*

In late June 1989, soon after the tragic event in Tiananmen Square, I predicted that China would enjoy an annual growth of real output of about 7.5% over the next decade. It is therefore reassuring to read in *China: Between Plan and Market* (World Bank Country Study, 1990) that "... the latent dynamism of [China's] productive sectors will enable the economy to continue growing during the 1990s at rates (once the contractionary policy is eased) that would be considered very respectable in most countries."

This well-written and informative report was prepared by a mission headed by Shahid Yusuf that visited China in 1989. It discusses economic trends since June 1989, the government's policy intentions, medium term economic prospects, and the country's credit-worthiness. It analyzes government proposals for further economic reforms and advances its own suggestions. A statistical annex provides 71 pages of tables on many important aspects of the Chinese economy to 1989.

In reviewing the onset and government response to the inflation crisis that preceded the Tiananmen Square events, the report recalls that in June 1988, the government announced plans for a major price reform to be implemented in 1989. Subsequently, inflation worsened as consumers switched in some panic from financial into real assets, and prices that had been rising at annualized rates of 10–15% in early 1988 soared to rates approaching 80% by August (for a short period). The government postponed further price liberalization and adopted a series of stabilization measures, including administrative guidelines to reduce state investment, a contractionary monetary policy based mainly on the administrative allocation of credit, and direct controls on prices and marketing.

These steps sharply cut the rate of inflation, and, together with curbs on imports of consumer goods, reversed a trade imbalance of about $6.7 billion in the third quarter of 1989 to a surplus of $4.54 billion in the first half of 1990. Industrial growth fell throughout 1989, becoming negative in the last quarter, but

---

*Reprinted by permission from *International Economic Insights*, vol. II, no. 3, pp. 32–34 (May/June 1991).

then recovered, rising to 2% in the first half of 1990. Urban unemployment worsened, reaching 2.7% by the end of 1989, and over 3.5% in the first half of 1990.

The report sums up the short-term implication of the events of June 1989 as: a somewhat lower growth rate; smaller trade and current deficits; greater unemployment; the possibility that certain reforms will be postponed for a longer time than was expected in May 1989; partial withdrawal of investors from OECD countries; a fall in tourist traffic from Western countries which has also forced a rescheduling of various hotel loans; and greatly reduced access to the international capital market, which is now compelling China to seek trade and current account surpluses to manage its external transactions.

Nevertheless, the World Bank team concludes that the country's growth as well as export potential are substantial and savings behavior is likely to remain stable. Furthermore, its study finds that projections based on reasonable assumptions regarding macroeconomic policies and the continuation of reform show credit-worthiness remaining secure over the 1990–1995 period.

The number of applications for foreign direct investment proposals fell after the events in June and, unless the earlier momentum is regained, this could affect capital inflows for a few years. Foreign investors have made a major contribution to the development of services, oil exploration, and export-oriented manufacturing industries, and the report underscores the importance to China's economic mod-ernization of the maintenance of these capital flows.

To revive interest among overseas investors, the authorities have begun leasing land for development purposes for up to 70 years in the "open cities" and Special Economic Zones. The government has also enhanced incentives for Sino-foreign equity joint ventures. However, the World Bank study points up such continuing difficulties as the time-consuming negotiations that precede any agreement; the high charges for land use, energy and infrastructure; and difficulties with the enforcement of contracts under China's legal system.

By and large, I agree with the descriptions and assessments of the World Bank study. What accounts, then, for "the latent dynamism" of China's productive sectors?

First, almost 60% of China's national product is from market-oriented produc-ers seeking profits including almost all of agricultural products (32.1% of national income in 1989; see 1990 *Statistical Yearbook of China*, p. 37), about 35% of industrial output (47.5% of national income) that is produced by private, rural collective and some urban collective and local government enterprises, about half of construction output (5.9% of national income) perhaps one-tenth of transportation (3.9%) and six-tenths of commerce (10.6%). Second, China is an open economy benefiting from foreign trade, with the total value of its exports and imports accounting for 28% of its GDP in 1989. Third, foreign investment is an important driving force.

Concerning foreign investment, I wrote in *Princeton Alumni Weekly* (Sept. 1989, p. 17) that "New Foreign investment has slackened not because of morality, but because investors are recalculating their risks. As long as investors believe that investment in China will be profitable and not unduly risky, they will continue to invest." This applies especially to the people in Hong Kong and Taiwan, even though they had much stronger emotional reaction to Tiananmen Square than others. Economic dependence on China is stronger in these two lands than elsewhere. Using low-cost labor in China, manufacturers in Hong Kong and Taiwan can compete effectively in the world market, so their entrepreneurs have powerful incentives to maintain their manufacturing facilities in China and to establish new ones. Investment and trade from other Asian nations, including Japan, South Korea, and Singapore, have been affected only slightly by the unrest.

The possible influence of Hong Kong investments on China's economic growth is summed up by a leading entrepreneur, Gordon Wu, who remarked in *Hong Kong Business* (January 1990, p. 4), "We can turn much of south and central China into a suburb of Hong Kong."

My view of the economic prospects of China has remained unchanged since late June, 1989, and my expectation is for an average annual growth rate of about 7.5%, a percentage point higher than the government's new five-year plan goals.

Worries are expressed about possible renewal of high inflation over the next several years, but I believe this is most unlikely. Inflation, together with corruption, contributed greatly to the political unrest in 1989, and the government will therefore make the utmost effort to prevent its renewal.

Direct controls, which China has used effectively to control inflation and would again if necessary, also have been used to help correct the trade imbalance. This has drawn criticism from trading partners, particularly the United States, where they have added fuel to the effort to remove Most Favored Nation status. Such retaliation, I believe, could do little more than moderate the growth of Chinese exports over the coming years, since so many of them enter world markets through third countries.

Many people continue to be concerned over political development in China. Political development is important in its own right, but it is unlikely to have much effect on the rate of economic growth in the 1990s. The rate of growth depends mainly on the nature of the existing economic institutions, which allow for substantial market-oriented (including foreign) profit seeking activities to take place. These resilient economic institutions, solidified by the vested interests of the rural, urban and especially coastal residents and bureaucrats who benefit from them, are unlikely to be seriously affected by foreseeable political changes. Attempts by central political authorities to achieve further economic reforms, or even to move the economic system backwards, are unlikely to change significantly these economic institutions in the 1990s.

CHAPTER 8

THE INTEGRATION OF CHINA AND OTHER
ASIAN COUNTRIES INTO THE WORLD ECONOMY*

8.1. Introduction

It is my pleasure to speak before this honored society of world citizens about world
economic integration. Our story began in the 18th century when the Industrial
Revolution took place in Europe, where people began to discover the possible
application of science and technology to improve their economic well-being. The
world could not remain stationary. Not only did changes in the means of production
lead to changes in economic, social and political institutions in Europe, but the
impact on the rest of the world was to take more than two centuries before the
majority of the non-Europeans could share the benefits of this great revolution.

There was a period of colonialism, of exploitation, which can be defined
as involuntary or even voluntary exchanges between the rich and the very poor,
and of imperialism. No wonder great thinkers like Karl Marx and his followers
associated capitalism with exploitation and imperialism. It was difficult for many
non-European countries to adjust their social and economic institutions to Western
impact. They were militarily weak as compared with the European powers armed
with technologically advanced weapons. Their social, political and cultural institutions were not ready to absorb western technology and western ideas. Science
was in conflict with the religions of many of these countries, as it was for Europe
and America which took some time to reconcile science and Christian religion.
The necessary rise of a commercial class ran counter to the interest of traditional
political power groups. The ideas of freedom, equality and democracy were foreign
and disruptive to the existing social and political order of many countries ruled by
emperors and aristocrats. Japan provided a rare example of a country successfully
transforming a traditional social and political order to take advantage of the impact
of the Western Industrial Revolution. It succeeded in adopting western technology

---

*Paper presented before the Mont Pèlerin Society 1992 General Meeting in Vancouver, August 31,
1992.

and certain aspects of capitalistic institutions while preserving much of its own cultural and social order. China and most other Asian nations did not succeed until much more recently.

After the end of the Second World War, with the collapse of the British Empire and the destruction of much of the industrial base of Europe, Third World countries began to gain political independence and world economic power began to shift towards Asia. The economic recovery and rapid growth of Japan was a significant chapter of this story. The economic successes of the NICs, with Taiwan, South Korea, Hong Kong and Singapore labeled four dragons, was an equally important chapter. The story demonstrated an obvious fact which some Western development economists up to the 1950s tended to overlook. It was that the adoption of science and technology and of market institutions to achieve rapid economic growth was not a Western monopoly. Many countries having a stable political order, a reasonably open society and an educated population can achieve it. The success of the NICs set an example for the political leaders of Mainland China to adopt economic reform, beginning in 1978, toward a more market-oriented economy with an open-door policy. The story of this essay is one of China and other Asian countries catching up with the pioneering Europeans in reaping the fruits of the Industrial Revolution. This is a very important component of world economic integration today.

Economic integration refers to the fairly free flow of goods, capital, ideas and people across national boundaries so that many nations form a single market. It is made possible by the advancement of technology and efficient working of economic institutions, which have reduced transportation costs, established international financial networks, improved communication systems and encouraged the migration of labor. Integrated international markets are the result of the spread of western technology to the rest of the world; they have also facilitated rapid economic growth in the LDCs which depended on the import of capital and technology, the adoption of new methods of management and the introduction of modern economic and financial institutions, as well as the export of their own products in the world market. It is therefore natural for me to begin my story by describing in Sec. 2 how Taiwan and Mainland China transformed their economies to achieve significant economic growth and become important partners in an integrated world economy. Section 3 presents a brief picture of intraregional economic integration of greater China and the interregional integration between some Asian countries and the United States. Section 4 deals with the role these Asian nations play in the world economy and the adjustment which the United States has to make.

8.2. Economic Growth and Transformation of Taiwan and the Chinese Mainland

Space permits only a very brief summary of the transformation of economic institutions and of the salient features of economic growth in Mainland China and Taiwan. It is well known that Taiwan's rapid growth took place earlier and set an example for the policy makers in Mainland China to follow. From 1961 to 1972, national production at constant prices (100 in 1976) in Taiwan increased from 25 to 74, implying an average annual growth rate of 10.37% (see *Statistical Yearbook of the Republic of China 1980*, pp. 462–463). From 1977 to 1988, the index of real national income (100 in 1952) in the Chinese Mainland increased from 403.7 to 1097.2 implying an average rate of growth of 9.52% (see *Statistical Yearbook of China 1991*, p. 33). The eleven years selected for both regions were years of rapid growth, after which sustained growth could be expected. The end of each eleven-year period was characterized by a brief period of inflation, caused by the world oil price shock in the case of Taiwan and a mismanaged macro policy on the Mainland. Although the two regions of China were different in many respects, it might be interesting to point out the common elements in their economic transformation and in the growth process.[1]

8.3. Interregional and Intraregional Economic Integration

Fueled by economic reform to allow private initiative and by an open-door policy and having transformed itself to a mostly market-oriented economy, China had taken off in its growth process by 1990. It has also integrated itself into the world economy. One important measure of the degree of international economic integration of a country is the fraction of world trade for which it is responsible.

Table 1 presents data on world merchandise trade for the top twenty-five countries in 1990 and 1991, in U.S. dollars and in percentage terms, as reported in *IMF Survey*, 13 April 1992, p. 117. In 1991, the top five exporters and importers are the United States, Germany, Japan, France and the United Kingdom, in that order, with the United States accounting for 12% and 13% of world exports and imports respectively. For exports, Hong Kong, Taiwan and the Chinese Mainland accounted for 2.8%, 2.2% and 2.0% of the world total and are ranked 10th, 17th and 16th respectively. Combining these three regions of China, one finds total exports to be 7% of world exports which would amount to the fourth place, below the 8.9% for Japan and above the 6.1% for France. Their total imports amount to 6.2% of the world total and would rank fifth, just below the 6.4% for France. The total trade volume of this greater China, with $246 billion of exports and $227 billion of imports, giving a total of $473 billion, would rank fourth in the world, above the $449 billion figure for France. If all three parts of China are consolidated into one country, some of the intraregional exports and imports would not be counted in its trade with the rest of the world and the above figures would represent overestimates of the volume of greater China's world trade (see two paragraphs below). Yet the above figures indicate that greater China is already a leading country in world trade.

Other important Asian countries besides Japan and China in world trade are the Republic of Korea, Singapore, Malaysia and Thailand, with 1991 combined exports accounting for 5.5% and combined imports accounting 8.0% of the world

---

[1] The five common features in the growth process of both parts of China and how China has transformed itself to being approximately 60% a market economy are already discussed in Sec. 3 of Chapter 2 and will not be repeated here.

Table 1.

Leading Exporters and Importers in World Merchandise Trade

(billion U.S. dollars and percent)

Rank 1990	Rank 1991	Exporters	1991 Value	1991 Share	Annual Change 1990	Annual Change 1991	Rank 1990	Rank 1991	Importers	1991 Value	1991 Share	Annual Change 1990	Annual Change 1991
2	1	United States	422	12.0	8	7.5	1	1	United States	509	13.0	5	1.5
1	2	Germany	403	11.4	16	-4.5	2	2	Germany	390	10.7	22	9.5
3	3	Japan	315	8.9	5	9.5	3	3	Japan	236	8.9	12	0.5
4	4	France	217	6.1	20.5	.	4	4	France	232	6.4	21.5	-1.0
5	5	United Kingdom	185	5.3	21.5	.	5	5	United Kingdom	210	5.7	13	-6.0
6	6	Italy	169	4.8	21	-1.0	6	6	Italy	183	5.0	19	0.5
7	7	Netherlands	133	3.8	22	1.0	7	7	Netherlands	124	3.4	2	2
8	8	Canada	129	3.7	5.5	2.0	8	8	Canada	124	3.4	21	-0.5
9	9	Belgium-Luxembourg	177	3.3	17.5	-0.5	10	9	Belgium-Luxembourg	120	3.3	21	.
11	10	Hong Kong[1]	98	2.8	12	19.5	12	10	Hong Kong[2]	100	2.7	14.5	21.0
10	11	U.S.S.R.[3]	78	2.2	-0.5	-25.0	11	11	Spain	93	2.6	22.5	-6.0
12	12	Taiwan, Pr. China	76	2.2	1.5	13.5	13	12	Korea, Rep. of	82	2.2	13.5	17.0
15	13	China	72	2.0	18	16.0	9	13	U.S.S.R.	70	1.9	5.5	-42.0
13	14	Korea, Rep. of	72	2.0	4	10.5	15	14	Switzerland	66	1.8	19.5	-4.5
14	15	Switzerland	62	1.7	24	-3.5	14	15	Singapore[2]	66	1.8	22.5	8.5
17	16	Spain	60	1.7	25	8.0	17	16	China	64	1.8	-10	19.5
18	17	Singapore[4]	59	1.7	18	12.0	18	17	Taiwan, Pr. China	63	1.7	4.5	14.5
16	18	Sweden	55	1.6	11.5	-4.0	16	18	Austria	51	1.4	26	3.5
19	19	Saudi Arabia	49	1.4	56.5	11.0	19	19	Mexico[5]	50	1.4	19.5	23.5
21	20	Mexico[5]	42	1.2	16	1.0	21	20	Sweden	50	1.4	11	-9.0
20	21	Austria	41	1.2	29.5	.	20	21	Australia	42	2.2	-6.5	-1.0
22	22	Australia	41	1.2	6	2.0	22	22	Thailand	38	2.0	28.5	15.5
23	23	Denmark	36	1.0	25	3.5	23	23	Malaysia	38	2.0	30	30.0
26	24	Malaysia	35	1.0	17.5	18.5	26	25	Denmark	33	0.9	19	3.0
24	25	Norway	34	0.9	25.5	0.5	24	25	Saudi Arabia	30	0.8	14	24.5
		Total	2,990	84.0	13.5	3.5			Total	3,064	83.8	13.5	1.5
		World	3,530	100.0	13.5	1.5			World	3,660	100.0	13.5	1.5

Includes re-exports. In 1991, they amounted to $69 billion compared with $53 billion in 1990.
Includes substantial imports for re-export.
Owing to valuation difficulties, the figures are only rough approximations. (See GATT, International Trade 1990-91, Vol. 1, Box 1.)
Includes re-exports. In 1991, they amounted to $21 billion compared with $18 billion in 1990.
Includes estimates of trade flows through processing zones.

Data: GATT1

totals; the former would give a ranking of 5 and the latter a ranking 4 among all countries excluding greater China. The combined trade of these four countries was about equal to that of greater China estimated above. In 1991 greater China and these four other Asian countries accounted for 12.5% of world exports and 14.2% of world imports, slightly above the 12.0% and 13.0% for the United States. The importance of these Asian countries is greater if one considers the rate of increase. In 1991, for example, the percentage changes in exports over the previous year were 19.5% for Hong Kong, 13.5% for Taiwan, 16.0% for Mainland China, 7.5% for the United States, 4.5% for Germany, 9.5% for Japan and 1.5% for the world total; the corresponding figures for imports were 21.0% for Hong Kong, 14.5% for Taiwan, 19.5% for Mainland China, −1.5% for the U.S., 9.5% for Germany, 0.5% for Japan and 1.5% for the world.

Concerning intraregional trade of greater China, large fractions of the exports and imports of Mainland China are with Hong Kong. In 1990, of the total exports of $62.9 billion, $26.65 billion or 42.9% went to Hong Kong. Of the 1990 imports of $53.34 billion, $14.26 billion or 26.7% were from Hong Kong (see *Statistical Yearbook of China 1991*, p. 620). This shows the high degree of economic integration within the three regions of China and the extent of overestimation of exports and imports of greater China with the rest of the world, simply by adding the corresponding figures for the three regions. However, to the extent that trade among the three regions of greater China represents international specialization and yields benefits by the principle of comparative advantage, it should be counted. If the nations of this world were to form one large country, the statistics of Table 1 would still be meaningful. If one reduces somewhat the total volume of trade of greater China with the rest of the world by eliminating certain fractions of intraregional flows, but allows for the rapid growth, one still reaches the conclusion that greater China is one of the five most important trading countries in the world.

Besides trade flows, economic integration among the three regions of China includes at least the flows of capital, technology, managerial skills, financial services, sharing of world markets and the migration of people. Such flows are an integral part of the growth process itself, which is propelled by export expansion, foreign investment and the adoption of new technology and methods of management. One useful measure of the flow of capital, technology and management skill to Mainland China is the amount of foreign loans and investment. *Statistical Yearbook of China 1991* (pp. 630–631) provides data on foreign capital actually utilized (as opposed to contracts signed) for 1989 and 1990 which include loans, direct investment and other investments. Among the total $10.06 billion of foreign capital utilized in 1989, $2.91 billion came from Hong Kong and Macao while $3.0 billion came from Japan. In 1990, Hong Kong and Macao accounted for $2.43 and Japan $3.02 of the total of $10.29 billion. The Japanese figures were mostly loans, being $2.60 and $2.50 billion in 1989 and 1990 respectively. The Hong Kong/Macao figures represent mainly investments of $2.34 and $2.12 billion in 1989 and 1990, which were large fractions of total foreign investments of $3.77 and $3.75 billion respectively. To assess the importance of foreign investment in the Mainland China's investment process in 1990, we refer to the total investment in fixed assets of 444.9 billion RMB, of which state enterprises accounted for 291.9 billion, collective enterprises for 52.9 billion and individuals for 100.1 billion (see *Statistical Yearbook of China 1991*, p.144). Using an exchange rate of 6 RMB for $1, which was approximately the market rate in 1990, total fixed investment was roughly $74.1 billion. The foreign investment of $3.75 billion accounted for about 5% of this total.

Although foreign investment was only a small percentage of total investment in Mainland China, it may have a large impact on growth by way of transfering technology and management skill to China and providing competition to domestic enterprises. It has stimulated rapid growth in the coastal provinces of China. The investment of Hong Kong stimulated the growth of the adjacent Guangdong

Province, as the investment from Taiwan residents stimulated the growth of nearby Fujian Province. Hong Kong entrepreneurs employed in 1991 approximately 700,000 manufacturing workers in Hong Kong itself and about three million workers in Guangdong Province. The economic success story of Guangdong has been well documented by Ezra Vogel (1989), who points out that industrial growth in Guangdong from 1978 to 1988 was unsurpassed by the best growth records of Taiwan, South Korea and Japan. Gross output values of industry and agriculture in 1981 were 37.0 billion 1980 RMB in Guangdong and 14.0 billion in Fujian respectively (*Statistical Yearbook of China 1981*, p. 19). The corresponding figures in 1990 were 250.3 billion current RMB for Guangdong and 76.0 billion for Fujian (*Statistical Yearbook of China 1991*, p. 58). The 1990 figures can be converted to 161.8 and 49.13 billion 1980 RMB, respectively, using the ratio .6464 of the implicit 1980 price index to the 1990 price index for gross output values of industry and agriculture (*Statistical Yearbook of China 1991*, pp. 54–55). These figures imply average annual rates of growth from 1981 to 1990 in total industry and agriculture gross output value in Guangdong and Fujian of respectively 17.8% and 15.0%. If we reduce the Guangdong and Fujian gross industry/agriculture output growth by 3 percentage points to estimate the growth rates for net output, the resulting growth rates would surpass the 10.38% annual growth rate of Taiwan in the period 1961–1972, reported at the beginning of Sec. 2.

Another aspect of economic integration is the transfer of ideas and ways of life from one region to another. Parts of such transfers take place when new technology and management methods are introduced through the investment process. The remainder takes place through personal travels among people in different regions, together with communications in the form of mail, reading material and telephone contacts. The transfer of ideas and ways of life from Hong Kong and Taiwan to the mainland provinces of Guangdong and Fujian are especially noteworthy. People in these provinces have adopted many of the ideas of entrepreneurship and of the market economy in general as well as the lifestyle of the people in Hong Kong and Taiwan. The latter includes clothing, hair-style, popular music, books, magazines and TV programs. Visiting Guangzhou, the capital of Guangdong Province, which is about two and a half hours from Hong Kong by train, a traveler would see similarities with Hong Kong in the streets, restaurants, shops and in the lifestyle of the people. The difference between lifestyles in Guangzhou and in Beijing may be about as great as between Guangzhou and Hong Kong. Economic integration has indeed taken place among the southern coastal provinces of China, Hong Kong, and Taiwan.

8.4. Impact on the United States

The rapid economic growth of Japan which has become an important economic power competing with the United States has caused concern and tension in both countries. The rise of China and other Asian countries will further weaken the leadership position of the United States as a world economic power. While the Japanese have taken much of the U.S. and the world markets in automobile and consumer electronics, China and other Asian countries have taken over parts of the market in textiles, clothing, shoes, sports equipment and other consumer products. There is also competition between Japan and greater China and other Asian countries for shares of world trade and investment.

The role of Asian imports in the United States can be seen by the data for 1991 from the *Survey of Current Business*, March 1992 (pp. 59 and 64). Of total U.S. merchandise imports of $490.1 billion in 1991, $91.6 billion or 18.7% came from Japan and $59.3 billion or 12.1% from Hong Kong, Taiwan, Republic of Korea and Singapore. Of the $91.6 billion from Japan, $32.7 billion was for automobiles and parts, $36.2 billion for other capital goods, and $12.5 billion for other (nonfood) consumer goods. Of the $59.3 billion from the four other regions of Asia, $28.7 billion was for (nonfood) consumer goods other than automobiles and $20.7 billion for capital goods other than automobiles. These Asian countries provide serious competition in the American consumer goods market, creating adjustment problems for the manufacturers and labor unions in the affected industries, and providing better and cheaper consumer goods and increasing the welfare for the general American consumer.

At the beginning of the paper, I suggested that we view the current world economic integration as the outcome of the Industrial Revolution in Europe over two centuries ago. In the last two centuries, Asian countries had to adjust themselves to Western impact. Except for Japan, other Asian countries went through very difficult periods of cultural, political, social and economic adjustments. By 1990, China and several other Asian countries had finally adjusted themselves to this impact and succeeded in sharing the process of economic growth and becoming important participants in the world economic community. It is natural that the rise in economic power of these Asian countries required some adjustments on the part of the United States and other Western countries which had achieved economic development earlier.

In the United States, the following aspects of the adjustments to the integration of Asian nations in the world economy have received much attention. First, as pointed out by several political leaders in the United States, Americans need to accept the fact that their country is no longer the leading and dominant economic power. They need to share economic influence with Japan, Germany and other Asian and European countries at the end of the 20th and in the 21th centuries. This requires a change in attitude, towards one of accepting our Asian and European friends as equals in economic relations. To maintain our competitiveness, we can no longer afford the inefficiency and waste in our political and economic system. The drags to our economic system are well-known but difficult to eliminate. There are too many entitlements which the American public is accustomed to extract from our government through the American democratic process. These include social security, medical and other welfare benefits and subsidies to agriculture. These excesses resulted from past political processes when the Americans believed that we could afford them. They can no longer afford them now if we are to remain economically efficient. The American legal system is also conductive to wastes, as the large expenditures on legal services have taken away our productive economic resources, human and nonhuman. The excesses of the unions in demanding high wages were less painful when the demand for American products in the domestic and world markets were strong, but have contributed to high production costs for American enterprises competing in the world market. American managers, hidden behind a board of directors not necessarily representative of stock-holders interests, have also shared the excesses, often receiving high and even increasing salaries when the economy is in a recession and when some workers get laid off. Government regulations have become hindrances to the functioning of private enterprises, while government manipulation of the tax rates in the name of stabilization policy has created an economic climate not conductive to private investment. The lack of U.S. government leadership is manifested in many forms that have received public attention in the 1990s. Among them are the failure to control the huge government deficit, neglect of American economic infrastructure and failure to provide incentives and leadership in education and in research in science and technology. American travellers to Hong Kong and Taiwan cannot help but reflect on the deteriorating roads and other capital stocks in the U.S., the use of a slow mail system and outdated computers and other office equipment rather than fax machines and more modern personal computers.

Besides the need to adjust to international competition in domestic and world markets, Americans have also to adjust to the international migration of labor. The influx of Asians into the United States is a part of the world economic integration process and has intensified racial tensions in American communities. Americans in the 1990s are recognizing the cultural diversity in our society, its costs and benefits. Economic integration had provided problems as well as opportunities. Just as the flows of goods and capital have provided opportunities for American traders and investors and benefits to American consumers, the flows of ideas and people have enriched American cultural life. Americans have taken advantage of all these opportunities in trading, investing, consuming and enriching their cultural and social life. As the leader in higher education and in scientific research, America has influenced and enriched the educational systems and cultural lives of many countries in the world.

It is outside the scope of this paper to discuss in detail the structural strengths and weaknesses of the American economic, legal and political system and the reforms required to take advantage of all the opportunities provided by world economic integration. Changes in the American system are required for America to remain a leader in the world economy of the 21st century. How the American people and the American government will take up this challenge will determine to an important extent the history of the United States and of the world in the first half of the 21st century. It is a topic to which members of this honored society can devote some attention.

References

Chow, G. C., 1985, *The Chinese Economy*, New York: Harper & Row; 2nd edn., 1987, Singapore: World Scientific.

———, 1987, Development of a more market-oriented economy in China, *Science* **235**, 295–299.

———, 1988, Market socialism and economic development in China, Princeton University Econometric Research Program, Research Memorandum 340; also in Chinese in *Wen Wei Po* (Hong Kong, 11 November 1988).

———, 1993, Capital formation and economic growth in China, *Quarterly J. of Econ.*

Kuo, Shirley W. Y., 1983, *The Taiwan Economy in Transition*, Boulder: Westview Press.

Li, K. T., 1976, *The Experience of Dynamic Economic Growth in Taiwan*, New York: Mei Ya Publications.

Lin, Justin Y. F., 1988, The household responsibility system in China's agricultural reform: A theoretical and empirical study, *Economic Development and Cultural Change*, S199–S224.

Scott, Maurice, 1979, Foreign trade, in Walter Galenson, ed., *Economic Growth and Structural Change in Taiwan*, Ithaca, NY: Cornell University Press.

Statistical Yearbook of China 1991, Beijing: State Statistics Bureau.

Statistical Yearbook of Republic of China, Taipei: Directorate-General of Budget, Accounting and Statistics, Executive Yuan.

Survey of Current Business, Washington, DC: U.S. Dept. of Commerce, Bureau of Business Economics.

Tsiang, S. C., 1980, Exchange rate, interest rate, and economic development, in L. R. Klein, M. Nerlove and S. C. Tsiang, eds., *Quantitative Economics and Development*, New York: Academic Press, pp. 309–346.

Vogel, Ezra, 1989, *One Step Ahead: Guangdong Under Reform*, Cambridge, MA: Harvard University Press.

CHAPTER 9

CAN CHINA AVOID SERIOUS INFLATION IN THE 1990S?*

I feel honored to be the speaker of this event which is sponsored by Lingnan College and the Hong Kong Economic Association. I was a primary school student of Lingnan at Stubbs Road — before the Japanese attacked Pearl Harbor and Hong Kong in December 1941 — and received a first rate education there. The Hong Kong Economic Association has been active in recent years to promote friendship as well as scholarship among economists in Hong Kong. I would like to thank all of you for coming here this evening to share with me our common concern about possible inflation in China.

Can China avoid serious inflation in the 1990s? This is an important question for all of us concerned with the economic future of China because inflation can destroy the economic fabric of a society and hinder economic development. If it is serious enough, inflation can even destroy the political order of a country. Some people, including my former colleague, the late Professor Ta-chung Liu, have attributed the downfall of the government of the Republic of China in the Mainland in 1949 to hyperinflation resulting from mismanagement of monetary policy.

To answer this question, let us first consider what causes inflation. We then examine whether the Chinese political situation as of the 1990s is likely to generate the sources of inflation. As an economist, I can answer the first part of the question clearly and definitely. The second question depends on political judgment to which people may disagree. I will give reasons for arriving at my judgment. The answer is less definite than for the first part of the question, but a qualified answer is the best I can offer.

Inflation means rapid increase in the general price level. The price level can be measured by a price index which is an average of the prices of many commodities at a given time, as compared with a similar average at a base period. Two commonly

*Paper delivered in Hong Kong on January 12, 1994 in a lecture sponsored by Lingnan College and the Hong Kong Economic Association. The author would like to thank Paula K. Chow for helpful comments on an earlier draft, but has not succeeded in taking all her valuable criticisms into account in the revision.

used general price indices in the United States are the consumer price index (CPI) and the Gross National Product (GNP) deflator. The former is the average price of a standard bundle of consumer goods used by a typical household. It measures how the monetary cost of living of such households changes. The latter is an average of the prices of all commodities (including producer goods as well as consumer goods) and services that are produced by an economy in a given period. Its increase provides a broader definition of inflation than the increase in the CPI. Chinese official statistics as reported in the *Statistical Yearbook of China* include an index of the cost of living for staff and workers (similar in concept to a CPI for families of urban workers) and an index of retail prices (which differs from the GNP deflator by including the prices of only those goods traded in retail markets).

Since price is an exchange rate between units of money and units of a physical commodity or a service, prices would rise if there are more units of money chasing after (offered to buy) the same quantities of physical commodities and services. Let M be the total quantity of money in circulation (measured narrowly by the quantity of currency and demand deposits in commercial banks in the United States, and simply by the quantity of currency in China before checks drawn on bank deposits became widely used). Let y be the total quantity of all goods produced and offered for sale in the market during a year, each weighted by its price at the base period chosen in the construction of the output index y. The ratio M/y is the most important factor explaining a general price index P.

When I make the above statement about the relation between the ratio M/y and P, I can cite not only economic theory (supported by plenty of experiences of many countries) but also historical data of China itself after 1949. I have carried out a statistical study of the relation between M/y and P in the period 1952–1984 and found the relation capable of explaining the Chinese historical experiences. See G. C. Chow, "Money and price level determination in China", *J. of Comparative Economics*, **11** (1987), 319–333. To cite the first important episode reported in that study, in 1961 the retail price index (with 1950=100) increased to 147.0 from 126.5 in 1960. The main reason is that M/y increased rapidly because of the decrease in national output y in the denominator from 121.6 billion yuan in 1960 to 83.9 billion in 1961 as a result of the economic collapse following the Great Leap Forward Movement beginning in 1958. As a second episode inflation occurred in 1985, with the retail price index increased to 174.1 from 160.0 in 1984. We note the increase in currency in circulation M was 50% during the year 1984. Thirdly, somewhat more serious inflation occurred in 1988, at an annual rate of 18 percent during the entire year but reached some 30 percent per year in the fall of that year. In the meantime M increased by 48 percent during the year 1988. A similar situation occurred in the late spring of 1993, with the price index and the quantity of money both increasing rapidly. According to preliminary estimates, the annual inflation rate in the spring of 1993 was about 20 percent while the rates of increase in money supply were about 32 percent in 1992 and 35 percent in 1993 respectively. Vice Premier Zhu Rongji was appointed the head of People's Bank in June, 1993, in order to control the expansion of money and credit.

In order to understand why money supply sometimes increased excessively, let us consider the experience in 1984 which witnessed the first episode, since economic reforms had began in 1978, that currency in circulation in China increased at a rate much greater than the output. The 50 percent increase in money supply during 1984 was due to two factors. The first is the automatic tendency for Chinese banks to overextend credits under existing banking institutions. Before economic reforms, People's Bank played a passive role in the supply of money as it extended amount of credit to enterprises which were authorized by the economic planning authorities. After the reforms in the early 1980s, state enterprises were given some autonomy in production decisions and in profit retention. In January 1984 the People's Bank officially became a central bank while the specialized banks for agriculture, industry, commerce, construction, foreign trade, and investment under its control were given autonomy to extend credit to enterprises. For a discussion of the institutional change in the Chinese banking system see Gang Yi, "The money supply mechanism and monetary policy in China," *Journal of Asian Economics*, **3:2** (1992), pp. 217–238. Once given autonomy, these banks were under pressure from provincial and local government officials (some having influence over the appointments of bank managers) to extend credit in order to promote economic growth in their own regions. The bank managers themselves wanted to foster economic growth of their own regions, to supply credits to enterprise managers friendly to them, and to make profits for their own banks. After the credits are extended, the People's Bank was obliged to issue money to honour the payments resulting from the use of credits. Secondly, the existing mechanism of monetary control is imperfect and the central government which has influence over the People's Bank could fail to exercise the control required to counteract the natural tendency for local banks to extend credits as just described. These two factors also accounted for the inflation of 1988 and 1993.

The above historical experiences suggest that to control inflation, the government must control the increase in money supply. The question is whether the Chinese government is determined to and able to control money supply in China. The monetary explanation of inflation has been questioned by some economists who claim that money supply itself is not the ultimate cause. For example, the need to print money to finance government deficits by the Nationalist government in the 1940s is said to be the ultimate cause. Also, political pressure to bank managers as part of the first factor explaining the increase in money supply in China can be said to be an ultimate cause. But most economists agree that without going through the increase in money supply the other causes cannot generate inflation. Let us look again at the historical record and see if historical experiences can provide a guide to forecast the events in the rest of the 1990s. By historical record, I refer to both published information as well as observations from personal experiences which I obtained through working with Chinese government officials. Therefore part of the following account will be based on personal experiences.

From the historical record, we have observed that the Chinese government had a genuine desire to and was able (though not without flaws) to control inflation caused by excessive increases in money and credit. Consider in turn the experiences of 1985, 1988 and 1993. In the summers of 1984 and 1985, I was in Beijing conducting workshops on microeconomic and macroeconomic respectively which were sponsored by the Chinese Ministry of Education (becoming State Education Commission in 1985). While in China I observed that the Chinese government, then headed by Premier Zhao Ziyang, was seriously concerned about macroeconomic policy and about possible inflation. When I met Premier Zhao on July 5, 1984, during the microeconomic workshop, he asked me why the workshop was not on macroeconomics instead. My reply was that macroeconomics was planned for the summer of 1985. Besides, many of us in the economics profession believe that microeconomics can serve as the foundation of macroeconomics and should be learned first; I teach macroeconomics using the tools first developed in microeconomics. Premier Zhao believed that macroeconomics was very important for China. Later I discovered that the term macroeconomics means somewhat different things to the Premier and to me, but the desire of Premier Zhao to exercise control of the macroeconomy including inflation is unquestionable. This attitude of Chinese government leaders has prevailed through today as witnessed by the decision of the Third Plenary Session of the Fourteenth Congress of the Chinese Communist Party on November 11 to 14, 1993 to make reforming central banking and macroeconomic management one of the most important tasks for economic reform (the other two being the reforms of the tax system and of management and ownership of state enterprises).

In the summer of 1985, soon after I arrived in Beijing for the macroeconomics workshop, I received word from two economic staff members of Premier Zhao's office that the Premier would like to have a study of the effect of the rapid increase in money supply in 1984 on inflation in 1985 and afterwards. I used the opportunity of the macroeconomics workshop conducted at the People's University to discuss this problem with the students. I suggested how macroeconomic analysis and econometric methods can be applied to provide an answer to the inflation question, and presented a preliminary study in class, pointing out its possible shortcomings. This was in fact a preliminary version of my paper on price level determination in China (see Chapter 18). When Premier Zhao greeted me at his dinner party on July 15, 1985 his first remark was that he had received report of my preliminary estimate that inflation in 1985 was not likely to be above 9 percent, and he was somewhat relieved by it. Evidence reported below suggests that the concern to prevent inflation persists until today, including the appointment of Vice Premier Zhu to head the Central Bank and the Decision of the Fourteenth Congress of the Communist Party in 1993 to reform macro-management.

In August 1985, I wrote to Premier Zhao in reply to his suggestion made at the dinner party in July that I invite some overseas economists to work on economic reform. His response was the letter included in the Appendix. Translated into English, the text of the letter reads:

Your letter of August 13 has been received. Thank you.

Three problems mentioned in your letter, namely (1) establishment of a sound banking system, (2) money markets and stocks and bonds of enterprises, (3) the supply and control of foreign exchange, I believe can all in principle be discussed in a gathering of overseas and local scholars. Concerning this matter, please get in touch with Vice Chairman An Ziwen of the Commission for Restructuring the Economic System [with Premier Zhao as Chairman] and Vice President Liu Hongru of the People's Bank.

This is to reply. Also to wish you good health.

It is interesting to note that in my letter of August 13 I mentioned first the reform of state enterprises, but in his reply the Premier placed the establishment of a sound banking system first. This is similar to his wish to have macroeconomic management taught at the summer workshop first, before microeconomics. At the subsequent 4-day meeting with An Ziwen, Liu Hongru and several of the economic reform officials from Beijing which took place in Hong Kong on January 15–18, 1986, the above three problems were indeed discussed. According to written record, the reform of the banking system and the stability of the price level were treated as a very important topic not only in this Hong Kong meeting but also in our Beijing meeting on June 26 to 30, 1986, in which overseas economists John Fei, Anthony Koo, and Lawrence Lau also participated.

In the autumn of 1988 when inflation became serious, the government tried to restrict the increase in money and credit by assigning credit quotas to banks in different regions and provinces. In addition interest rates on bank deposits were raised to attract deposits and to reduce the quantity of money in circulation, thus making the price level lower than otherwise. Although administrative means such as the assignment of credit quotas to banks were employed because of the absence of a modern banking system for monetary control by economic means, the Chinese officials did use some economic tools such as raising interest rates to control inflation. Other overseas economists and I met with An Ziwen, Liu Hongru and a few other reform officials again in Hong Kong for three days in March 1989. The most important topic of discussion was inflation but we covered topics of economics reform as well.

The main points of our meeting were reported at a dinner party at the Lee Garden Hotel on March 16, 1989 hosted by the late J. K. Lee, former Chairman of the Board of Directors of the Lingnan Education Organization who contributed a great deal to financing Lingnan College. Guests included Edward Chen (of Hong Kong University), Hin-kwong Chiu, Allen Lee, Fook-shiu Li, Shiu-kit Ngai, Maria Tam, C. H. Tung, Philip Wong, Gordon Wu and James T. Wu. Economists reporting on results of the meeting with Chinese reform officials included S. C.

Tsiang, Anthony Koo, John Fei, Lawrence Lau and myself. I remember making the forecast at the dinner party that within a year from March 1988, inflation would be under control because effective means to control inflation would be applied by the Chinese government. Some guests at the party disagreed with me. Anthony Koo supported my forecast, which later turned out to be correct. Some people might attribute the slowing down of inflation later in 1989 partly to the reduction of demand (by foreign investors, for example) after the tragic event in Tiananmen Square on June 4. Others might consider Tiananmen contributory to inflation. While I was confident about the ability of the Chinese government to control inflation, Milton Friedman was forecasting economic chaos and high inflation soon after the event of Tiananmen Square. See his article in the *San Francisco Chronicle*, June 22, 1989, reprinted in *Friedman in China* (Hong Kong: The Chinese University Press, 1990).[a]

Regarding the third inflation episode in late spring 1993, the experience was so recent that all of us can remember very well. Administrative and economic means (controlling credit amounts of regional banks and raising interest rates) similar to those used in the 1988–89 episode were applied. A strong and reputable administrator in the person of Zhu Rongji was appointed to head the People's Bank. Inflation did slow down in July soon after the appointment, as witnessed by the swap exchange rate in Shanghai dropping from about 13.5 Chinese Renminbi (RMB) per U.S. dollar to about 8.5 per dollar. This exchange rate is a rough measure of the general price level in China. The fact that the rate has not returned to its high point of 13.5 for half a year by now is a sign that the control of credit has been partly successful.

In summary, historical records on the policies to deal with inflation in 1985, 1988 and 1993 show that the Chinese government was able to control inflation each time. The question is, will the Chinese government continue to do so in the future, at least in the remaining years of the 1990s. My answer is a qualified yes, subject to some uncertainty.

The qualified positive answer is based on the two important observations that Chinese government leaders take inflation seriously, as documented above by public as well as personal information, and that they have successfully applied the means at their disposal (however imperfectly) to stop inflation in three historical episodes. Government officials do change, but they have all been concerned about inflation. My most recent encounter is a meeting with Chairman Li Tieying of the Commission on Restructuring the Economic System on July 19, 1993 in which

---

[a] After receiving a copy of the book, I wrote to Friedman on January 22, 1991, pointing out that: "Perhaps your Chapter 10 written on June 22, 1989, might be slightly too pessimistic, especially your remarks on p. 143 concerning the future." Friedman's reply of February 7 was quite admirable, stating in part: "Re your letter of January 22, you are entirely right that the column I wrote in 1989 shortly after Tiananmen Square was not 'slightly' but much too pessimistic, especially my predictions about inflation. That is certainly not one of my better predictions and it should teach me not to predict where my knowledge is as limited as it is about China."

he included monetary reform and price stability as a most important task. Recall also the November 1993 Decision of the Fourteenth Congress of the Communist Party on reform of the banking system mentioned above. The qualification in my answer is due to two factors. First, because of recent decentralization of economic and political power (the latter including the transfer of revenue sources from the central to the provincial governments), the People's Bank might loose some of its power of administrative and economic control. Hence effective control of money and credit might become difficult to achieve. Although some might hope that the institutional reform of the monetary system stressed in the November 1993 decision of the Community Party Congress would improve the ability of the People's Bank to exercise control, such institutional reforms take time and are unlikely to yield significant improvements on monetary control in the 1990s. Second, government leaders might yield to political pressure to stimulate rapid growth. For instance, in November 1993 when Deng Xiaoping stated that rapid growth should be the country's policy objective, some officials might have interpreted the statement to mean increasing credit rapidly to promote growth. To an economist, this interpretation of Deng's objective is incorrect. Serious inflation will destroy economic and perhaps even political order and thus hinder rather than promote economic growth. We understand that monetary stimulation can be successful only if applied occasionally and under the environment of a stable price level. As Milton Friedman has put the point aptly by an analogy. Increasing money supply to an economy is like feeding alcoholic drinks to a person. A small quantity used when the economy or the person is in a normal and stable condition does sometimes help to stimulate, but continued usage of a large quantity will lead to malfunctioning and collapse. I hope that most Chinese government officials appreciate this point.

中华人民共和国国务院

邹至庄教授：

　　八月十三日来信收到，谢谢。

　　信中提出的三个问题，即（1）建立健全的银行制度问题，（2）金融市场和企业的股票债券问题，（3）外汇的供给和控制问题，我认为原则上都可以邀集海内外学者共同研讨。有关事宜，请与国家经济体制改革委员会安志文副主任和中国人民银行刘鸿儒副行长联系。

　　此复。顺颂

大安！

一九八五年八月二十四日

Part III
Data and Tools of Analysis

CHAPTER 10

CHINESE STATISTICS*†

This article points out that the development of statistics in China is a part of the modernization process. It reviews the scope and the quality of Chinese statistics and discusses the statistics of consumption and national income in particular. The future prospects of Chinese statistics are also indicated.

10.1. Introduction

The Chinese economy has changed more rapidly in the early 1980s than any informed observer in 1976 could have imagined. Examples of the change include: the introduction of the responsibility system in agriculture, which essentially redistributed land to the individual farm households and permitted them to sell their products in the market after paying certain quantities of the products to the commune; reforms in state-owned enterprises, which allowed managers some autonomy in the production of outputs, the procurement of inputs, and the use of retained profits for investment and distribution to workers, encouragement of individually and collectively owned enterprises; expansion of rural and urban markets; rapid increase in foreign trade; inducement of foreign investment, including not only joint ventures but entirely foreign-owned enterprises in special economic zones and in certain large cities; and large-scale importing of modern technology and management training. On October 20, 1984, the Central Committee of the Chinese Communist Party announced further reforms to promote autonomy of state enterprises and decontrol prices. These changes were made to achieve modernization. One important aspect of modernization is the change in the collection, use, and dissemination of statistics. Chinese economic statistics were guarded as secrets for two decades up to the end of the 1970s. The sudden release of many official statistics in 1980 was as surprising to an informed observer as some of the aforementioned changes.

When I visited China in the summer of 1980 as a guest of the Chinese Academy of Social Sciences, I tried to find some published facts and data about the Chinese economy. Searching in bookstores in several cities and libraries at several major

*Originally published in *The American Statistician*, vol. 40, no. 3 (August 1986), pp. 191–196.
†This research was supported by National Science Foundation Grant SES-8012582. The author is grateful to a referee and an associate editor for helpful comments.

universities, I found none. My colleagues in China told me that there was simply no published material on how the Chinese economy actually functioned. In October 1980, after returning to the United States, I received a copy of *Survey of the First Lathe Factory of Beijing* from its senior author Ma Hong (then Vice President and later President of the Chinese Academy of Social Sciences). This volume was prepared and written by a survey team in 1961 but not published until 1980. Its publication signifies the change in government policy to publish facts and data about the Chinese economy. In 1981–1982 we witnessed the publication of three important statistical yearbooks, *Agricultural Yearbook of China* (Ministry of Agriculture 1981), *Almanac of China's Economy* (Economic Research Center 1982), and *Statistical Yearbook of China* (State Statistical Bureau 1982).

In this article, I will comment on the scope of Chinese official statistics (Sec. 2), their quality (Sec. 3), what the statistics on consumption and income reveal (Sec. 4), and the future development of statistics in China (Sec. 5).

10.2. Scope

Let me start with the *Statistical Yearbook of China 1984* (State Statistical Bureau 1985). Table 1 is abstracted from a table of the same title in the *Yearbook* (pp. 12–15). It conveys the coverage and some important statistics concerning the Chinese economy. The sections of the *Yearbook* follow closely the sections of Table 1.

Among the important data available in the Chinese State Statistical Bureau but only partially revealed in the *Statistical Yearbook*, mention should be made of the population data and the family budget data. The Chinese government conducted censuses of the population in the years 1953, 1964, and 1982. A major census and a major fertility survey were conducted in 1982 with technical assistance from the United Nations. More and more of these data have been made available to foreign scholars. Coale (1984) is an analysis of these data. A computer tape containing the 1982 census and survey data was made available in 1985 to scholars in the East–West Center in Hawaii who were collaborating with Chinese scholars in demographic research. More research results on Chinese population are forthcoming. Since the 1950s, the Chinese government has collected surveys of income and expenditures from several thousand households of staff and workers in the cities and from more than 30,000 farm households [see *Statistical Yearbook 1984* (State Statistical Bureau 1985), pp. 462–471 for some details]. These data have not been adequately analyzed. I have explored with officials of the Chinese State Statistical Bureau means for organizing and releasing some of these data for research by Chinese and foreign scholars.

Besides the three yearbooks mentioned here, official economic data can be found in newspapers, including *People's Daily* (*Renmin Ribao*) and *Economics Daily* (*Jinji Ribao*) numerous journals published by universities, research institutions, and professional organizations, and weekly or monthly periodicals, including *Market Reports*, (*Shichang Bao*) in particular, which contains information on prices and other market and economic information. Since 1980 the proliferation of journals related to economics has been astounding. More and more space in these journals is devoted

Table 1. Main Indicators of the Chinese Economy

Item	Unit	1952	1957	1965	1978	1983
Population						
Year-end population	10 thousand	57,482	64,653	72,538	96,259	102,495
Labor force employed in economy (year-end)	10 thousand person	20,729	23,771	28,670	39,856	46,004
Of which: staff and workers	10 thousand person	1,603	3,101	4,965	9,499	11,515
Index of total product of society (1952 = 100)	%	100.0	170.9	258.2	725.8	1,074.6
Of which: index of gross output value of agriculture and industry (1952 = 100)	%	100.0	167.8	268.3	779.0	1,138.5
National income						
Index of national income (1952 = 100)	%	100.0	153.0	197.5	453.2	639.4
Accumulation rate	%	21.4	24.9	27.1	36.5	30.0
Agricultural production						
Index of gross agricultural output value (1952 = 100)	%	100.0	124.8	137.1	229.6	335.9
Output of major farm products						
Grain	10 thousand tons	16,392	19,505	19,453	30,477	38,728
Cotton	10 thousand tons	130.4	164.0	209.8	216.7	463.7
Oil-bearing crops	10 thousand tons	419.3	419.6	362.5	521.8	1,055.0
Afforested area	10 thousand hectares	108.5	435.5	342.6	449.6	632.4
Pork, beef, and mutton	10 thousand tons	338.5	398.5	551.0	856.3	1,402.1
Industrial production						
Index of gross industrial output value (1952 = 100)	%	100.0	228.6	452.9	1,601.6	2,340.1
Light industry	%	100.0	183.2	344.7	970.6	1,651.2
Heavy industry	%	100.0	310.7	651.0	2,780.4	3,571.3
Output of major industrial products						
Cloth	100 million meters	38.3	50.5	62.8	110.3	148.8
Bicycles	10 thousand	8.0	80.6	183.8	854.0	2,758.2
Sewing machines	10 thousand	6.6	27.8	123.8	486.5	1,087.2
Wrist watches	10 thousand			.04	100.8	1,351.1	3,469.0
Coal	100 million tons	.66	1.31	2.32	6.18	7.15
Crude oil	10 thousand tons	44	146	1,131	10,405	10,607
Electricity	100 million kwh	73	193	676	2,566	3,514
Steel	10 thousand tons	135	535	1,223	3,178	4,002
Index of overall labor productivity of state-owned independent accounting industrial enterprises (1952 = 100)	%	100.0	152.1	214.6	266.0	311.9
Principal financial items of state-owned independent accounting industrial enterprises						
Original value of fixed assets (year-end)	Rmb 100 million	148.8	334.6	1,040.0	3,193.4	4,767.8
Total fund	Rmb 100 million	146.8	330.3	1,037.3	3,273.0	4,452.5
Net value of fixed assets (year-end)	Rmb 100 million	100.8	239.8	777.2	2,225.7	3,161.0
Quota circulating fund	Rmb 100 million	46.0	90.5	260.1	1,047.3	1,291.5
Profits and taxes	Rmb 100 million	37.4	115.1	309.2	790.7	1,032.8
Transport, posts, and telecommunications						
Volume of freight traffic	100 million ton-km	762	1,810	3,463	9,829	14,044
Railways	100 million ton-km	602	1,346	2,698	5,345	6,646
Highways	100 million ton-km	14	48	95	274	1,084
Waterways	100 million ton-km	146	416	670	3,779	5,788
Civil aviation	100 million ton-km		.1	.3	1.0	2.3
Volume of passenger traffic	100 million person-km	248.4	496.3	697.1	1,743	3,095
Railways	100 million person-km	201	361	479	1,093	1,776
Highways	100 million person-km	22.7	88.1	168.2	521	1,106
Waterways	100 million person-km	24.5	46.4	47.4	101	154
Civil aviation	100 million person-km	.2	.8	2.5	28	59
Cargo handled at principal seaports	10 thousand tons	1,440	3,727	7,181	19,834	24,952
Service revenue of posts and telecommunications	Rmb 100 million	1.64	2.94	6.28	11.65	22.26
Letters delivered	100 million	8.09	16.41	21.76	28.35	35.21
Newspapers and magazines circulated	10 thousand copies	1,363	3,264	5,621	11,250	22,933
Investment in fixed assets of state-owned units						
Total investment in fixed assets	Rmb 100 million	43.56	151.23	216.90	668.72	951.96
Of which: investment in capital construction	Rmb 100 million	43.56	143.32	179.61	500.99	594.13
Newly increased fixed assets through capital construction	Rmb 100 million	31.14	133.92	168.09	372.30	453.10
Rate of fixed assets turned over to use	%	71.5	93.4	93.6	74.3	76.3
Index of overall labor productivity of state-owned constructing units (1952 = 100)	%	100.0	123.8	133.5	173.6	241.3
Domestic trade						
Total value of retail sales	Rmb 100 million	276.8	474.2	670.3	1,558.6	2,849.4
Volume of retail sales of major commodities						
Grain	10 thousand tons	2,961	3,724	3,682	4,750	7,095.0
Bicycles	10 thousand	33.5	84.7	176.2	809.6	2,620.7

Table 1. (continued)

Item	Unit	1952	1957	1965	1978	1983
Foreign trade						
Total value of exports and imports	Rmb 100 million	64.6	104.5	118.4	355.1	860.1
Exports	Rmb 100 million	27.1	54.5	63.1	167.7	438.3
Imports	Rmb 100 million	37.5	50.0	55.3	187.4	421.8
Public finance						
Revenue	Rmb 100 million	183.7	310.2	473.3	1,121.1	1,249.0
Expenditure	Rmb 100 million	176.0	304.2	466.3	1,111.0	1,292.5
Price indexes						
General index of purchasing prices of farm and sideline products	%	100.0	120.2	154.5	178.8	264.2
General index of retail prices	%	100.0	108.5	120.4	121.6	139.3
General index of cost-of-living prices of staff and workers	%	100.0	109.6	120.3	125.3	146.3
Wages of staff and workers						
Average annual wage of staff and workers in state-owned units	Rmb	446	637	652	644	865
Education and culture						
Students enrolled in institutions of higher learning	10 thousand	19.1	44.1	67.4	85.6	120.7
Students enrolled in secondary specialized schools	10 thousand	63.6	77.8	54.7	88.9	114.3
Students enrolled in regular secondary schools	10 thousand	249.0	628.1	933.8	6,548.3	4,397.7
Students enrolled in primary schools	10 thousand	5,110	6,428	11,621	14,624	13,578
Public health						
Hospital beds	10 thousand	16.0	29.5	76.6	185.6	211.0
Professional medical personnel	10 thousand	69.0	103.9	153.2	246.4	325.3
Of which: doctors	10 thousand	42.5	54.7	76.3	103.3	135.3

Source: State Statistical Bureau (1985, pp. 12–15). Reprinted by permission of Economic Information & Agency, Hong Kong.

to economic analysis of actual problems in China rather than to economic ideology. A list of economic periodicals can be found in Sec. 2 of the appendix to *Almanac of China's Economy, 1984* (Economic Research Center 1984). Furthermore, provincial almanacs are also available, including those issued by Beijing, Shanghai, Tianjin, Guangzhou, Jiangsu, Liaoning, Anhui, Hunan, and Shanxi.

In spite of the large increase in economic statistics now available, the scope of the coverage is still limited. For example, the national income data available are far from being as detailed as those provided by the United States Department of Commerce in its *Survey of Current Business*. The *Statistical Yearbook of China* is much less complete in coverage than the *Statistical Abstract* of the United States. Two reasons account for the paucity of published economic statistics in China compared with what is available in an economically advanced economy. First, partly because of the Cultural Revolution, the collection of statistics is underdeveloped and many important data are simply not available. Second, among the available data, some are classified as state secrets and not made available to the public. For example, several institutions in China, including the Academy of Social Sciences, have constructed input–output tables, but these tables are regarded as confidential material.

10.3. Quality

In discussing the quality of statistics from China, I am unable to provide quantitative measurements of the errors in particular statistical series and will confine myself to inferences from such characteristics as sources of data and quality of personnel. The quality of particular statistical series will depend on the circumstances in which they are constructed. Several factors in the collection of Chinese statistics will affect their quality. First, as of the early or middle 1980s, both the quantity and the quality of the technical personnel engaged in the collection of statistics are limited. The State Statistical Bureau in the State Council (or executive branch) of the Chinese government is responsible for directing all activities in connection with the collection, storage, and distribution of statistics. Technical personnel working in this bureau and all of its supporting units at provincial and county levels are in short supply, affecting the quality of some statistical series. Few of these people are trained in statistical sampling methods. Second, on the positive side, the Chinese government has tighter control over its population down to the level of street blocks and families. The local units of the Chinese Communist Party and the Chinese government can extract information from the population in ways that cannot be done by the federal, state, and local governments of the United States or by private information-gathering agencies. Third, in the past, especially during the period of the Great Leap Forward, there were political pressures to falsify statistics. For example, rural communes, which had unrealistic production targets to fulfill, often overstated their outputs. Industrial enterprises might count as their output those products that could not be used. Political pressures still exist today in some areas. For example, the movement to promote one-child families has led to some killing of female infants. Reports only show much smaller numbers of female births than male births. *People's Daily*, April 7, 1983, reports that in 1981 the percentage of female births in Huaiyuan County in Anhui Province was only 41.8%; in four selected communes in this county, the percentages were 24.8, 36.5, 37.2 and 42.5 out of total births of 133, 104, 231, and 285, respectively. It is my judgment, to be justified forthwith, that by and large Chinese statistics officials are honest. They would make an attempt to correct the data when false reporting is easily detected.

My judgment concerning the honesty of Chinese statistical officials is based on personal contact, internal statistical evidence, and an announced government policy. I have spent most of the summers of 1980, 1982, 1984, and 1985 in China meeting and working with officials at different levels from various parts of the government, universities, and the Chinese Academy of Social Sciences. The problems involved include economic reform, economic education, promotion of research, and the improvement of economic statistics. I spent countless hours with officials from the State Statistical Bureau, the State Commission on Education (formerly the Ministry of Education), the State Planning Commission, the Economic Reform Commission, several Economic Research Centers at the State Council, several provincial and municipal governments, and many universities. In the 1980s, the Chinese government has placed educated and well-meaning people in responsible positions. This statement can be verified only by foreigners who have had extensive contacts with them.

From internal evidence, let me cite several examples. In *Almanac of China's Economy, 1981* (Economic Research Center 1982) footnote 2 accompanying the table on population and natural resources states that "cultivated land acreage may be underestimated, awaiting confirmation by further survey" (p. VI-3). As communes had to surrender farm outputs at fixed, below-market prices to government purchasing departments according to cultivated land acreage, there was an incentive for the communes to underreport land acreage. The previously quoted footnote shows an awareness of this and an attempt to correct the error. I have mentioned the honest reporting of deaths of female infants. *Statistical Yearbook, 1984* (State Statistical Bureau 1985, pp. 30 and 83) shows a drop in national income in constant prices from 199.2 in 1960 to 130.9 in 1962 and an increase in the death rate from 10.80 (per thousand) in 1958 to 25.43 in 1960. Both facts are honest reporting of the economic catastrophe of the Great Leap Forward. Third, as will be pointed out in Sec. 5, honest statistical reporting is required by a new law and failure to comply is subject to punishment. It is the policy of the Chinese government to improve the quality of its statistics. The State Statistical Bureau has sought the collaboration of the American Statistical Association (ASA) to train statisticians in China by upgrading the statistics curriculum at major Chinese universities. George Tiao of the University of Chicago is assisting ASA in this activity.

From the aforementioned considerations, one can conclude that if a certain statistical series does not require much technical sophistication in its collection and is not likely to be subject to false reporting under political pressure, it is less likely to be in error. In this category I would include data such as the numbers of economic units, including communes (and brigades and work teams within communes), state-owned and collectively owned enterprises, numbers of employees of different types, total wage bill and average wage per worker, numbers of educational institutions and student enrollments at different levels, numbers of health-care units and different medical personnel, and mileages of railroad trunks and waterways. Construction of price indexes requires more sophistication in the selection of the commodities to be included and in designing a set of weights for the individual components that may be changing through time.

Similarly, any statistics in constant prices requiring adjustment by appropriate price indexes may be subject to question. These statistics include national income in constant 1952 prices and consumption in constant prices. Income, consumption, and production data during the worst years, 1961–1962, following the Great Leap Forward may be subject to a larger margin of error than in other years. Data on Chinese population obtained from the 1982 census are probably reliable because of the special attention given to them by the Chinese government and the technical assistance from the United Nations in their collection and tabulation. Coale (1984) pointed out that although marriage rates and birth rates by ages of women reported by Chinese official sources are very accurate, official data on birth and death rates have understated the true numbers by a considerable margin.

One element that affects the quality of some Chinese economic statistics from the viewpoint of the user is the incomplete description of the method of construction. Examples are price indexes and indexes of national income in constant prices of selected years. Documentation and description of sources and methods of construction for national income data are much less detailed than can be found in the statistical appendixes of the "National Income" issues of the *Survey of Current Business*. The poor standard of documentation is one aspect of the underdeveloped state of statistical work in China. In addition, detailed documentation of certain statistical series may reveal information regarded as confidential by the Chinese government.

10.4. Statistics of Consumption and National Income

In spite of the limitations of Chinese economic data both in scope and in quality, much has been revealed by the data made available since 1980. I will discuss briefly the trends of consumption and income in the last three decades.

There were some disagreements among observers of the Chinese scene concerning the improvement in living standards since 1949. The published data have revealed a clear picture. Let us consider in turn the trends in per capita consumption for the urban and rural populations, the latter being about 85% of the total. According to Chinese official data, the real wage of all state-owned enterprises in China in 1975 was some 13% lower than in 1957. Average annual wage was 637 yuan in 1957 and 613 yuan in 1975, as reported in *Statistical Yearbook of China 1981* (State Statistical Bureau 1982, pp. 435–436). Deflated by the cost-of-living index of staff and workers, which equals 126.6 for 1957 and 139.5 for 1975 (State Statistical Bureau 1982, pp. 411–412), the annual wage became 503 and 439, respectively, in 1950 prices. According to *Almanac of China's Economy, 1981* (Economic Research Center 1982, p. 895), however, private consumption per capita of the nonagricultural population increased from 126.3 in 1957 to 181.1 in 1975, or by about 43%, in spite of the decline in the real wage rate. The explanation is that the proportion of urban population employed increased during this period, mainly because of increasing participation of women. Rawski (1980, pp. 29–30) reported that the ratio of employed to total urban population was about 33% in 1957 and it rose to about 50% in 1975. The increase from 33% to 50% of urban population employed would by itself raise the wage income per capita by a factor of 50/33, or 51.5%. From 1957 to 1975, average real wages decreased from 503 to 439 yuan in 1950 prices. These two factors combined yield a factor of $(50/33) \times (439/503)$, or 1.32, for the ratio of real wage per capita for the urban population between 1975 and 1957. This figure is not far from the increase of 43% in nonagricultural per capita consumption reported in *Almanac of China's Economy, 1981*.

An official index of per capita private consumption of all peasants shows an increase from 117.1 in 1957 to 143.1 in 1975, or about 22% (Economic Research Center 1982, p. 895). Thus the improvement of consumption per capita from 1957 to 1975 was only moderate, being somewhat larger in urban areas than in rural areas as a result of an increased percentage of the urban population being employed.

Concerning the trend of national income, Chinese official data (State Statistical Bureau 1982, p. 20) show that an index of national income in 1952 prices increased from 100 in 1952 to 510.1 in 1981, or to an average annual rate of about

6.0%. In 1952 the ratio of the price of industrial products to the price of agricultural products was about three times as high as in 1980. With 1950 as base, the official general ex-factory price index of industrial products declined from 113.2 in 1952 to 83.4 in 1980, whereas the official general purchasing price index of farm and sideline products rose from 121.6 to 284.4 (State Statistical Bureau 1982, pp. 411–412). Therefore, in computing national output in 1952 prices, the relative weight given to industrial output compared with agricultural output is about three times the relative weight applied when 1980 prices are used. Chow (1985a) estimated the annual growth rate of industry to be about 11% and that of agriculture and other sectors to be about 1.9%, using official data. A large weight given to industry can produce a high rate of growth of 6.0% per year. By using 1980 prices and thus giving a small weight to industrial output, one would obtain an average rate of growth in real national income between 1952 and 1980 of 3.9% per year instead of 6.0%. The 3.9% growth rate is more meaningful because the high prices assigned to industrial products in 1952 are arbitrary and because the growth of future real output will be measured by using prices close to 1980 prices. It is interesting to note that, according to the Central Intelligence Agency of the United States (1979), Gross National Product of the People's Republic of China was estimated to be $99 billion in 1952 and $444 billion in 1978, implying an annual growth rate of 5.94%.

Chow (1985a, Chaps. 5 and 6) presented statistical analyses using official data on consumption and income. Cross-section analyses were performed to find out the relations between total consumption expenditures and expenditures on four categories of consumption — food, clothing, housing, and miscellaneous items. A sample survey in 1981 on the expenditure patterns of Chinese peasants was used (State Statistical Bureau 1982, pp. 445–446). The statistical relationships obtained are reasonable. Annual time series data on aggregate consumption and investment were used in Chow (1985b) to construct a very simple econometric model of the Chinese economy. The model is a multiplier–accelerator model consisting of a consumption equation and an investment equation. The consumption equation is consistent with the life-cycle-permanent-income hypothesis as formulated by Hall (1978). The investment equation is consistent with the acceleration principle, which explains aggregate investment expenditures in a given year by the change in national income in that year and investment expenditures of the preceding year. The estimated model appears reasonable. One may conclude that the consumption and investment relations were stable relations for the Chinese economy in spite of the political upheavals of the periods of the Great Leap Forward (1958–1961) and the Cultural Revolution (1966–1976); the model does show larger residuals for some of these years, which measure the effects of the political shocks on the economy. One may also conclude that the Chinese official consumption and income data, by and large, are accurate enough for use in econometric analysis. I have estimated other economic relationships, including a production function in Chow (1985a, p. 123) and an equation explaining the general retail price index by the money supply and real output (unpublished), which show the reasonableness of the official data used.

By further econometric analyses, we will find out more about the quality of Chinese statistics.

10.5. Future of Chinese Statistics

In the early 1980s, the quality and availability of Chinese statistics were subject to rapid changes, as was the Chinese economic system. Ansley Coale of Princeton University, who has been studying Chinese population problems using Chinese official data since 1980, likened the arrival of new sets of Chinese demographic data to the arrival of new personal computers — soon after one has chosen a set for his or her work, a new and better set becomes available. As of 1986, one can expect that the quality and quantity of Chinese statistics will continue to improve for some time, as a part of the modernization process.

It is noteworthy that on December 8, 1983, the third meeting of the Executive Committee of the Sixth National People's Congress of the People's Republic of China (PRC) passed a "Law on Statistics of the PRC." This law was published on page 2 of *People's Daily*, December 10, 1983. Chapter 1 of the law states the general principles, pointing out the purposes of the law: to promote the effective organization of statistical work, to safeguard the accuracy and timeliness of statistical data, and to enhance the use of statistics in understanding the state of the nation and thus guiding China's economic and social development. The functions of statistical work are stated to be to provide statistical data on the country's social and economic conditions, to perform statistical analysis, and to practice statistical supervision. All government, state-owned, collectively owned, and individually owned units must obey this law in providing the necessary statistical information accurately. All statistical work is directed by the State Statistical Bureau of the State Council. Statistical personnel are responsible not only for honest reporting and actively detecting statistical errors of others but also for keeping state secrets.

Chapter 2 of the "Law of Statistics of the PRC" deals with statistical survey planning and the statistical system, delegating responsibilities to the appropriate government agencies at different levels. Chapter 3 is concerned with the administration and dissemination of statistical information, also delegating responsibility to different agencies or units. Chapter 4, on statistical organization and personnel, establishes statistical organizations in the provincial and county levels and specifies their organization and responsibilities. Chapter 5 states the legal responsibilities and punishment of violation of this law, including falsification of statistics, interfering with proper functioning of statistical personnel, and the publication of secret statistical data. In Chapter 6, the appendix, it is pointed out that the State Statistics Bureau can issue orders and rules based on the principles of this law, subject to the approval of the State Council.

The seriousness of the Chinese government in promoting and administering its statistical work is a positive factor in the future development of statistics in China. In China, the direction of statistical activities is more centralized than in the United States. Although ministries of the State Council other than the State Statistical Bureau and many agencies of the provincial and local government collect statistics, the State Statistical Bureau has the responsibility of overall direction and control. One possible shortcoming of central control is the discouragement and, often, prevention of the parallel collection of statistics by independent agencies. For example, the Institute of Economic Research of Nankai University was well known for the price indexes that it compiled in the 1930s and 1940s but had difficulties in compiling similar indexes in the early 1980s as long as official price indexes were available. Perhaps such parallel efforts should not be prohibited.

With the opening of China, the development of Chinese statistics will depend not only on the efforts made in China but on the cooperation and assistance of scholars and statisticians abroad as well. The 1982 population census and fertility survey are outstanding illustrations of this point. The Chinese government has encouraged the World Bank to study its economics development problems and make recommendations by providing the latter with a large quantity of economic data. Two lengthy reports by the World Bank (1983, 1985) resulted. In July 1985, Premier Zhao Ziyang asked me to encourage and invite foreign scholars to study Chinese economic development problems. I responded by suggesting that Chinese economic data be made available in a Data Center to be established at the Chinese People's University for use by foreign as well as Chinese scholars and students. The Premier quickly approved the suggestion. We can look forward to the establishment of this Data Center. Further opening of Chinese data sources and further statistical and econometric analyses of these data by Chinese and foreign scholars, individually or cooperatively, can only help to improve the quality of Chinese statistics in the future.

In summary, statistical activities are a part of China's modernization process. The Chinese government has committed itself to this process, and we can expect to see improved quality and quantity of statistics as a result of government effort. The improvement will also depend on the cooperation and interest of foreign scholars and statisticians.

References

Central Intelligence Agency of the United States, 1979, *China: A Statistical Compendium*, Washington, DC: U.S. Government Printing Office.

Chow, G. C., 1985a, *The Chinese Economy*, New York: Harper & Row; 2nd edn., 1987, Singapore: World Scientific.

———, 1985b, A model of Chinese national income determination, *J. Pol. Econ.* **93**, 782–792.

Coale, A. J., 1984, *Rapid Population Change in China, 1952–1982*, Washington, DC: National Academy Press.

Economic Research Center, State Council of the People's Republic of China, 1982, *Almanac of China's Economy, 1981*, Hong Kong: Modern Cultural Co.

———, 1984, *Almanac of China's Economy, 1984*, Hong Kong: Modern Cultural Co.

Hall, R. E., 1978, Stochastic implications of the life cycle-permanent income hypothesis: Theory and evidence, *J. Pol. Econ.* **86**, 971–987.

Agricultural Yearbook of China 1981, 1982, Ministry of Agriculture, State Council of the People's Republic of China, Beijing: Agricultural Press.

Rawski, T. G., 1980, *Economic Growth and Employment in China*, New York: Oxford University Press.

Statistical Yearbook of China 1981, 1982, State Statistics Bureau, Hong Kong: Hong Kong Economic Review Publishing House.

Statistical Yearbook of China 1984, 1985, State Statistics Bureau, Hong Kong: Economic Information & Agency.

Survey of the First Lathe Factory of Beijing, 1980, prepared by the Survey Team of Beijing's First Lathe Factory, Beijing: Chinese Social Publishing Company.

China: Socialist Economic Development, Vols. 1–3, 1983, Washington, DC: World Bank.

China: Long-Term Issues and Options, Washington, DC: World Bank.

CHAPTER 11

ECONOMIC RESEARCH IN CHINA*

The purpose of this paper is to survey the state of economic research in China as of 1984. Some information contained herein was obtained in the summer of 1984 when the author organized a six-week microeconomics workshop at Peking University on behalf of the Chinese Ministry of Education. This survey may be useful to general readers interested in China, as well as to economists outside China who are interested in research on China and possibly in cooperative research with Chinese economists. To economists in China, an outside view concerning their work and its future prospects might also be of interest. In 1984 the state of economic research is in the process of rapid change, as is the state of the Chinese economic system itself. Where and how fast it will go depends on the actions to be taken by Chinese economists and on the cooperation of economists outside China. It is therefore timely to survey the current state of economic research, to indicate its possible future directions, and to suggest where outside cooperation might be useful.

11.1. State of Economic Science in China

Before discussing economic research, it is necessary to describe the state of economics as a social science in China. Prior to the establishment of the People's Republic of China in 1949, economics as taught at Chinese universities followed mainly the European–American tradition, and most Chinese universities had adopted the essential features of the Euro-American system. In 1956, soon after China had embarked upon the First Five-Year Plan along the Soviet lines, the university system was also modeled after the Soviet Union. Instead of a liberal college education with emphasis on introducing basic ideas and developing methods of thinking, students were given a professional training in a narrow field, with very limited electives from other fields. The universities themselves were reorganized and became more specialized. Engineering colleges and sometimes economics and finance departments were separated from their former universities to become independent institutions. Music schools were also separated, making it difficult for the students in the university to organize a symphony orchestra.

Social sciences were changed more drastically. Sociology and psychology failed to keep up with modern trends and became essentially dormant. Economics became

*Financial support from the International Program of the National Science Foundation through Grant no. INT84-12790 is gratefully acknowledged.

112

predominantly Marxian. Students were expected to find truths about economics mainly by studying the classical works of Marx, Engel, Lenin, Stalin, and Chairman Mao. Much of the economic curriculum was on economic philosophy and ideology. Methods of economic analysis introduced after Marx were ignored. Empirical economic research by faculty members and students virtually disappeared. Students were supposed to know the economic world, past and present, by appealing mainly to Marxian theory, without having to examine the facts carefully. When I visited China in the summer of 1980, I could not find a single empirical study published in China on any aspect of the Chinese economy since the 1950s. The absence of such empirical studies at that time was confirmed by my colleagues at Chinese universities and research institutions.

The abandonment in the middle 1950s of modern post-Marxian economic analysis was sufficient to create a large gap in economic research between China and the outside world. The gap was widened by two additional factors: The Cultural Revolution of 1965–1975, which severely disrupted the Chinese educational system, and the great advances in modern economics in the rest of the world. From September 1966 to February 1972, all universities in China were closed. From February 1972 to autumn of 1976, although universities were open again, admissions were granted by political considerations rather than by scholastic qualifications. Youths from workers' and peasants' families having insufficient academic qualifications were assigned by their units to attend universities. The quality of instruction was below standard. Even after 1978, when admission to a university was based on merit, university professors were still inhibited in their teaching as many of them had been physically and mentally abused during the Cultural Revolution. Furthermore, from 1949 onward, modern economics had greatly advanced in the rest of the world. Economic research in China did not make much progress for three decades while economic science in the rest of the world went many steps forward.

In 1979, there was an important factor influencing the development of economic science and of the economic system in China. From thirty years of experience, Chinese economists and economic planners had learned the shortcomings of centralized economic planning and the inadequacies of Marxian economics as a practical guide to economic development. Chinese economists involved with planning had accumulated much experience on how a centrally planned economy works. The valuable experiences are now documented in books, including Xue Muqiao, *China's Socialist Economy*, Ma Hong and Sun Shangqing, eds., *Zhongguo Jingji Jiegou Wenti Yanjiu* (*Studies of problems of China's economic structure*), and others. Failing to discover adequate answers from Marxian economics to the important and urgent questions of economic planning and development, economists in China are very eager to learn new tools. Xu Dixin, a noted Marxian economic theorist and Vice President of the Chinese Academy of Social Science (CASS), directed the efforts of CASS in academic economic exchanges with the West, inviting a group of American economists to lecture on econometrics in 1980, and initiating the establishment of the Friendship Publishing Company to publish books by outside authors on economics, literature, art, and other social sciences.

In 1979, China began to absorb post-Marxian economic ideas. Economists from the United States and other developed countries have been invited to lecture in China. New courses on capitalist economies have been introduced in universities, as well as courses on management, accounting, statistics and econometrics. Economics books from the west have been translated, including Paul Samuelson's *Economics* and Milton Friedman's *Free to Choose*. Scholars and graduate students from China have been sent abroad to study and do research in economics. By 1984, five years later, economic science has grown rapidly. One witnesses a revival of interest among older economists who were trained in the West before the middle 1950s and the development of new interest among young scholars originally specializing in economics or in other fields, such as engineering and applied mathematics. Some of them have returned from recent studies abroad. Others have learned by attending courses and lectures given in China by visiting economists, or by self-study. By 1984, one can find a small number of economists, perhaps somewhat between 150 and 200, who are familiar with some modern tools of economic analysis and are able to apply them to empirical research.

To summarize the state of economic science in China as of 1984, one can say that there were three decades of stagnation and interruptions up to 1978, and rapid progress since 1979. In 1984, Marxian economics remains the most important part of the economic curriculum at Chinese universities, but post-Marxian modern economics has been introduced to various degrees at different institutions, depending partly on the availability of economics teachers. While Marxian economics is the main subject in departments of political economy, modern economics topics are taught also in departments of world economy, departments of economic management, and departments of system science or operations research. As long as China remains a socialist country, it will draw from Marxian ideas to build a philosophical and intellectual foundation for the society. Marxian writing will be seriously studied at Chinese universities. At the same time, to the extent that modern economics is capable of providing useful tools for understanding the working of the Chinese and other economies, and for planning Chinese economic development, it will also be studied seriously in China and applied to economic research and economic planning. This viewpoint is reflected in the following statement by Party Secretary-General Hu Yaobang in his report to the Twelfth National Congress of the Communist Party of China on September 1, 1982: "We must improve our study and application of economics and scientific business management, and countinuously raise the level of economic planning and administration and the operation and management of enterprises and institutions."

11.2. The State of Economic Research

As the ideas of modern economic analysis were revived and introduced in China, and as teaching and research resumed, the quantity and quality of economic research have changed. A great deal of research output can be found in the newly published journals, numbering over one hundred in 1984. Universities, schools of finance and economics, government research organizations including CASS and its affiliates, the Planning Commission, the Economic Commission and Ministries of the State Council, and professional economic associations (numbering over one hundred) are conducting economic research and publishing economics journals. The *Almanac of China's Economy, 1984*, Chinese edition, pp. XI-15-23, lists 169 "Important" economic journals divided into the following nine categories: (1) Economics and economic management, 55; (2) industrial economics, 34; (3) agricultural economics, 10; (4) financial and commercial economics, 21; (5) technical economics and modern management, 11; (6) finance and accounting , 9; (7) statistics, 3; (8) merchandising and market information, 21; and (9) transportation and communications, 5. Although some of these journals may be closer to trade journals than research journals, all except twenty-five began publication after 1979, showing the rapid growth of economic research since that year.

The subject areas of economic research related to the Chinese economy can be broadly classified under three headings from the viewpoint of modern economic analysis. The first deals with some theoretical issues of the Chinese economy by offering the authors's opinion based on general experience or interpretation of Marxian writings. The second presents some factual analyses of the Chinese economic situation without relying on the tools of modern economics. The third is a piece of economic research using modern, post-Marxian tools of economic analysis.

The first type of research can be illustrated by articles on aspects of the Chinese economic system or possible directions for Chinese economic reform with the authors's recommendations. There are numerous articles offering Marxian views on current Chinese economic issues, such as the role of prices, of markets, of central planning, and of collective and individual enterprises as compared with state-owned enterprises. Many of these articles are attempts by Marxian economists to understand the current Chinese economic situation and to offer solutions to the many problems of China's economic development. To the extent that they are concerned with the pressing problems of developing China's economy, rather than with predicting the downfall of capitalism outside China or with philosophical issues not relevant to the Chinese economy, they will contribute to the accumulation of economic knowledge in China. Although most contemporary economists believe that Marxian economic analysis has been improved upon, an old tool may still be valuable for understanding certain important economic problems in China.

The second type of economic research consists of factual reporting and simple analysis of certain aspects of the Chinese economy. For example, in the annual *Almanac of China's Economy*, one finds reports on many aspects of China's economy in the year concerned, including population, national income, consumption, agriculture, industry, construction, commerce and trade transportation, education, health, foreign trade and investment. Somewhat more technical papers can be found, for example, in the journal *Price Theory and Practice* published by the Economic Research Institute of Nankai University. In this journal certain facts about prices and pricing in China are presented, and simple analyses are offered. The second type of research might have been motivated by the often quoted Chinese official policy "to discover truths from facts." I have separated it from the first type because of its emphasis on facts and the absence (nearly) of preconceived theoretical notions, Marxian or modern, employed in interpreting the facts. Much statistical data on the Chinese economy published since 1980 can be included in this type of research, although the selection and construction of economic statistics are colored by the researcher's preconceived notions of what should be measured.

The third type of economic research is based on modern economic analysis. Input–output analysis was attempted to a limited extent in the 1950s and the 1960s, but most of modern economic research in China today has its origin after 1979. It is practised by the few older economists who learned modern economics before the 1950s but did not use it for over two decades, and by a small but growing number of bright, energetic and hardworking younger economists who have acquired the tools since 1979. Examples of such research are an econometric model of the Chinese economy appearing in the october 1984 issue of *Economic Research (Jing Ji Yan Jiu)*, published by the Institute of Economics of CASS, and an estimation of linear expenditure systems using urban family budget data of Hubei province, appearing in the first 1983 issue of *Economic Management Research (Jing Ji Guan Li Yan Jiu)*, published by the Department of Economic Management of Wuhan University. Because of the late start and the lack of economists trained in modern tools, economic research in this category is limited in both quantity and quality, but is rapidly improving.

Some economists, Chinese and foreign, have questioned the usefulness of modern economic tools for the study of the Chinese economy. The above discussion implies the view that such tools are useful. Some of my Chinese colleagues refer to modern economics as Western economics and believe that it is applicable only to the study of capitalist economies. First, the term Western economics is inappropriate because Marxian economics is also Western, but not modern. Terminology aside, modern economics consists of methods of thinking and analysis and of the specific applications of such methods to build models of economic behavior and economic institutions. Some models may have more general applicability than others. For example, models of consumer behavior based on utility maximization, with or without the institution of rationing, appear to be applicable to capitalist economies as well as socialist planned economies. Models built for U.S. financial markets may not be applicable to China where the financial institutions are different. Different economic models are built to explain and predict economic phenomena under different institutional arrangements, just as different buildings are constructed to satisfy different needs. Different economic models may be required for the Chinese economy and the American economy, but the methods of model construction and of economic theorizing may be applicable to both. As in the case of architecture, the same set of tools may be useful in China and in the United States, but the specific buildings constructed may be different as the needs are different. This observation will also answer my American colleagues who believe that the Chinese social, cultural and political environment is so different from the American that modern economics has only limited applicability. They may be saying that different economic models are required. Yet the same methods of economic analysis are useful in constructing different models. Sections 14.4.2 and 14.4.3 illustrate this point.

To go a step further, it may be argued that even the tools themselves are colored by the institutional setting of the economists who invented them. Therefore, economists living in Western, economically developed, capitalist economies are likely to have invented methods of thinking and analysis which are applicable mainly, if not only, to such economies. My Chinese colleagues who have accepted Marxian economic thinking cannot take this argument too seriously. While this argument may have some validity, it by no means implies that tools developed by scholars of Western cultures are inapplicable to non-Western societies. Tools of sociology, anthropology and psychology developed in the Western world would then all have to be abandoned in the study of non-Western Societies. Chinese economists have applied modern economic tools to study the Chinese economy, as I have reported earlier. The Chinese Ministry of Education has sponsored workshops on modern economics for university teachers, graduate students, and government research economists in China, and as of 1984, is in the process of sending a large number of students to pursue graduate work in economics in American and Canadian universities. This indicates that the usefulness of modern economic tools to the solution of Chinese economic problems has gained substantial acceptance in China. To say that such tools are useful neither means that they are useful for all Chinese economic problems nor that they should not and will not be modified, improved upon, or even replaced by new tools to be developed through studying the Chinese economy.

The three types of economic research, theoretical-Marxian, purely empirical and modern analytical, coexist in China today, each playing its part in enhancing our understanding of the Chinese economy. The third type is gaining importance. The existence of different schools of thought often creates conflicts, and the situation with Chinese economic research is not an exception. Especially because the possible conflict between the first and the third modes of thinking is not easily separated from the conflict between Marxian and capitalist political ideology, and China is a Communist country, such conflict may hinder the development of modern economics in China. As I see it, the top leadership and its supporters in China are determined to build a "Chinese-style socialist economy" using whatever means that are available. Tools of modern economic analysis are accepted, or at least not excluded, by them as possibly useful tools as the experience in the rest of the world has demonstrated. However, many Chinese economists and government officials are more doctrinaire and perhaps less open-minded about the acceptance of modern economic tools. Thus conflicts remain. This and other problems in the development of economic research in China will be discussed in Sec. 5.

11.3. Organizations of Economic Research

The Almanac of China's Economy 1984, Chinese edition, pp. XI-1–14, provides a list of 206 important economic research organizations in China. Under the State Council of the Chinese central government are seven economic research centers, for economics, technical economics, economic laws, prices, agricultural development, economic problems under the State Planning Commission and economic management problems under the State Economic Commission. Under CASS are six economic research institutes, for economics, industrial economics, agricultural economics, financial and resource economics, world economics and politics, and quantitative and technical economics. There are also economic research institutes under the State Planning Commission, the State Economic Commission, the People's Bank, the Bank of China, Chinese People's Development Bank, China's Agricultural Bank, the Ministry of Finance, Commerce, Foreign Trade, Agriculture and Fishery, and of several industries. Government organizations of provinces and municipalities have their economic research institutes. Finally, universities and colleges of finance and economics at both the national and provincial levels may have economic research institutes.

We have seen that economic research centers or institutes are administered by different organizations in China, including the State Council, its Commissions and Ministries, CASS, provincial and municipal government units, universities under the Ministry of Education and colleges under the jurisdiction of provincial and municipal governments. Since different administrative units have their own jurisdictions, control over these economic research institutes is dispersed. Accordingly, different research institutes are engaged in different types of research following the guidelines set by their own sponsors. The styles of research can differ among different institutions. Some may be heavily Marxian-oriented. Others are engaged in factual analyses. Still others are applying the tools of modern economics. Furthermore, there is room for separate research efforts on the same research topics. For example, different research centers of the State Council, and research institutes under CASS and universities, are engaged in building econometric models of China. While official price statistics are published by the State Statistics Bureau of the State Council, the Nankai Institute of Economic Research, is engaged in research in the collection of price statistics. Overlapping research efforts are not left entirely uncontrolled, but they do exist to a significant extent in China.

The diversity of research approaches and the existence of parallel efforts are the desirable characteristics of the dispersed administration of economic research in China. On the negative side, the communication among research workers in different organizations is somewhat limited. This partly reflects the lack of communication among many Chinese government agencies, each having its specific responsibilities, following directions from the unit immediately above it but having no need to cooperate with units on the same level. However, as economic reforms are introduced in China giving state enterprises more autonomy and requiring them to deal with sister institutions, cooperation or at least communication among different organizations will be enhanced. In the case of economic research, the proliferation of professional associations can only improve the communication among Chinese economists. These professional economic associations hold meetings in which members present papers on their research. For example, in October 1984, the Chinese Association of Quantitative Economics held its second annual meeting in which over 150 papers were presented, with many dealing with the construction of econometric models.

11.4. Problems and Prospects

In Sec. 2 we have pointed out that Chinese government policy is to encourage and promote economic research by whatever means that would yield useful results for the purpose of the economic development of China. We have also pointed out one obstacle to progress in economic research, namely, the possible interference of some traditional ideologists who are reluctant to use modern economic analysis or who may even be obstructing others from using it. There is always resistance to new ideas everywhere in the world. It is difficult to judge how serious this problem is in China. The vested interests of some traditional ideologists may be strong and some of them are holding important positions in economic research and teaching. On the other hand, the desire is great among the young people in China for learning new ideas that might provide useful solutions to the development problems in China. Having observed the Chinese youth while teaching modern economics in China in 1980, 1982 and 1984, I believe that the young people in China will win out. They will learn, and some of them have learned, useful tools of economic analysis. Marxian or otherwise, that can be applied to the solution of Chinese economic problems. In the meantime, what else is hindering the progress of economics research in China?

First and foremost, well-trained researchers and teachers of economics are in very short supply. It is encouraging to learn that the Chinese Ministry of Education is selecting "some one hundred best-qualified students" majoring in different disciplines from about thirty major universities to study economics in the United States and Canada beginning the Fall of 1985. It also welcomes distinguished economists to lecture in China, organizing special workshops or placing them at various Chinese universities. Sending students and visiting scholars abroad and welcoming lecturers to teach in China are two obvious ways to train economists.

Second, there are institutional obstacles to fully utilizing the existing human and material resources in economic research. Some economic data are guarded as state secrets, including input–output tables. Many important economic research results are classified. Some economic reports have limited circulation and are available to people with specified ranking. Foreign exchange is under strict control. An economic research institute wishing to buy foreign books, material or equipment has to apply for foreign exchange through the supervising central authority. The material supplies available to individual scholars are even more restricted. Some of these institutional obstacles may be gradually removed as China's economic reform gains momentum.

Third, freedom of inquiry and of expression in the area of economic research is still restricted in China, although the improvement in this respect in the early 1980s has been remarkable. Researchers still have fears that if they freely express their views, they may be severely criticized and punished. In 1983, there was for a time a movement against "spiritual pollution" from Western ideas. Fortunately this movement was stopped, but Chinese intellectuals are still uncertain as to what ideas would be regarded as polluted and what ideas would not. This fear inhibits their expression and intellectual inquiry. For those who dare express unconventional views in writing, prospective publishers may be inhibited from publishing their work. The publishers too are uncertain as to what material is publishable, and would tend to reject a manuscript if there is doubt. Until the Chinese government guarantees the freedom of expression and prevents political ideologists from interfering with it, Chinese intellectuals including economists will be inhibited in their research and writing activities.

In spite of the above obstacles, the environment in China as of 1984 is such that economic research will flourish in the coming decades. The Chinese government promotes it and the Chinese intellectuals are eager for it.

11.5. Possible Cooperation with Outside Economists

Given the policy of the Chinese government to promote teaching and research in modern economics and the eagerness of the Chinese intellectuals to participate in these activities, there are plenty of opportunities for economists outside China to cooperate with the Chinese for the benefits of both. More opportunities to cooperate are made available as of 1984 than one or two years before, and more will become available in the near future. Therefore, the position of a potential outside participant is more favorable now than one or two years ago. A change in the attitudes of the outside participants may be called for. As for 1982 and 1983, it was not uncommon for American economists negotiating exchange activities with the Chinese to take a stance of bargaining rather than cooperation. From 1984 on, a cooperative stance will be more fruitful and pleasant.

Until recently, outside social scientists wishing to do work in China often felt that opportunities were limited, and that they had to negotiate hard with the Chinese to get what they wanted in terms of access to Chinese personnel, facilities and materials. This attitude was justified by the reality of the time. The opening of China had just begun. The Chinese were as inexperienced in dealing with foreigners as the latter were with them. Chinese personnel, facilities and material which were of interest to foreign social scientists were extremely limited. In economics, the usefulness of modern analytical tools was not yet clear in China. In general, China was less open one or two years ago than it is today. On the part of outside social scientists who had not had access to China for decades, there was a lot of unsatisfied demand for the access accumulated through the years. When demand greatly exceeds supply, the suppliers can set their conditions in allocating the available slots and the demanders feel that they have to bargain for what they can get.

The situation has changed, especially in economics. The Chinese are offering more opportunities for outside economists to do teaching and research. They have recognized the usefulness of modern economics. They are interested in cooperation. More Chinese personnel, facilities and material related to modern economic research are available, although these are still very limited by the standards of a developed economy. In the meantime, some of the accumulated demands for access by foreign social scientists have already been satisfied. To my knowledge, qualified economists interested in teaching and research in China are likely to succeed in finding suitable opportunities in China. There is no need for hard bargaining since there are plenty of arrangements which will be beneficial to both sides.

Let me spell out what these arrangements might be. First, in terms of financial reward to an outside economist, the Chinese government is still offering little, in order to economize on its foreign exchange. Whatever an outsider's view on this policy might be, the Chinese government will probably continue practicing it as long as outside economists are available to satisfy its needs. The Chinese government has been seeking outside assistance to finance the visiting economists. Support has come from the United States and Canadian governments, the Committee on Scholarly Communications with the People's Republic of China (CSCPRC), the United Nations and organizations affiliated with it, private foundations including Ford and Luce, and other sources. Most visiting economists are paid from funds so obtained, with the Chinese hosts paying for the local expenses.

Financial rewards aside, what opportunities are available? Opportunities for teaching are plenty. Chinese universities, financial and economic colleges, the Academy of Social Sciences and government agencies requiring economics training for their staff would all welcome qualified economists to teach if satisfactory financial agreements could be made, either by the hosting institutions or by the visitors. Research opportunities are more limited, but many are still available to interested and qualified researchers. Chinese government economic agencies and universities are trying to improve the quality and quantity of their economic research, and are willing to cooperate with foreign economists in such activities. For example, Lawrence Klein of the University of Pennsylvania is cooperating with the Institute of Technical and Quantitative Economics of CASS to build an econometric model. Teh-wei Hu of Pennsylvania State University has coauthored with colleagues at Nankai University on a study of household expenditure patterns in the city of Tianjin, based on survey data from 500 households of that city in 1982. Herbert

Simon of Carnegie-Mellon University has collaborated with Chinese colleagues in Peking on experimental research in psychology. These are just a few illustrative cases to show that the Chinese are interested in cooperative research with foreign social scientists and economists.

What areas in cooperative economic research are fruitful to pursue? The areas of interest to the Chinese are broad, covering almost all aspects of modern economics. Problems of pricing, resource allocation, consumer behavior, enterprise behavior and welfare in microeconomics, problems of economic growth and fluctuations, inflation, unemployment and productivity in macroeconomics, problems of banking and finance, of foreign trade and investment, of population, labor and human capital, and public finance are obviously important for China's economic development and therefore considered important research problems by the Chinese. In *The Chinese Economy* (1985), I discuss these problems in the context of the Chinese economy and suggest some topics for research. Research economists in any of these and other important areas can think of research topics which are of mutual interest to the Chinese and researchers themselves.

How does a foreign economist interested in research on any of these topics find a Chinese counterpart or a Chinese host? The same question can be asked of an American economists interested in research on the British or French economy. In the latter cases, information is more readily available, through published material or personal contacts. Both sources of information are more limited in the Chinese case for most American economists. The published material includes bulletins of the universities and their research institutes, and economics journals where one can find out what interesting research is being done at what institution and by whom. Published information alone is insufficient for locating a suitable hosting institution or a good collaborator. Personal contacts are required to obtain better information on a potential hosting institution and its staff, and to generate an acceptable invitation from it, as when an economist is searching inside his or her own country. Unlike the situation in the earlier 1980s, an individual foreign economist can find his or her contacts and deal directly with Chinese research institutions and universities.

Some of the better known economic research institutes affiliated with Chinese universities include the population research institutes at Peking, Nankai, Jilin, Lanzhou, Fudan, Nanking, Xiamen, Wuhan, Zhongshan, Sichuan and People's Universities; the institutes related to studies of the American economic system reported in Teh-wei Hu's report *The State of American Economic Studies in the PRC* the economic research institutes at Nankai, Fudan, Xiamen and Wuhan Universities, among others. Since teaching and research in modern economics is growing in China, almost all major Chinese universities provide opportunities for economic research. However, for Chinese and foreign economists alike, the research environment is less attractive than in an economically developed country, in terms of computer and library facilities, data available and accommodation. On the positive side, the economic research problems are challenging, the students and research assistants are bright, eager and hard-working, the potential collaborators are friendly, and the possible impact of economic research on the advancement of economic science and on the economic development of China can be great, not to mention the rewarding experience of being associated with the Chinese culture. Under these circumstances, one can expect that many foreign economists will find their way to doing research in or on China in the coming years. They will benefit personally and professionally from the experience, and China as a nation will benefit from their research efforts.

References

Almanac of China's Economy 1984, Chinese edn., Beijing: Economic Management Publishing Company.

Chow, G. C., 1985, *The Chinese Economy*, New York: Harper & Row; 2nd edn. 1987, Singapore: World Scientific.

_____, 1987, Development of a more market-oriented economy in China, *Science* **235**, 295–299.

Ma, Hong, and Sun, S., eds., 1982 *Zhongguo Jingji Jiegou Wenti Yanjiu (Studies of Problems of China's Economic Structure)*, vols. 1 & 2 (Beijing: People's Publishing Society).

Xue, M., 1981, *China's Socialist Economy*, Beijing: The Foreign Language Press.

CHAPTER 12

ECONOMIC ANALYSIS OF
THE PEOPLE'S REPUBLIC OF CHINA[*][†]

How much of economic analysis is applicable to China? Most, I believe. Some illustrations are presented in this paper.

12.1. Production Functions

The relation between output and major inputs in Chinese industry can be studied by using a production function. A Cobb–Douglas production function relating industrial output Y to labor input X_1 and capital input X_2 takes the form

$$Y = \alpha X_1^{\beta} X_2^{(1-\beta)}$$

which implies

$$\frac{Y}{X_1} = \alpha \left(\frac{X_2}{X_1} \right)^{(1-\beta)}$$

Data on output per person Y/X_1 (in 1970 yuan) and on original value of fixed assets per person X_2/X_1 in state-owned industrial enterprises are available for the seven years 1952, 1957, 1965, 1975, and 1979–1981 (see Chow, 1985, Table 4.1, p. 121). Using these seven annual observations, the following regression was estimated

$$\log \left(\frac{Y}{X_1} \right) = 3.762 + \underset{(.028)}{.602} \ \log \left(\frac{X_2}{X_1} \right) \qquad \begin{array}{l} R^2 = .9896 \\ s \ \ = .0445 \end{array} \qquad (1)$$

where the number in parentheses is the standard error of the corresponding regression coefficient. The fit was very good, as shown by Fig. 1.

After Eq. (1) was estimated, data on Y/X_1, X_1, and X_2 for 1982, 1983, and 1984 have become available, as found in *Statistical Yearbook of China 1985* (pp. 382,

[*] *Journal of Economic Education*, vol. 19, pp. XX, (Winter 1988). Reprinted with permission of the Helen Dwight Reid Educational Foundation. Published by Heldref Publications, 1319 18th Street, N. W., Washington, DC 20036–1802. Copyright 1988.

[†]The author would like to thank Hirschel Kasper for helpful comments and The Garfield Foundation for financial support in the preparation of this paper.

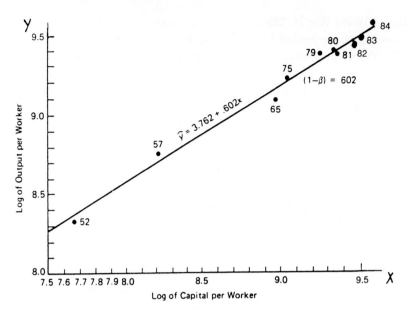

Fig. 1. Regression of gross output per worker on capital per worker

224, and 374 respectively). Y/X_1 for these three years are 12,084, 12,996, and 14,013 1970-yuan; X_2/X_1 are 12,849, 13,423, and 14,393 yuan per person. These three data paints are also plotted in Fig. 1. The differences between the observed $\log(Y/X_1)$ and the predicted values by Eq. (1) for 1982–1984 are respectively $-.038$, $-.009$, and $.025$. These prediction errors are small, even compared with the standard error of the regression $s = .0445$, not to mention the larger standard errors of the predictions themselves. The evidence has suggested that the Cobb–Douglas production function fits the data for Chinese state-owned industry very well; and that, in spite of the economic reforms introduced in the 1980s, the production function in state-owned industry did not change, implying that there was no visible increase in production efficiency in this sector in 1982–1984. This result agrees with the casual observation that economic reforms' in China improved economic efficiency in the agricultural sector but not in the state-owned industrial sector. For a discussion of the institutional aspects of Chinese economic reforms, the reader may refer to Chow (1987a).

12.2. Theory of Consumer Behavior

The economic theory of consumer behavior states that consumers act as if they were maximizing a utility function of quantities of consumer goods subject to a budget constraint. The theory implies that if the relative price of a commodity goes up, given real income, the demand for it will decrease. This theory appears to be universal, being applicable to China as well as other countries.

In urban China, rationing of food grain, vegetable oil, meat, sugar and cotton cloth has existed in various degrees in the last three decades. Rationing also existed in developed market economies including Great Britain and the United

States during World War II. There is a well-developed theory of consumer behavior under rationing as expounded by Neary and Roberts (1980) which is applicable to China. This theory is related to the standard theory without rationing by using the concept of virtual prices. Let x and y (possibly vectors) denote quantities of the non-rationed and rationed commodities respectively, p and q their unit prices, and I denote money income of the consumer. We are interested in two demand functions under rationing, one using money income, and the other using real income or utility as an argument, namely

$$x = g(\mathbf{y}, p, q, I) \tag{2}$$
$$x = g^c(\mathbf{y}, p, q, u) \tag{3}$$

where $\mathbf{y}$ denotes the ration quantity, u denotes utility, and the superscript c signifies that g^c is a compensated demand function.

Define the virtual price $\mathbf{q}$ as that price of the rationed commodity which, if there were no rationing, would make the compensated demands for x and y the same as under rationing. Denoting the compensated demand function for x in free market by $f^c(\ )$, we have, by this definition of virtual price,

$$f^c(p, \mathbf{q}, u) = g^c(\mathbf{y}, p, q, u) . \tag{4}$$

The ordinary demand function (2) under rationing is related to the ordinary demand function $f(\ )$ without rationing by the following equation

$$f(p, \mathbf{q}, I + [\mathbf{q} - q]\mathbf{y}) = g(\mathbf{y}, p, q, I) . \tag{5}$$

The justification of (5) is that, if the price of the rationed goods is increased from q to $\mathbf{q}$, to keep the consumer's real income under a free market the same as under rationing, his money income must be increased by $(\mathbf{q} - q)\mathbf{y}$ to enable him to buy the same quantities $(x, \mathbf{y})$ of consumer goods as before. By Eq. (5) this free-market demand is the same as the demand for x under rationing at prices (p, q) and income I, and with $\mathbf{y}$ as the ration quantity.

To illustrate possible applications to China, assume that we have estimated demand functions for China before rationing was introduced in the middle 1950s. For concreteness, and as suggested by Neary and Roberts (1980, pp. 40–41), let these demand functions satisfy a linear expenditure system, with the non-rationed goods numbered $1, 2, \ldots, n-1$, and the nth goods being rationed. The n demand functions are, with γ_i and β_i as parameters,

$$p_i x_i = p_i \gamma_i + \beta_i \left(I - \sum_{j=1}^{n-1} p_j \gamma_j - q\gamma_n \right) \qquad i = 1, \ldots, n-1 \tag{6}$$

$$qy = q\gamma_n + \beta_n \left(I - \sum_{j=1}^{n-1} p_j \gamma_j - q\gamma_n \right) .$$

From these free-market demand functions, we can derive the demand functions under rationing with $y = \mathbf{y}$. The latter demand functions g with $\mathbf{y}, p, q$, and I as arguments are the same as the former demand functions f with I increased by $(\mathbf{q} - q)\mathbf{y}$ and q raised to $\mathbf{q}$ to make the free-market demand for y equal to $\mathbf{y}$. Making these changes to (6) yields

$$p_i x_i = p_i \gamma_i + \beta_i \left[I + (\mathbf{q} - q)\mathbf{y} - \sum_{j=1}^{n-1} p_j \gamma_j - \mathbf{q}\gamma_n \right] \qquad i = 1, \ldots, n-1 \qquad (7)$$

$$\mathbf{q}\mathbf{y} = \mathbf{q}\gamma_n + \beta_n \left[I + (\mathbf{q} - q)\mathbf{y} - \sum_{j=1}^{n-1} p_j \gamma_j - \mathbf{q}\gamma_n \right] \, .$$

The virtual price $\mathbf{q}$ can be found by solving the last equation of (7):

$$\mathbf{q} = \frac{\beta_n}{(1 - \beta_n)(\mathbf{y} - \gamma_n)} \left[I - \sum_{j=1}^{n-1} p_j \gamma_j - q\mathbf{y} \right] \, . \qquad (8)$$

Substituting (8) for $\mathbf{q}$ in the first $n - 1$ equations of (7) gives the demand functions under rationing:

$$p_i x_i = p_i \gamma_i + \frac{\beta_i}{1 - \beta_n} \left(I - \sum_j p_j \gamma_j - q\mathbf{y} \right) \qquad i = 1, \ldots, n-1 \, . \qquad (9)$$

Equation (8) itself is useful for China because it tells how high the free-market price of the rationed goods would be if the government should decide to abandon rationing and not to increase the supply of the rationed goods. From it the government can find out how much to compensate the urban population to keep their real income constant after derationing, the amount being $(\mathbf{q} - q)\mathbf{y}$.

Theory and methods for studying household expenditure patterns are universal. Houthakker (1957) presents a study of this topic using data on four categories of expenditures — food, clothing, housing, and other miscellaneous items — for some thirty-three countries. Houthakker wrote (p. 532):

> Few dates in the history of econometrics are more significant than 1857. In that year Ernst Engel (1821–1896) published a study on the conditions of production and consumption in the Kingdom of Saxony, in which he formulated an empirical law concerning the relation between income and expenditure on food. Engel's law, as it has since become known, states that the proportion of income spent on food declines as income rises. Its original statement was mainly based on an examination of about two hundred budgets of Belgian laborers collected by Ducpétiaux. Since that date the law has been found to hold in many other budget surveys; similar laws have also been formulated for other items of expenditure.

He found the total-expenditure elasticities for food, clothing, housing, and all other items to be, respectively, about .6, 1.2, .8, and 1.6 for many countries.

Using per-capita data on Chinese peasant families from 28 provinces and municipalities in 1981, I have estimated the following regressions of log per-capita expenditures y_i for the above four categories on log per-capita total expenditure x (see Chow, 1985, pp. 165–166):

Food
$$\log y_1 = 0.587 + 0.790 \ \log x, \qquad R^2 = .872 \qquad (10)$$
$$(.313) \quad (.059) \qquad\qquad s^2 = .00650$$

Clothing
$$\log y_2 = -.962 + 0.789 \ \log x, \qquad R^2 = .535 \qquad (11)$$
$$(.760) \quad (.144) \qquad\qquad s^2 = .0383$$

Housing and Fuel
$$\log y_3 = -6.073 + 1.783 \ \log x, \qquad R^2 = .843 \qquad (12)$$
$$(.794) \quad (.151) \qquad\qquad s^2 = .0418$$

Miscellaneous
$$\log y_4 = -3.378 + 1.248 \ \log x, \qquad R^2 = .797 \qquad (13)$$
$$(.650) \quad (.123) \qquad\qquad s^2 = .028 \ .$$

Thus, the total-expenditure elasticities of demand for food, clothing, housing (including fuel), and all other items, based on a sample survey of Chinese peasants in 1981, are estimated to be .79, .79, 1.78, and 1.25 respectively.

The total-expenditure elasticity of demand for food estimated from the survey of Chinese peasants is somewhat higher than the .6 figure proposed by Houthakker. This difference may be explained by the suggestion of Houthakker (p. 547) that "the elasticity for food with respect to total expenditure might be higher for the countries and time periods with lower total expenditure, though the evidence is equivocal." The estimate of the elasticity for clothing is somewhat lower, and for housing somewhat higher, in the case of the Chinese peasants surveyed in 1981, than the corresponding average figures used by Houthakker. Two related explanations for the differences can be offered. First, the surveys used by Houthakker are mainly for urban families, and it is reasonable to suppose that urban people tend to spend more on clothing than peasants do as their incomes increase. To the extent that people spend less on clothing, they will spend more on other things, including housing. Secondly, the demand for housing by Chinese farmers is perhaps subject to fewer restrictions than the demand for clothing. Chinese peasants are relatively free to build their own houses, while the supply of clothing may be more limited. The elasticities for clothing and housing estimated from urban families in Peiping (in 1927) and in Shanghai (in 1929–1930) as given in Table III of Houthakker (p. 546) are much closer to the international averages. The higher elasticity for clothing in Shanghai than in Peiping is noteworthy because the residents of the cultural city of Peiping in the late 1920s were known to dress more modestly than the residents of the cosmopolitan Shanghai. There is no reason to believe, and no evidence to suggest, that the consumption behavior of the Chinese people is very different from that of the other people in the world. Bai, Hu, and Shi (1987) presents a more recent study of family budgets of Chinese urban families.

12.3. Law of Supply in Agriculture

As a part of the Great Leap Forward Movement introduced in 1958, agricultural communes were rapidly organized between April and September 1958. In a commune, peasant workers, students, and members of the army engaged in agriculture, fishing, forestry, industrial sideline and construction activities. Labor was mobilized to perform the important tasks of supplying food and materials for industrialization and building roads, bridges, irrigation systems and other construction projects. Each commune was headed by an administrative committee. In the 1960s, a commune was divided, on the average, into about nine brigades, and each brigade into eight work teams (see Chow, 1985, p. 98). Construction projects were carried out by brigades and farming was performed by the smaller work teams, which often corresponded to traditional villages. Farming was performed by command, with the central planners deciding on the crops to grow, the output targets and the quantities each commune was obligated to deliver to the government purchasing units at compulsory procurement prices. Yet the law of supply continued to operate in Chinese agriculture, as discussed in Chow (1985, pp. 107–112).

By the law of supply, in order to call forth more output, price has to increase. The law is ordinarily derived for a competitive industry in which individual firms attempt to maximize profits under the condition of increasing marginal costs. In a Chinese commune, land was assigned to each work team. Inputs were distributed at non-market prices and workers were not necessarily paid the values of their marginal products under a "work point" system. Even when the inputs were not appropriately priced, each production unit still performed its cost calculations using the misguided data. It still had a marginal cost curve where the cost figures were calculated by using whatever prices of inputs it had to pay. Its marginal cost was still an increasing function of output. If the government paid a compulsory procurement price below the production unit's marginal cost, the more the unit produced the more money it would lose. It became difficult for the government to force the production units to increase output without paying a higher price for it because no unit wanted to produce more and earn less. A clear piece of evidence that the law of supply worked in China is that in the late 1970s, the Chinese government raised the procurement prices of farm products several times to increase agricultural production, the official general index of purchasing prices of farm and sideline products in 1978–1981 being respectively 217.4, 165.5, 184.4, and 301.2 (see *Statistical Yearbook of China 1981*, p. 411). There are also sufficient data in the *Statistical Yearbook of China* of recent years to study the responses of Chinese farmers to the relative prices of various farm products in their supply decisions. For example, there appear to be positive relations between the relative purchasing prices of various commercial crops and the sown areas in 1978–1983 (see *Statistical Yearbook of China 1984*, pp. 138–139 and 434). A statistical study of such relations would be of interest.

12.4. Money and Price Level Determination

The quantity theory of money can provide a crude explanation of the price level in many countries including China. It is based on the quantity equation

$$Mv = Py \tag{14}$$

where M is the stock of money, P is the price level, y is national income in real terms, and v is income velocity. The quantity equation (14) can be interpreted merely as an identity which defines the velocity v as the ratio of national income Py in money terms to the stock of money M. The quantity theory of money is derived from Eq. (14) on the condition that velocity v is nearly constant empirically. Under this condition, the theory provides an explanation for the price level P.

There are many reasons why the constancy of v is at best a rough approximation to reality. A well-known one is the Keynesian argument that when prices are rigid an increase in M will lead to a downward movement in the rate of interest and a reduction in v, rather than a rise in P. How good is the assumption of the constancy of v? This question has been answered both theoretically and empirically mainly by reinterpreting (14) as a demand equation for money:

$$\frac{M}{P} = ky \tag{15}$$

where $k = v^{-1}$. If the demand for real money balances, M/P is approximately proportional to real income y, or if (15) is a good approximation to reality, k, or its inverse v, can be treated as a constant approximately.

However, assuming that Eq. (15) fits the data reasonably well by some standard, one cannot thereby conclude that an increase in M, given y, will lead to a proportional increase in P. To see this, suppose that the data for M and y satisfy the relation $M = ky$, or

$$\log M = \log k + \log y$$

and that $\log P$ is generated as an independent, identically distributed random variable ε. We have

$$\log \left(\frac{M}{P} \right) = \log k + \log y - \varepsilon \ .$$

A regression of $\log(M/P)$ on $\log y$ may yield a coefficient of unity and possibly a high R^2, supporting the hypothesis (15) and yet changes in M do not affect changes in P. Hence by studying the demand for real money balance through Eq. (15), one learns little about how money supply affects the price level. Nevertheless, the demand for money is itself a subject of interest.

To apply the quantity theory of money to explain the price level P, we rewrite (14) as

$$P = v \left(\frac{M}{Y} \right) \ . \tag{16}$$

If v were close to being constant, regressing $\log P$ on $\log(M/P)$ would yield a coefficient of unity and a good fit. If v itself is negatively associated with (M/y), changes in P will be less than proportional to changes in (M/y). As long as an increase in (M/y) is not completely offset by a proportional reduction in v, it will have a positive effect on P. How well Eq. (16) explains P may differ from how well Eq. (15) explains M/P.

In Chow (1987b), I have estimated the following demand equation for money, using annual data on currency for M, an official retail price index for P, and a real national income variable for y from 1952 to 1983:

$$\ln\left(\frac{M}{P}\right) = -3.927 + 1.162 \ \ln y, \qquad \begin{array}{ll} R^2 & = .9083 \\ s & = .1971 \\ \mathrm{DW} & = .7847 \ . \end{array} \tag{17}$$
$$\phantom{\ln\left(\frac{M}{P}\right) = } (.492) \quad (.067)$$

This demand for money equation appears reasonably good except for the facts that the coefficient of $\ln y$, or the income elasticity of demand for money, is larger than unity, contradicting the quantity theory, and that the Durbin–Watson statistic is low, signifying positive serial correlation in the residuals. Both of these characteristics have been found in demand for money equations estimated using data for the United States (see Chow, 1966). A simple way to account for the positive serial correlation in the residuals is to assume that $\ln y$ explains only the equilibrium level of $\ln(M/P)$, and that the actual change in $\ln(M/P)$ is only a fraction of the difference between this equilibrium level and the actual level, leading to the equation, for 1953–1983:

$$\ln\left(\frac{M}{P}\right)_t = -1.322 + .3504 \ \ln y + .7409 \ \ln\left(\frac{M}{P}\right)_{t-1}, \qquad \begin{array}{ll} R^2 & = .9749 \\ s & = .1024 \\ \mathrm{DW} & = 2.101 \ . \end{array} \tag{18}$$
$$\phantom{\ln\left(\frac{M}{P}\right)_t = } (.394) \quad (.0966) \qquad\quad (.0813)$$

The positive serial correlation in the residuals is eliminated in Eq. (18) as seen from the Durbin–Watson statistic. Thus the quantity theory as formulated in Eq. (15) provides a reasonable first approximation in explaining the demand for money in China.

To find out how well the price level can be explained, we take logarithms of both sides of (16) and regress $\ln p$ on $\ln(M/y)$ using annual data from 1952 to 1983, obtaining

$$\ln P = .9445 + .2687 \ \ln\left(\frac{M}{P}\right), \qquad \begin{array}{ll} R^2 & = .8217 \\ s & = .0363 \\ \mathrm{DW} & = 1.003 \ . \end{array} \tag{19}$$
$$ (.0567) \quad (.0229)$$

Equation (19) shows that the ratio M/y does provide a good explanation of the price level P, as the quantity theory predicts. The t statistic for the coefficient of $\ln(M/y)$ is $.2687/.0229$ or 11.76, and the R^2 is fairly high. However, the coefficient of $\ln(M/y)$ is only .2687 and very much below unity, contradicting the quantity theory. The conclusion is that although the ratio M/y can explain the price level

P fairly well, changes in M/y lead to less than proportional changes in P. This can happen if v is negatively associated with M/y so that when M/y increases, its effect is partly absorbed by the reduction in v and only partly reflected in an increase in P. A second shortcoming of Eq. (19) is the low Durbin–Watson statistic, suggesting a positive serial correlation in the regression residuals. To overcome this shortcoming, short-run dynamics was introduced in Chow (1987b) and the following equation was found to be consistent with the data

$$\ln P = .3604 + .8404 \ln P_{-1} - .2175 \ln P_{-2} + .1430 \ln \left(\frac{M}{y} \right) - .0417 \ln \left(\frac{M}{y} \right)_{-1} . \quad (20)$$

When the sample was divided into two subsamples, the second using observations from 1979 to 1983, the Chow test showed that the parameters of this equation are stable after 1979, in spite of the introduction of economic reforms. The equation forecasts well in the post-sample year 1984. Equations (19) and (20) were found to fit the Chinese data slightly better than similar equations fit the United States data for the years 1922–1953.

12.5. The Acceleration Principle and National Income Determination

A multiplier–accelerator model of national income determination can be derived from a Harrod–Domar model of economic growth. Let Y_t, C_t and I_t denote, respectively, national income, consumption, and investment in year t, all in constant prices. The Harrod–Domar model consists of two equations. First, the savings function explains aggregate savings $S_t = Y_t - C_t$ as a fraction σ of national income,

$$S_t = Y_t - C_t = \sigma Y_t$$

implying the consumption function

$$C_t = (1 - \sigma)Y_t = \gamma Y_t . \quad (21)$$

Second, the ratio of capital stock K_t to output Y_t is assumed to be a constant,

$$K_t = \alpha Y_t . \quad (22)$$

When simple distributed lags are introduced, Eqs. (21) and (22) become

$$C_t = \gamma_0 + \gamma_1 Y_t + \gamma_2 C_{t-1} \quad (23)$$
$$K_t = \alpha_0 + \alpha_1 Y_t + \alpha_2 K_{t-1} . \quad (24)$$

Equation (24) is converted to an investment function by using the identity $I_t = \Delta K_t = (K_t - K_{t-1})$, where I_t stands for net investment, and by first differencing

$$I_t = \alpha_1 \Delta Y_t + \alpha_2 I_{t-1} . \quad (25)$$

The multiplier–accelerator model consists of Eqs. (23) and (25) and the identity

$$Y_t = C_t + I_t . \quad (26)$$

The method of two-stage least squares was applied in Chow (1985) to estimate Eqs. (23) and (25) using the 30 annual Chinese data from 1953 to 1982. The analysis is now updated to include the data for 1983. In the first stage, Y_t is regressed on C_{t-1} and I_{t-1} to obtain the estimated $\hat{Y}_t$. The regressions obtained in the second stage using $\hat{Y}_t$ as an instrumental variable for Y_t are

$$C_t = -5.7448 - .1123\, Y_t + 1.2862\, C_{t-1}, \qquad \begin{aligned} R^2 &= .9929 \\ s &= 5.140 \\ DW &= 1.760 \end{aligned} \qquad (27)$$
$$(3.0520) \quad (.1595) \qquad (.2626)$$

$$I_t = 1.6979 + .6541\,(Y_t - Y_{t-1}) + .8906\, I_{t-1}, \qquad \begin{aligned} R^2 &= 3.819 \\ s &= 3.819 \\ DW &= 1.401 \end{aligned} \qquad (28)$$
$$(1.3471) \quad (.0890) \qquad\qquad (.0272)$$

Originally, I had formulated a consumption function (23) with income and lagged consumption as explanatory variables. This consumption function is consistent with the permanent income hypothesis as expounded by Friedman (1957). When this consumption function was estimated in Eq. (27), I found the current income variable insignificant. Equation (27) is consistent with the stochastic version of the permanent income hypothesis suggested by Hall (1978). According to Hall, as a first approximation, consumption evolves according to a random walk; no variable apart from C_{t-1} should be of any value in predicting C_t, as Eq. (27) suggests. Indeed, C_{t-2}, I_{t-1}, and I_{t-2} were all found to be insignificant in predicting C_t given C_{t-1}. Equation (28) is consistent with the acceleration principle, showing the importance of $(Y_t - Y_{t-1})$ in explaining current investment, apart from I_{t-1}.

The acceleration principle is another universal law in economics. It states that investment is a function of the rate of change in income. In an equation explaining net investment, the coefficients of Y_t and Y_{t-1} should be positive and negative, respectively but equal in absolute value. This was found for the United States and China as well (see Chow, 1967, 1968, and 1985a, p. 236).

12.6. Conclusion

The above examples have illustrated the proposition that most of existing economic analysis is applicable to China. Mention should also be made of the theories of international trade and finance. For example, the Ricardian theory of comparative advantage shows the possible gain from international trade when the marginal rate of substitution in domestic production of two commodities differs from their price ratio in the international market. It is applicable to any economy including China, although some governments may prevent the possible gain from being realized. Our proposition does not imply that no new economic tools are required or are desirable for studying the Chinese economy. Tools of economic analysis have been developed for the study of real economic problems. Before new tools are developed for China, one should understand the usefulness as well as the limitations of the existing tools.

References

Bai, Jushan, Hu, Teh-wei and Shi, Shuzhong, 1987, Household consumption analysis in Tianjin, 1982–1984, *China Quarterly*, forthcoming.

Chow, G. C., 1967, Multiplier, accelerator, and liquidity preference in the determination of National Income in the United States, *The Review of Economics and Statistics*, **XLIV**, 1–15; also in M. G. Mueller, ed., 1971, *Readings in Macroeconomics*, Holt, Rinehart and Winston, 412–429.

———, 1968, The acceleration principle and the nature of business cycles, *Quarterly Journal of Economics*, **LXXXII**, 403–418.

———, 1985a, *The Chinese Economy*, New York: Harper & Row; 2nd edn., 1987 Singapore: World Scientific.

———, 1985b, A model of Chinese National Income determination, *Journal of Political Economy*, **93**, 782–792.

———, 1987a, Development of a more money-oriented economy in China, *Science*, **235**, 295–299.

———, 1987b, Money and price level determination in China, *Journal of Comparative Economics*, forthcoming.

Friedman, M., 1987, A Theory of the Consumption Function, New Jersey: Princeton University Press, for N.E.B.R.

Hall, R. E., 1978, Stochastic implications of the life cycle — permanent income hypothesis: Theory and evidence, *Journal of Political Economy*, **86**, 971–987.

Houthakker, H. S., 1957, An international comparison of Household expenditure patterns, commemorating the centenary of Engel's law, *Econometrica*, **25**, 532–551.

Neary, J. P. and Roberts, K. W. S., 1980, The theory of household behavior under rationing, *European Economic Review*, **13**, 25–42.

Part IV

Modeling Economic Behavior

CHAPTER 13

MARKET SOCIALISM AND
ECONOMIC DEVELOPMENT IN CHINA*

"Can socialism work? Of course it can."
Joseph A. Schumpeter, *Capitalism, Socialism and Democracy*, Harper & Brothers, 1947,
p. 167.

"I have always said that if any country in the world can make communism work, China
is the country, but I do not believe it can either."
Milton Friedman, *The Invisible Hand in Economics and Politics*, Academia Sinica
lecture, Taipei, 1981.

Can socialism work in the promotion of a fairly rapid rate of economic development
in China? I think it can. Socialism did not work satisfactorily in China from 1949
to 1978, according to the consensus of the Chinese people and their political leaders
who embarked upon major economic reforms in late 1978. However, it can and
is likely to work in the second and third decades after the economic reforms. In
Sec. 1 of this Chapter I will characterize the Chinese economic system as it has
evolved up to 1988. In Sec. 2, I will evaluate, from a theoretical point of view, the
performance of such a system. In Sec. 3, the historical performance of the Chinese
economy in the last decade will be briefly reviewed, and the prospects for its future
development will be examined under the assumption that economic institutions will
not be changed substantially in the next two decades. The analysis is confined to
a purely economic point of view, leaving many important political and social issues
untouched.

13.1. Characterizing the Chinese Economic System

The Chinese economy is a socialist economy. By the definition of socialism,
most of the means of production are controlled by the state. It is not a highly
centralized socialist economy. Although in the 1950s the Chinese government tried
to adopt Soviet-style central planning, with the First Five-Year Plan starting in
1953, observers question the degree to which China practiced centralized economic

---

*Originally Research Memorandum no. 340, Econometric Research Program, Princeton University,
December 1988.

planning from the 1950s to the 1970s. Central economic planning penetrated mainly into the urban industrial sector for a selected number of products. The economic power of local authorities existed all through this period. Furthermore, planning was interrupted by the Great Leap Forward Movement, in 1958–1962 and the Cultural Revolution of 1966–1976. The limited degree of central planning has been reduced further since the economic reforms initiated by the Third Plenary Session of the 11th Central Committee of the Communist Party in December 1978. See Chow (1985, pp. 50–69) for a discussion of the limited degree of central planning and the introduction of economic reforms. As of 1988, the Chinese economy is to a significant extent a decentralized (socialist) market economy, even though most of the means of production are controlled by the state. To characterize the Chinese economy, I will consider in turn its domestic microeconomy, its foreign trade and investment, and its macroeconomy.

13.1.1. *Domestic microeconomic institutions*

According to *Statistical Yearbook of China* (*SYC for short*) *1987*, p. 41, the five major sectors — agriculture, industry, construction, transport and commerce respectively — accounted for 34.9, 45.6, 6.3, 3.6, and 9.6 percent of China's national income in 1986. While agriculture accounted for 34.9 percent of national income, 73.67 percent of the total population engaged in farming, animal husbandry, forestry and fishery (p. 86). As is well known, after economic reforms Chinese agriculture has been characterized by household farming, with each household assigned a piece of land. The household is required to sell a fixed amount of its farm output to the government procurement department at a fixed purchase price (usually below market price), but is allowed to sell the remaining output in the free market at market price. The above "responsibility system" amounts to the government collecting a fixed rent for the land assigned to the farm household. The short-run maximizing behavior of the farm household is identical to that prevailing in a market economy.

In practice, the farm household can transfer its right to the use of the land to another household, that is, the right to land use can be bought and sold. However, the right to use the land is not permanent (usually assigned for 10 to 15 years) and the farmers are not certain of a stable land assignment policy. These two factors have affected the incentives of the farmers in investing to improve the land, thus behaving differently from the farmers owning their land in a market economy. The incentive to save by Chinese farmers operating in a market farm economy in the early 1950s after the land reform is documented in Chow (1985, p. 93): "The ratio of saving to income in the agriculture sector is found to be 13.0 percent in 1952, 3.7 percent in 1957 [when most farm households had been organized into advanced cooperatives], 7.7 percent in 1965 [when the period of economic adjustment after the Great Leap allowed some free markets in the rural sector] and 6.9 percent in 1979 [as the responsibility system had just been introduced in Chinese agriculture]." In summary, except for the very small fraction of output produced by state farms, essentially market-oriented institutions in the agricultural sector are responsible for producing about 34 percent of national income in China.

Consider next the industrial sector which accounts for 45.6 percent of national income. It is dominated by state-owned enterprises, while collective and individual enterprises also exists. In 1986, there were 499,300 industrial enterprises, of which (1) 96,800 or 19.4 percent were state-owned, (2) 80.1 percent were collective-owned (49 percent being township enterprises) and (3) the remaining 0.5 percent being of other forms, including joint state-collective, joint state-private, joint collective-private, joint ventures with foreigners, and enterprises run by overseas Chinese and by foreign investment (*SYC 1987*, p. 187). The above three types of industrial enterprises account respectively for 73.12, 25.61 (9.93 for townships), and 1.27 percent of net industrial output value (*SYC 1987*, p. 223). Collective enterprises may belong to local governments or to individuals. Accordingly the incentives of their managers may differ. To a significant extent, they are operated for profit as enterprises of market economies. From the fact that 26.88 percent of net industrial output is produced by the second and third types of enterprises, it appears that perhaps about 20 percent of industrial output in China, or 9.12 percent of national income, is produced by enterprises operating somewhat like those of a market economy.

The construction sector, accounting for 6.3 percent of national income, employed 18 million persons in 1986, with state-owned enterprises, collective-owned enterprises in cities and towns, and rural construction teams employing respectively 6.2, 3.8 and 8.1 million (*SYC 1987*, p. 381). Net output values of the first two categories were respectively 16.0 and 6.4 billion RMB. In view of the large numbers of persons employed in the second and third categories, it seems plausible to count about 50 percent of national income contributed by the construction sector as being produced by enterprises with management incentives somewhat similar to those prevailing in a market economy.

The transport, post and communication sector, accounting for 3.6 percent of national income, is mainly state-owned, although highway transportation by private vehicles (of the 3.6 million civil motor vehicles in 1986, 347,000 or about 10 percent are private, *SYC 1987* pp. 342 and 344) and waterway transportation by private boats belong to the market-oriented sector of the economy. Perhaps 0.3 of the 3.6 percent of national income can be so included. Of the 9.6 percent of national income originating from commerce, perhaps 6.0 percent can be so included. This estimate is based on the following facts: In retail trade, of the 18.4 million engaged in 1986, 3.1 million are in state-owned units, 6.5 million in collective-owned units, 33,000 in jointly owned, and 8.8 million in individually owned units; in catering trade, the corresponding four categories have 524,000, 1.1 million, 29,000 and 2.2 million persons respectively; in service trade, they are 626,000, 1.1 million, 43,000 and 1.9 million respectively (*SYC 1987*, p. 452); and in retail trade, the values of retail sales by the four categories are respectively 195.10, 180.40, 1.52 and 80.48 million yuan, while retail sales by peasant to non-agricultural residents amount to 37.50 million (p. 484).

Adding up the percentages 34.0, 9.1, 3.2, 0.3, and 6.9 of national income produced by market-oriented units in the five sectors, I conclude that these units produced about 52.6 percent of China's national income in 1986. Assuming that the remaining production units are state enterprises, or are collective enterprises behaving like state enterprises, I next ask to what extent these enterprises may also behave like enterprises of a private market economy.

Before the economic reform initiated in 1978, Chinese state enterprises were designed to operate as enterprises in a centralized planned economy, following instructions on prices, output and employment from the ministry which controls them, receiving supplies of materials from a bureau of material supplies and delivering products as directed by the central authority. Reform of state enterprises was initiated in 1979 by allowing 6,600 industrial enterprises to make certain market decisions. By June 1980, these units produced 45 percent in value of the output of all state enterprises, surpassing in profits and in revenue those enterprises run under the old system of central planning. In August 1980, the Chinese People's Congress approved legislation to follow the principle of regulation through planning combined with the regulation of the market. See Chow (1985, p. 149).

A major landmark of economic reform was the Decision of the Central Committee of the Communist party of China on Reform of the Economic Structure of October 20, 1984. The Decision includes the following major components concerning the operation of the domestic economy.

First, "We should extend the decision-making power of enterprises owned by the whole people ... on the premise of following the state plans and subjecting itself to state control, the enterprise has the power to adopt flexible and diversified forms of operation; plans its production, supply and marketing; keep and budget funds it is entitled to retain; appoint, remove, employ or elect its own personnel according to relevant regulations; decide on how to recruit and use [note: not explicitly "dismiss"] its work force, and on wages and rewards; set the prices of its products within the limits prescribed by the state; and so on. In short, the enterprise should be truly made a relatively independent economic entity and ... responsible for its own profit and loss and ... act as a legal person with certain rights and duties."

Second, concerning central planning, "The socialist state institutions must manage, inspect, guide and regulate the activities of the enterprises, as is necessary, through planning and by economic, administrative and legal means; ... it must designate, appoint and remove the principal leading members of he enterprises or approve their appointment and election ... for a considerably long time to come, our national economic plans on the whole can only be rough and elastic and ... we can do no more than, by striking an overall balance in planning and through regulation by economic means, exercise effective control over major issues while allowing flexibility on minor ones ... the socialist planned economy is a planned commodity economy based on public ownership, in which the law of value must be consciously followed and applied."

Third, concerning price reform, "The irrational system of pricing is closely related to the irrational system of price control. In readjusting prices, we must reform the over-centralized system of price control, gradually reducing the scope of uniform prices set by the state and appropriately enlarging the scope of floating prices within certain limits and of free prices. Thus prices will respond rather quickly to changes in labor productivity and the relation between market supply and demand ... " However, market price determination was somewhat restricted. "All enterprises should achieve better economic results through efforts to improve management and operation and should never try to increase their income by price increases. It is absolutely impermissible for any unit or person to boost prices at will by taking advantage of the reform, deliberately generating a tendency towards a general rise in prices, disrupt the socialist market and harm the interests of the states and the consumers." The Decision also allowed the market sector of collective and individual enterprises to expand. Wage rates were to be differentiated enough "to apply fully the principle of rewarding the diligent and good, punishing the lazy and bad, and of giving more pay for more work and less pay for less work ... "

Under the Decision of October 1984, the responsibility system in agriculture was to be introduced in the management of state enterprises by allowing subunits of each enterprise to act independently, while using the resources allotted to them by the enterprise. This provision should be distinguished from the policy of allowing the enterprise itself to have financial independence after paying a fixed rental to the state as in the case of individual farms. The distinction was made partly because the state enterprises are much larger than the individual farms and the management of these enterprises could not be permitted to use the possibly very large profits as freely as the individual farm households could. It was not until 1986 that a major attempt was made to introduce the responsibility system to the level of the state enterprises themselves rather than their subunits. By 1986, some small state-owned commercial and industrial enterprises were leased to the managers who were given almost complete control of the profits after paying rent to the government. A number of successful cases, with tremendous increases in outputs and profits, were well publicized in the news media. The "contract responsibility system" was then introduced in 1987. The main feature of this system is to let the management and workers sign a contract with the state or provincial government to lease the enterprise, paying fixed amounts of taxes in the forthcoming years (often five) of the contract and keeping the remaining profits for distribution among the management and workers in a way agreed upon by their mutual consent. By the end of 1987, over 90 percent of state enterprises were placed under this system. Even though this system looks attractive on paper, in practice the results are not entirely satisfactory. The management and workers often complain that the fixed taxes imposed by the state or local government are too large, leaving too little profit for them; they would prefer to pay a fixed percentage from their profits, thus avoiding the risk of paying taxes when the enterprise is operating at a loss.

In summary, over 50 percent of the national income in China is produced by production units having incentives similar to those of enterprises in a private market economy. The state enterprises responsible for producing the remaining part of national income are decentralized. They are given certain autonomy and incentives, while commodity prices are partly determined by market forces, so that these enterprises too may behave to some, smaller, extent like enterprises of a market economy. How efficient these enterprises are is a subject of Sec. 2.

13.1.2. *Foreign trade and investment*

A very important component of China's economic reform is the open-door policy, which is a drastic change from Chairman Mao Zedong's policy of closing China's door to the outside world. China's exports increased from 5.6 percent of national income in 1978 to 13.9 percent in 1986 (*SYC 1987*, pp. 38 and 519). The amount of foreign capital utilized, in the form of foreign loans or foreign investments, increased steadily from 1979 to 1986, totaling $29.23 billion during these eight years, with $20.92 billion being loans and $8.31 billion being foreign investment. In the year 1986, foreign loans utilized amounted to $5.01 billion and foreign investments $2.24 billion (p. 531). Of the $2.24 billion of foreign investment utilized in 1986, however, $1.33 billion came from Hong Kong (p. 532) while $0.86 billion went to Guangdong Province (p. 533). Foreign investment has gone mainly to coastal areas.

The significance of foreign trade and foreign investment for China's economic system is three-fold. First, foreign investment augments domestic investment in the process of capital accumulation while foreign trade expands China's production possibility frontier inclusive of trade. Second, foreign investment and trade are channels through which updated technology and management practices are introduced into China in the process of learning by doing. Third, and not least, joint venture, foreign enterprises, and foreign trade provide competition to Chinese state and collective enterprises, forcing them to be more efficient, and at the same time putting pressure on the Chinese price system to reflect the forces of demand and supply.

13.1.3. *Macroeconomic management*

A slogan used by Chinese reform officials since 1985 was "Invigorate the microeconomic units and control by macroeconomic means." This is another way of describing the policy stated in the Decision of October 1984 to change from compulsory planning to guidance planning: "A planned economy does not necessarily mean the predominance of mandatory planning, both mandatory and guidance planning being its specific forms ... guidance plans are fulfilled mainly by use of economic levers; mandatory plans have to be implemented, but even then the law of value must be observed." While state enterprises are given more autonomy to make economic decisions and are asked to be responsible for their own profits, regulation of the economy is to be achieved by the use of the levers of fiscal and monetary policies. However, macroeconomic policies in China include some direct control of microeconomic units, more so than in the United States, as the quotations in Sec. 1.1 from the Decision of October 1984 indicate. (In the United States, direct control of microeconomic units is not entirely absent, as evidenced by the introduction of price and wage controls in 1972–1973 proposed by Federal Reserve Chairman Arthur Burns in the first administration of President Richard Nixon.)

Under the system of Soviet-style central planning, fiscal control of the macroeconomy was automatically achieved when production and investment quotas for the state enterprises were determined. Revenues and expenditures of state enterprises were parts of government revenues and expenditures. In 1980, about 43 percent of the revenues of the central government were incomes from state enterprises (Chow, 1985, p. 230). For most of the three decades up to 1979, the annual state budget was nearly balanced. In 1983, when state enterprises became financially more independent, their revenues were no longer automatically government revenues and they were required to pay taxes to the government. When state enterprises are allowed to make their own investment decisions, rather than seeking approval from the planning authorities, total investment expenditures are no longer under the direct control of the central government. A suitable macroeconomic control mechanism is yet to be designed to control total investment expenditures.

The lack of a suitable control mechanism also applies to the control of total money supply and credit in the conduct of monetary policy. In 1983, while state enterprises were given more autonomy in their investment decisions, the People's Bank had just been reorganized to become a central bank and its branch banks were given autonomy to make loans to state and collective enterprises. While an appropriate mechanism of monetary control under the central banking system — such as by effectively imposing a fractional reserve requirement to the branch banks — was not firmly established, local banks extended credits freely to the state and collective enterprises requesting them. After the loans were made, the central bank had no alternative but to honor the loans and to provide currency to the borrowers on demand. As a result, the total quantity of currency in circulation increased from 52.98 billion RMB at the end of 1983 to 79.21 billion at the end of 1984, or by 50 percent in one year (*SYC 1987*, p. 565). In 1985, realizing the rapid increase in money supply occurring in the previous year, the central bank tried to tighten credit by issuing credit quotas to the branch banks. Depositors were sometimes not permitted to withdraw funds from their own accounts. This incident illustrates the fact that China has not established appropriate economic institutions to implement the stated objective of the Decision of October 1984 to apply the economic levels of interest and tax rates for monetary and fiscal control to the macroeconomy. In the meantime, government authorities have exercised control by using quotas as under the former system of central planning.

The same situation prevails today, in October 1988. Without appropriate control, currency in circulation in China continued to increase, being 98.78 billion RMB at the end of 1985, 121.84 billion at the end of 1986, 145.45 billion at 1987 (*SYC 1987*, p. 565 and *China Statistics Monthly*, April 1988, p. 152). The percentage increases in these three years are respectively 24.7, 23.3 and 19.4, following the 50 percent increase in 1984. Not surprisingly, inflation had become serious by the Spring of 1988, with the increase in the official index of the prices of consumer goods reaching an annual rate of 20 percent, the true inflation rate being claimed by residents to be higher. The statistical relation between money supply and inflation has been investigated in Chow (1987b). At the end of September 1988, the Central Committee of the Chinese Communist Party met and decided to tighten control of the macroeconomy. The Central Committee declared that "the major effort required in improving the economic environment is to reduce the total social demand and curb inflation and ... to put an end to confusion existing in economic activities, especially in the sphere of circulation." Prime Minister Li Peng stated: "Government at every level must go all out to improve links in circulation by checking up on and reorganizing various corporations and companies, putting a firm stop to all unauthorized price hikes and, in accordance with law, banning and cracking down on such illegal activities as jacking up prices, hoarding, speculation, profiteering, and extortion by middlemen." (*New York Times*, October 1, 1988, pp. 1 and 4). These statements echoed the provisions for restricting price increases stipulated in the October 1984 Decision of the Central Committee on Reform of the Economic Structure quoted in Sec. 1.1 (third paragraph from end of section).

13.2. Evaluating the Chinese Economic System

In this section I will try to evaluate the Chinese economic system as characterized in Sec. 1. Short of very drastic and unexpected political changes, this system is unlikely to be greatly changed in the next decade. Reform of economic institutions is unlikely to be reversed. Chinese farmers are much happier with the system of individual farming than with collective farming under the Commune system, and government officials are pleased with the performance of the agricultural sector. Having more vitality than state enterprises, the collective and individual enterprises are likely to account for larger shares of national income in the future. The state enterprises are unlikely to return to the former mode of Soviet-style central planning as Chinese leaders have become firmly convinced of its many shortcomings through years of experience before the reform. The open door will not and cannot be closed. At the same time, one cannot expect a very rapid progress in institutional reform. The basic characteristics of the economic system to be achieved were already outlined in the Central Committee Decision of October 20, 1984, and there has been no indication that these basic characteristics will be significantly changed (the introduction, after 1984, of the contract responsibility system to the level of state enterprises possibly being classified as a mild exception). In review, the basic characteristics include limited central planning combined with autonomous state enterprises, a gradual change of the price system to reflect significantly the market forces of demand and supply, and a differential wage system to reflect productivity. The techniques of central planning and macroeconomic control, the functioning of financial institutions including the banking system, the operation of state enterprises, and the working of the price system can be expected to improve only slowly for reasons of institutional inertia, bureaucratic resistance, and the slow process of training personnel at all levels to improve their performance. The two well-known dependency problems under Chinese socialism of the workers on the enterprise for job security (the iron rice bowl) and of the enterprise on the state, in spite of the attempted institution of bankruptcy laws, are difficult to solve. Therefore, for the purpose of predicting the performance of the Chinese economy in the next two decades, it is realistic to evaluate the Chinese economic system as it exists today. For those readers who believe that the Chinese economic system may change significantly, my prediction of performance is conditional on the system remaining approximately constant. In any case, it is of interest to evaluate the Chinese economic system as it exists today.

My conclusion is that the present Chinese economic system, with proper management, is capable of achieving a fairly high level of performance to generate a reasonably rapid rate of economic development. This conclusion is based on the following three propositions, each to be discussed in turn.

Proposition 1. A decentralized socialist market economy, if properly designed, can perform somewhat between 60 and 100 percent as efficiently as a capitalist market economy. By "60 percent efficiency" is meant producing 60 percent of the output using the same amount of resources.

The analysis below is essentially static while economic development is a dynamic process. To apply the analysis to economic growth, consider for example the Harrod–Domar model consisting of production function $Y_t = \Theta K_t$ and a savings function $\Delta K_t = I_t = \sigma Y_t = \sigma \Theta K_t$, implying output growth by $Y_t = (1 - \sigma\Theta)^{-1} Y_{t-1}$. A 60 percent efficiency statistic means changing Θ to $.6\Theta$ in the above model. A similar analysis applies to a different model.

Whether a decentralized socialist market economy ("market" meaning the respect for the price system) can perform as well as a capitalist market economy in terms of economic efficiency (ignoring other possible virtues of socialism) is a controversial question in economics which has been intensely debated in the literature. In the literature written in English, the best known proponents of the proposition that market socialism can perform equally well are Lange and Taylor (1983) and Schumpeter (1947, Part III). Schumpeter (1947, pp. 172–173) refers to earlier proponents including Vilfredo Pareto and his student Enrico Barone. A recent defender of market socialism is Yunker (1988). L. von Mises (paper in von Hayek, ed., 1935) is a well-known opponent of this proposition. So are the majority of American economists including in particular Milton Friedman (1962).

I put the upper limit at 100 percent in Proposition 1 because arguments supporting a higher percentage appear to me as weak as those supporting a percentage below 60, and there is no historical example to support it. Most economists believe, and history has demonstrated, that decentralized economic decisions by independent producing units maximizing profits under the institution of market prices are capable of yielding efficient economic performance. The main point of the opponents of market socialism is that under public ownership the enterprise managers, even when instructed by the central authority, have no incentive to maximize profits, or to take an optimum risk in investing. This argument has much merit to it. How serious the incentive problem is depends on how well market socialism is designed.

Consider a small enterprise, one which employs not more than 300 employees. Its management can be given a lease by the state and required to pay a market rental. Such an enterprise can be expected to perform almost as well as the case of private ownership under capitalism. This point has been demonstrated by the performance of some small commercial (mainly retail) and industrial enterprises leased to the managers in China under the contract responsibility system. The incentive problem for the management of a medium-sized or a large state enterprise is more difficult to solve. One suggested solution is the leasing arrangement similar to that for a small enterprise, but such an arrangement might not work well because the management may not be willing or able to bear the financial risk when the large enterprise is operating at a loss. The Chinese have experimented with a "contract responsibility system" for medium-sized and large state enterprises. The system does not work very well, partly because, lacking a market for capital goods, the government officials do not know the appropriate amount of tax or rental to charge. Sometimes the government officials are too greedy, trying to extract too much tax from the lease. The management and labor signing the contract complain that the fixed tax is too high and they would prefer to pay a percentage of profits as tax so that they do not have to bear the risk. Also they often suspect that if profits become higher, taxes may increase.

A second proposed solution is to diversify the ownership of state enterprises and let the stockholder, through a board of directors, control the management as in the case of a corporation in a capitalist economy. It has been suggested that bureaucrats of economic ministries will not do a good job (have wrong incentives) in controlling state enterprises, including the appointment and rewarding of their managers. As a solution, the state ministry in charge can be required to issue up to 49 percent of the stocks of each enterprises to the public, and much of the remaining 51 percent mostly to other ministries and provincial government agencies. Enterprises management will be subject to the control of board of directors elected by stockholders as in the case of a private market economy. Even takeover by new management team (good or bad) is possible if the team can buy up sufficient stocks from the public and/or convince the stockholders representing government agencies to vote for it. Under such an arrangement, the management of a state enterprise will have incentives similar to those of corporate executives in a capitalist economy, and will behave about as efficiently. Whether managers of state enterprises need to be as highly paid as corporate executives in a capitalist system is a debatable question. University presidents in the United States are not as highly paid and do not maximize profit, and yet some are highly motivated in their work.

The above discussion suggests that a state enterprise under market socialism can be made about as efficient as a corporation in a capitalist economy. Since this is a debatable point, and since my conclusion is that market socialism can work, I ought to underestimate its performance by asserting in Proposition 1 that it can work between 60 to 100 percent as efficiently as capitalism. To be conservative, I will use a figure of 75 percent in the following discussion.

Proposition 1 asserts that market socialism can work reasonably well, leaving the Chinese case aside. In terms of remuneration for management of state enterprises, and of partial privatization and decentralization of ownership (through the use of many public stockholders) of state enterprises, there are discrepancies between the second solution suggested above and the current thinking of many Chinese leaders. By examining the provisions of the Central Committee's Decision of October 1984 which are politically feasible and considered by the Chinese Communist Party leaders to be most desirable, I conclude, based partly on the interferences with the market mechanism provided in the Decision, that the state enterprises under the desired form of Chinese socialism as stated in the Decision are perhaps about 80 percent as efficient as under an ideal form of market socialism. The difference lies in the remuneration of management, the degree of diversification of stock ownership, and the job security provided to the workers. These characteristics of Chinese socialism may be desirable from a point of view other than pure economic efficiency.

Proposition 2. The combination of economic planning with market socialism or capitalism can make the economic system work about as well, if not better, than pure market socialism or capitalism.

Economic planning exists in every economy. The differences among countries are in the extent to which it exists. In capitalist economies, macroeconomic planning is prevalent, while government-directed activities affecting the microeconomy are less so. In the United States, for example, national defense, the federal highway network and national parks are among the public goods subject to central planning. It is difficult to decide the optimal amount of central planning and the particular areas to which it should apply. In developing economies where markets are not yet highly developed and where highly trained and experienced entrepreneurs are scarce, it may be reasonable for the government to establish and operate some state enterprises for the purpose of developing certain industries, leading and setting examples for private enterprises but not monopolizing the industry. To compete in the international market, it may be beneficial for the government to set up larger enterprises than can be financed by private funds. The above propositions are questioned by advocates of a "pure" market economy, often citing Hong Kong as an example to illustrate the benefits of the absence of government economic planning. Yet even Hong Kong practices planning for public goods such as education services, roads and harbors. Just as a large multinational and multiproduct corporation can used central planning effectively in operating its branches, so can the economic ministry of a mixed planned-market economy.

Two conditions should be observed to make central planning effective. First, government directed productive activities by state enterprises should be subject to the law of prices in the same way as autonomous state enterprises and private enterprises. For example, in the building of railroads, a government enterprise following the direction of central planning should pay for the steel at market price so that the cost of the project can be accurately ascertained under rational central planning. The October 1984 Decision of the Central Committee shows some appreciation of this point, as suggested by the quotation cited in Sec. 1.1 concerning central planning that "the law of value must be consciously followed and applied." Secondly, as much as possible, competition from independently operated state enterprises in the form of alternative bids or of producing competitive products should be encouraged in order to ensure the efficiency of government projects.

Proposition 3. Monopolistic and rent-seeking behavior on the part of state enterprise managers and government bureaucrats in China affects the distribution of income but might not seriously affect the efficient working of the market.

Large state enterprises in China often take advantage of their monopoly power and reap high profits. This is partly the result of monopolistic pricing and the lack of capital markets to evaluate the cost of capital goods. This situation can be improved by making further progress in the proposed price reform of the Decision of October 20, 1984, and by allowing for more competition by foreign corporations, potential or existing provincial and collective enterprises. Bureaucrats and enterprises managers in China take advantage of their positions to obtain bribes in various forms (money, foreign goods and travel, foreign scholarships for their children, returning favors, etc.) when approving licenses, signing contracts and making other economic decisions affecting the welfare of their clients. Such practices prevail in many countries to various degrees. Hong Kong (especially in the 1960s and 1970s, but less so today) and Taiwan government officials received bribes when issuing construction permits. The Chinese case is bad, but is probably not much worse than in some other developing countries. The situation will improve when the compensation and income of government officials increase and as the market sector expands. Higher income reduces the desire to take bribes. When the market sector expands, fewer economic activities are subject to government control or to the authority of government bureaucrats, and competition from the market sector will reduce the monopoly power of state enterprise managers. Bribery results in an unfair distribution of income if one believes that the officials taking bribes do not deserve (they do not work for) the side payments which they receive, but not if one considers the payments as "commissions" for their jobs, paid by the users of their services rather than by their employers. Insofar as useful economic activities are carried on after the required payments are made to government officials, the system may function fairly efficiently.

Socialism is characterized by state ownership of most economic resources. Under either state ownership or private ownership in the case of capitalism, resources are always controlled by people. The difference lies in the ways people obtain control of resources and are supposed to use them. Under capitalism, a person obtains control of resources by competition in the market, by advancing one's position in a private enterprise, and less frequently in a government bureau, by personal transfers including inheritance, and by transfers from the state through welfare programs. Under socialism, a person obtains resources by competition in the market sector, by advancing in a state enterprise or in a government bureau, by joining the ruling political party, and by transfers. Under capitalism or socialism, a person controlling the resources owned by the state is supposed to use the resources entirely for the benefit of the state, however the benefit is defined, but in practice the person often takes advantage of his or her position for personal gains, such as taking bribes. If the person thinks he is well compensated, he is less likely to take bribes. Taking bribes is ethically wrong and affects the distribution of income. In many occasions, it might not seriously affect the efficient functioning of the economy.

Consider an example of a purchasing agent of a state or private enterprise offering to pay $100,000 to buy a certain product from another state or private enterprise and asking for $5,000 as bribe. In effect, the purchasing enterprise pays $100,000, $95,000 to the seller and $5,000 to its own agent. If the purchasing agent happens to be the owner of the first enterprise, he pays, and the second enterprise receives $95,000 for the goods sold. Nothing is wrong. Something is wrong when he does not own the enterprise because the owner of the enterprise in effect pays him $5,000 to which he is not entitled. Also nothing is wrong if the owner or the seller willingly and openly offers the purchasing agent $5,000 commission for the transaction, as in the case of someone buying a $100,000 house in the United States. Bribery is considered bad because it is paid to a person who is not entitled to it or who does not deserve it.

The problem of entitlement is more serious under socialism because most resources are publicly owned and the persons controlling them are not entitled to them. The problem of enterprise executives not deserving the side payment is also more serious under socialism because, in practice, it is the ethnical judgement of the advocates of socialism that enterprise managers and staff members should not be highly paid and should not receive commissions for conducting economic transactions. Bribes paid to government officials issuing licenses of various kinds have similar economic effects as increase in licence fees which are then paid to certain employees of the licensing bureaus. Leaving the ethical question of bribery aside, much of economic efficiency is already achieved when, in contrast with central planning, state enterprises are allowed to make autonomous market transactions, if prices are set by market forces and if sufficient incentives are provided to the workers and managers. Bribery might be a secondary issue in terms of economic efficiency, although it is a very serious issue for political and moral reasons. The validity of this comment, and of Proposition 3, is illustrated by the fact that Taiwan, Hong Kong and Singapore succeeded in rapid economic development in spite of such practices.

Let me now apply these propositions to evaluate the economic efficiency of present-day Chinese socialism which uses a combination of planning and market forces. Propositions 1 and 2 show that market socialism, combined with a certain degree of central planning, can work about 75 percent (conservatively) as efficiently as capitalism. The state sector of the Chinese system to be established under the principles stated in the October 1984 Decision on Economic Reform of the Central Committee of China's Communist Party may attain about four-fifths of this 75 percent efficiency, or 60 percent of the efficiency of ideal capitalism. As of today, in October 1988, the Chinese government has made important progress, say about 65 percent of the way, in price reform and in the reform state enterprises suggested by the Decision. In the next decade, momentum itself will carry the reform process forward to something like the 70 percent mark, in spite of the present policy to curb inflation which is necessary and desirable. Inflation control will not jeopardize the reform of state enterprises or even slow down price reform, since under present conditions, it can provide a more stable economic environment for future reform to take place. If we apply the 70 percent to the 60 percent efficiency of the desired Chinese socialism of the 1984 Decision as compared with ideal capitalism, we may obtain 42 percent for the efficiency of the state sector of the present Chinese system. This evaluation is not meaningful because the present Chinese system should not be compared with an ideal but unachievable system. Even if one assumes that the capitalist system is more efficient and that hypothetically the Chinese leaders decide to adopt its economic institutions for the present state industrial sector, it will take time for large private corporations to be established and to operate efficiently. Institutional inertia, ideological resistance on the part of Communist Party members and the lack of trained personnel would prevent large enterprises in China from becoming as efficient as modern corporations. Rather than using ideal capitalism as 100 percent to evaluate the state sector under Chinese socialism in the next two decades, it is more reasonable to use 70 percent of ideal capitalism as something achievable. Our evaluation of the Chinese state sector is more like 42 percent divided by 70 percent, or 60 percent, of the feasible ideal. For the Chinese economy as a whole, we apply 100 percent efficiency to the individual and collective sector, which accounts for 52.6 percent of national income, and 60 percent efficiency to the remaining 47.4 percent for the state enterprises, obtaining a final measure of 81 percent efficiency as compared with an ideal and feasible economic system. If the reader disagrees with some of the percentage figures used above, she or he may revise the calculations and use a figure somewhat different from 60 percent for the efficiency of the state sector. Since the state sector accounts for only 47.4 percent of total output, my conclusion concerning the Chinese economy as a whole will not be seriously affected.

13.3. Retrospect and Prospect

A strong supporting evidence for the conclusion that a mixed planned and market economy under Chinese socialism functions well is the historical growth of the Chinese economy during the first decade of reform from 1979 to 1988. An official index of national income at constant prices (1952 = 100) increased from 484.9 in 1979 to 884.1 in 1986, or at an average annual rate of 8.96 percent (*SYC 1987*, p. 39), as compared with an annual increase of about 6.0 percent from 1952 to 1979. In per capita terms, it amounts to 7.71 percent per year (p. 67 for population figures). National income contributed by the industrial sector, which is dominated by state enterprises, increased from 48.6 percent of the index of 484.9 in 1979 to 45.6 percent of the index of 884.1 in 1986, or at an annual rate of 7.97 percent. One has to be careful in attributing economic growth to economic reform since a part of it was probably due to the recovery after the Cultural Revolution. However, the effect of recovery is not the main story, as one can observe the enthusiasm and behavior of the farmers and compare this recovery with past recoveries. For a more detailed documentation of the Chinese economic record since reform, the reader is referred to Robert Dernberger (1987). For a discussion and assessment of the reform process, see Lardy (1987) and Perkins (1988). The agreement among these authors and other knowledgeable observers is that the first decade of China 's economic reform, in spite of some shortcomings, is essentially a success story, especially in view of the condition China was in before the reform.

The fact that the Chinese economy has grown substantially in the last decade is not sufficient to justify the conclusion that it will grow at similar rates in the next two decades. Some reservations have been voiced. First, the economic momentum generated by the reform will run out of steam. In particular, reform in agriculture increased efficiency in terms of raising output per capita as compared with farming under the Commune system, but once the level of output per capita is raised, no further increase is expected. In fact, the record of agricultural output since 1985 has been poor. This is a valid point, except that the energy of the farmers unleashed by the present system (in spite of the uncertainty about the right of long-term land use) has been applied to work in light industry, and in commercial and other more productive pursuits in the rural areas, and that the process of technological change in the form of the changing occupation and production mix in China's countryside has continued and is expected to continue, thus helping to raise output per capita in rural areas.

Second, inexperienced macroeconomic management in an environment of imperfect macroeconomic institutions may destroy the economic fabric for further growth. This is a serious possibility. Like other observers, I am concerned about the current inflation, but it is my judgment that the Chinese government will succeed in preventing it from getting out of hand, even if some arbitrary controls might be applied and the progress of price reform might be slower than in the absence of inflation. Like many economists who appreciate the distinction between the flexibility of relative prices and the control of the (average) price index, I believe that it is possible for the Chinese government to control inflation while allowing prices of individual products to remain fairly free. One well-known experience is the control of the inflation in Taiwan in the 1950s, when aggregate demand for consumer goods and the velocity of currency circulation were reduced significantly by raising the rates of interest, following advice given by Sho-chieh Tsiang to the Taiwan government. High interest rates from "real goods saving deposits" and "real unit bonds" were also used in the People's Republic of China in 1949, and they helped to curb inflation rapidly in 1950 (see Tsiang, 1980, p. 311). A similar device can be used today. There is no need to estimate the rate of inflation in order to determine the rate of interest for deposits. One can try a monthly rate of 4 percent, for example, and observe the inflow of deposits to the banking system. The rate can be adjusted monthly depending on observed results. Furthermore, the increase in money supply in the last five years at rates quoted at the end of Sec. 1.3, though excessive, was not large enough to cause runaway inflation, if the rapid increase is to slow down under the present policy of curbing inflation. High interest rates as recommended above, in order to be effective, have to be accompanied by stopping the rapid increase in money supply.

Third, some observers are concerned that the reform process will stop. As I have argued above, reasonable economic progress in China can occur without significant further reforms in economic institutions. The present system is good enough, although it can be better under Chinese socialism as put forward by the October 1984 Decision. Supporting this argument further is the open-door policy, which will continue to provide energy to China's economic growth in the form of capital and technology import, and of setting examples for and providing competition to Chinese State enterprises. The contribution to economic growth of foreign investment, and of collective and private enterprises, has been evident in the province of Guangdong, neighboring Hong Kong. Vogel (1989) is a detailed and interesting account of the economic success of Guangdong in the last decade. Comparing with Japan, South Korea, and Taiwan, the author asserts that Guangdong "has made a more dramatic turnaround than any of those countries, and its annual rate of industrial progress compares favorably with the periods of fastest growth in any of the East Asian countries." (See Vogel's letter in the *New York Times*, March 15, 1988.) Observing China's recent experience and inferring from theory, one can expect that China will continue its reasonably rapid economic growth in the next two decades. One can also expect its coastal provinces, including Guangdong, to develop more rapidly, serving as leaders to economic development in China as a whole. China may be slow in correcting the present deficiencies of the economic system. These deficiencies include the dependency of labor on the iron rice bowl, the dependency of state enterprises on the government for financial help, a certain amount of corruption, the lack of proficiency in economic planning and macroeconomic management, and the poor environment for foreign investment.

It is my conclusion that market socialism combined with a certain degree of central planning will succeed in modernizing China. This conclusion does not rule out the possibility that capitalism may be better than socialism under other circumstances. Most people living in a capitalist society prefer capitalism as a form of economic organization. China has a very different historical experience from the United States. How feasible and desirable capitalism is under China's political and economic situation are difficult questions to answer. Many Chinese leaders believe that socialism is more desirable for China, although many young people in China are questioning this view. Since the end of the Second World War, under the leadership of the United States and Soviet Union, capitalist and communist countries have been engaged in a cold war. People and intellectuals on each side have criticized the other system while arguing the superiority of their own. The Chinese economic experiment, by combining socialism with market incentives, may help resolve the conflict in economic ideas and hasten the end of the Cold War.

References

China Statistics Monthly, April 1988, Chicago: University of Illinois.

Chow, G. C., 1985, *The Chinese Economy*, New York: Harper & Row; 2nd edn. 1987, Singapore: World Scientific.

———, 1987a, Development of a more market-oriented economy in China, *Science* **235**, 295–299.

———, 1987b, Money and price level determination in China, *J. Comparative Econ.* **11**, 319–333.

Dernberger, R., 1987, The drive for economics modernization and growth, paper presented before the International Conference "A Decade of Reform Under Deng Xiaoping", Brown University, November 4–7 1987.

Friedman, M., 1962, *Capitalism and Freedom*, Chicago: University of Chicago Press.

———, 1981, The invisible hand in economics and politics, Taipei: Institute of Economics, Academia Sinica, Chung-Hua Series of Lectures by Invited Eminent Economists, no. 3.

Lange, O., and Taylor, F. M., 1938, *On the Economics of Socialism*.

Lardy, N. R., 1987, Recasting the economics system, paper presented before the International Conference " A Decade of Reform Under Deng Xiaoping", Brown University, November 4–7 1987.

Perkins, D., 1988, Reforming China's economic system, *J. Econ. Lit.* **26**, 601–645.

Schumpeter, J. A., 1947, *Capitalism, Socialism and Democracy*, New York: Harper & Brothers.

Statistical Yearbook of China, Beijing: State Statistic Bureau.

Tsiang, S. C, 1980, Exchange rate, interest rate, and economic development, in

Klein, L. R., Nerlove, M. and Tsiang, S. C. eds., *Quantitative Economics and Development*, New York: Academic Press, pp. 309–346.

Vogel, E., 1989, *One Step Ahead: Guangdong Under Reform*, Cambridge, MA: Harvard University Press.

von Hayek, F. A., ed., 1935, *Collective Economic Planning*.

Yunker, J. A., 1988, A general equilibrium evaluation of capitalism versus pragmatic market socialism, Western Illinois University mimeograph.

CHAPTER 14

RIGHTS TO ASSETS AND ECONOMIC BEHAVIOR
UNDER CHINESE SOCIALISM*†

A basic hypothesis of asset management is advanced that an asset manager will try to derive the most benefit from the management. It is used to derive laws of asset management which can explain the behavior observed in China in managing one's own person, one's nonhuman assets for own use, one's nonhuman assets for use by others, and collections of assets in the form of state enterprises. Two models of management behavior for state enterprises before and after economic reforms in the early 1980s are provided. They are models of maximizing behavior, but the objective function and the constraints vary according to economic institution.

Private property is a fundamental institution of capitalism. Accordingly, existing theory for explaining economic behavior in a capitalist society takes private property for granted. Under socialism, much of wealth is publicly owned. Public ownership leads to different economic behavior in a socialist society. This paper is an attempt to explain economic behavior in China as it is affected by the rights to assets which the Chinese people are permitted to have under existing economic institutions. Under capitalism or socialism, all assets are managed by people. Assets include human and nonhuman assets, consumption goods and physical capital as well as enterprises and parts thereof which are collections of assets. In a socialist society the rights of people to manage the assets under their control, including their own persons, physical assets and collections of assets are different from the rights in a capitalist society with private ownership. The economic hypothesis here adopted is capable of explaining behavior in the managing of all kinds of assets in different societies, although this paper is confined to explaining the behavior observed in contemporary China.

*Originally appeared in *Academia Economic Papers*, vol. 20, no. 2, part I, pp. 267–290, (September 1992).

†The author would like to thank Abhijit Banerjee, William Baumol and Walter Oi for helpful comments and the Center for International Studies of Princeton University for financial support. This paper was prepared for the USAID sponsored Institute for the Study of Free Enterprise Systems' May 1991 conference "The Economic Contest between Capitalism and Communism: What's Ahead?" held at the State University of New York at Buffalo.

I will adopt the following hypothesis to which most economists would readily agree and which will be called *the hypothesis of asset management: A person managing an asset will, to the best of his or her knowledge, try to derive the most benefit from it, in (a) utilizing its services directly himself or herself, (b) allowing others to use its services, or (c) delivering it to others.*

In Sec. 1 four laws of economic behavior will be stated which are immediate implications of this hypothesis. These laws will be applied to the management of one's own person (Sec. 2) and to the management of an individual physical asset (Sec. 3). Section 4 deals with collections of assets including parts of an enterprise and an entire enterprise. It will present two models of managerial behavior in state enterprises in China before and after the urban economic reforms beginning in the early 1980s. Institutional arrangements affect the objective function which the enterprise management seeks to maximize and the production function constraints to which it is subject, and hence the behavior of the enterprise.

14.1. Laws of Asset Management

The basic model is that of an asset manager who is given control over an asset and some limited rights in the use of the asset. Under socialism, the rights to use economic assets and to derive benefits from them are more limited than under capitalism. Our hypothesis is that an individual managing an asset will try to derive the most benefit from it. Two assumptions are made. First, in order to produce service S from the asset (which may be a physical asset or simply the human asset of the manager), labor L from the asset manager is required, through a production function $S = S(L)$, with $dS/dL > 0$. In the case of managing one's own person, $S = L$. In the case of managing a physical asset, labor from the manager is required to extract from it in the form of physical handling, supervision, maintenance, etc. Second, there exists a utility function $u(S, L)$ which the asset manager tries to maximize, with $\partial u/\partial S \geqslant 0$, $-\partial u/\partial L > 0$, and the marginal disutility of labor $-\partial u/\partial L$ being an increasing function of L. The socialist institution specifies $\partial u/\partial S$, that is, how much benefit the asset manager obtains by providing additional service.

The equilibrium condition resulting from the asset manager maximizing utility is

$$\frac{\partial u}{\partial S} \cdot \frac{dS}{dL} = -\frac{\partial u}{\partial L} \tag{1}$$

From this simple condition and our assumptions concerning u, four laws of economic behavior are readily deduced, depending on the institutional setup.

14.1.1. *Law of supply of asset service*

When the marginal benefit from providing the service of an asset is smaller (larger), the asset manager will supply less (more) of its service.

Here we envisage the asset manager keeping control of the asset and adding her own labor in producing a stream of services which would yield her some benefit. Starting with equilibrium condition (1), when the marginal benefit $\partial u/\partial S$

is reduced, the marginal disutility of labor $-\partial u/\partial L$ has to be reduced by decreasing L to maintain equilibrium, thus reducing service S through the production function. In the case of supply of labor service, $S = L$ and this law is related to, but different from the law of supply of labor. The latter is concerned with the relation between labor supply and the wage rate, assuming that the rate of payment per unit of labor service is given. Reducing the wage rate does not necessarily lead to a reduction in labor supply. The present law is concerned with the relation between labor supply and the marginal benefit of supplying an additional unit of service. To relate this law to the law of labor supply, let $u(C, L)$ be the utility function, with consumption $C = wS$ where w is the wage rate. The equilibrium condition is

$$\frac{\partial u}{\partial C} \cdot w = -\frac{\partial u}{\partial L} . \tag{2}$$

By our law, given $w = 1$, reducing $\partial u/\partial C$ leads to reducing $-\partial u/\partial L$ and reducing L. By the law of labor supply, reducing w might not lead to reducing $-\partial u/\partial L$ because $\partial u/\partial C$ evaluated at $C = wS$ may increase as a result of diminishing marginal utility of consumption.

14.1.2. *Law of asset delivery*

When the marginal benefit from delivery or surrendering an asset to others is smaller (larger), the asset manager will be less (more) willing to deliver it, possibly reducing the qualities of delivery in the form of delays or lower product quality.

The situation envisaged is that of an asset manager whose task is to deliver the asset, such as a producer good or a certain raw material, to a potential user. Interpreting S to be delivery service, one can use equilibrium condition (1) to derive this law in the same way as law A.

14.1.3. *Law of asset maintenance*

When the benefit of managing an asset, either through the use of its service or through surrendering it to others, is smaller (larger), the manager will be less (more) willing to maintain it or to improve upon it.

This law corresponds to a statement concerning optimum investment policy in a capitalist society. Maintenance expenditures for an asset and addition to the asset will be small if the asset provides little income in the future. Without introducing a dynamic framework explicitly, one can simply define S in the equilibrium condition (1) to mean the service to maintain or to improve upon an asset to derive this law.

14.1.4. *Law of rent seeking*

When opportunities to extract payment or benefit from providing the service of an asset or from delivering it to others are available and not unduly risky, the manager will take advantage of them.

This proposition follows directly from our hypothesis of asset management. In terms of the equilibrium condition (1), there are choices of $\partial u/\partial S$ available to the manager. Some, such as taking bribes, may be risky and lead to punishment if caught. Often the rule of a socialist society assigns no extra benefit to an asset manager for providing additional services and hence he requires compensation from the user for providing the services. Any illegal payment that he can extract from the user can be considered rent.

14.1.5. *Welfare effects of restrictions on asset use*

Besides the four laws of economic behavior in asset management, I would like to state the following proposition concerning the welfare effects of restrictions on the use of assets: When restrictions are placed on the use of an asset's service or on the delivery of an asset, leading to less benefit to its manager, the manager will reduce the quality of its service or the quality of the asset delivered. The net welfare effect of such restrictions on society is negative unless the use of the asset is harmful to society, or unless the government is able to redirect the use of the asset for social gains which outweigh the loss of benefits to its manager and the reduction of quality of its service to the users.

The above laws will be illustrated by economic behavior in China.

14.2. Managing One's Own Person

14.2.1. *Eating from a large rice pot*

As an application of the law of supply of asset service, consider the low quality of the services provided by the farmers under the Commune system before 1978 and the workers in state enterprises. The poor performance is sometimes attributed to the Iron Rice Bowl, the implication being that, given job security which guarantees sufficient food to eat from an unbreakable rice bowl, farmers and workers have no need to work hard. The real reason for poor performance is not job security alone, but rather the lack of additional remuneration when one tries to work harder. Under the Commune system, when the farmer worked harder to increase output, he or she would get very little additional benefit because the output is shared by the entire work team consisting of some fifty farmers on average. That Chinese farmers respond to material incentives has been documented by Lin (1988), McMillan, Whalley and Zhu (1989), and Putterman (1990). Lin (1988) models the team with supervision as maximizing average net income per worker assuming each worker to maximize his own utility function of income and effort, with the return to effort differing according to institutional arrangements. McMillan, Whalley and Zhu (1989) also employ a utility function of income and effort for the farmer and find that Chinese farmers responded to income incentives provided after reform. Putterman (1990) found that even working under the system of a production team, Chinese farmers increased their work effort when a larger fraction of the team output was distributed to them.

The remuneration system for the workers is also such that by working harder a person receives little additional benefit. The services of retail store clerks, waiters in restaurants, public transportation personnel and all government officials dealing with people are known to be extremely poor in China. The problem of the Iron Rice Bowl is related to the problem of "eating from a large rice pot." People have the right to share without having to put in additional work, just like the farmers working collectively under the Commune system.

14.2.2. *Restriction of labor mobility*

The lack of labor mobility has been recognized to be a serious problem in China. The farmers in the communes could not move to other locations. The urban population needed residence permits to reside in a given city. Without the permit, one could not obtain rationed food items and clothing if he moved to another city. The situation improved in the 1980s as the Commune system was abolished in 1983 and as market supplies of food and clothing became more abundant, and rationing was no longer needed. Opportunities became available for urban migration. Another aspect of the restriction is the power given to labor bureaus to assign jobs to the urban population, and to university administrators to assign jobs to college graduates. The restriction of opportunities for an individual to seek the best job and the best location has limited the usefulness of his services to himself and to society. This is an illustration of the negative welfare effects of restrictions on asset use.

14.2.3. *Poor investment in human capital*

When the opportunities to use human services are restricted, there is less incentive for students in schools and laborers in the work force to improve themselves through education and training. In the meantime, one can increase the benefits from his labor by joining the Communist Party or by establishing personal connections in order to obtain a better job assignment. Such efforts replace the efforts to study and to obtain additional training. This is an illustration of the law of asset maintenance.

14.3. Managing Physical Assets

14.3.1. *Assets for own use*

Chinese urban residential housing deteriorated rapidly from the 1950s to the 1980s partly because of the poor maintenance by its tenants. A tenant, in China and in the rest of the world, puts little effort in maintaining a rental apartment if the benefit from maintaining it is small. Although some tenants in urban China may expect to stay in the same apartment for some time, many tenants try to move to better apartments through negotiations with administrators and hence have limited incentive to maintain the current apartment. On the other hand, the rural population in China, especially after the introduction of economic reforms in 1978, was allowed to build their own housing which turned out to be of good quality and well maintained. Farmers in China allegedly do not take sufficient care of the land assigned to them partly because the future benefits from farming the land are uncertain. The government, realizing this uncertainty, has instituted policies to make the right of land use inheritable to children, although the credibility of this policy might be questioned by the farmers. The limited care devoted to maintain and improve the stock of housing, farm land (ceasing crop rotation) and other productive assets is an illustration of the law of asset maintenance.

14.3.2. *Assets for use by others*

1. *Poor quality of services*
A widespread phenomenon in China is the poor quality of the services rendered by persons controlling physical assets when the services provided yield no benefit to the persons rendering them. One example is the poor maintenance of residential housing by the staff of the housing bureaus. Other examples are the poor services provided by the personnel servicing publicly owned retail stores, restaurants, transportation facilities, etc. To illustrate this point from a personal experience, when I was scheduled to give a lecture at a university in 1982, I asked my host, the chairman of the economics department, to show me the lecture room. He presented my request to the bureaucrat in charge of room assignment and was first rejected on the ground that he allegedly had not filled out the appropriate forms to apply for the use of the room. After pleading with the bureaucrat, my host finally obtained approval to use the room, which was empty most of the time. As a favor, the bureaucrat unlocked the door and showed us the room before my lecture.

The above story is typical of the way assets are managed by bureaucrats in China. Each bureaucrat abuses his right in managing assets and provides poor services to those requesting for them if the services provided yield no benefit to him. Poor services are provided partly to reduce demand and thus to reduce the workload of the bureaucrat. This is an important reason why life in China is so miserable, especially before economic reforms. The people are humiliated continuously by bureaucrats who control the assets yielding services necessary for daily living. The same bureaucratic behavior is observed in other societies under similar circumstances, including, for example, that of the bureaucrats managing subsidized faculty housing at universities. Such bureaucratic behavior elsewhere is sometimes not as bad as in China when there are alternatives provided by the market. Having to deal constantly with bureaucratic behavior for survival, the Chinese in the Mainland have learned ways to beat the system and to fend for their self interests. Such behavior is not looked upon favorably by foreign hosts when the Chinese practice it in foreign countries as visitors or immigrants.

2. *Rent-seeking behavior by bureaucrats*
Examples abound to illustrate the law of rent seeking. When opportunity arises, the asset manager will try to extract rent, often illegally, for the services rendered.

Bribery in China and the rest of the world occurs when bureaucrats in charge of assets extract rents for their use, and the users are willing to pay for the services. Some of the assets being managed are rights to issue permits for engaging in economic activities, such as import and export licenses, inspection permits to build a house, etc. Bribery is a form of corruption which is widespread in China after the economic reforms. Economic reforms increased economic opportunities and hence the demand for the services from assets managed by the bureaucrats. The increase in demand raises the price of the services and the quantity supplies, if it is paid for by bribes.

3. *Poor quality of asset delivery*
The poor service provided to nonpaying users and the desire to extract payment for using the service of an asset also prevail in the delivery of an asset to others. Without compensation, one finds poor quality in the delivery, in the form of delays or physical defects. This explains why the material inputs delivered by the bureaucrats managing the supply of materials to state-owned industrial and commercial enterprises are often defective in physical terms or in delivery time. It also explains the extraction of rent by the asset managers in the form of return favors or outright payments. The products being delivered include producer goods (physical capital and materials) or consumer goods (airplane tickets, train tickets, food and nonfood items distributed to consumers).

4. *Nonmarket trading of services and goods (Guan-xi)*
The manager of an asset providing service or for delivery can trade the service or the asset with managers of other assets. In a capitalist economy, the trade often takes place in the market for money. If the manager is not allowed to receive money for providing services or supplying goods under his control, he will try to extract services and goods in return. Spot exchange does not take place frequently because the user of the services or goods provided by the asset manager may not have something immediately useful to the latter to pay in return, if money payment is not allowed. Payment often takes the form of credit, not explicitly recorded, to be settled in the future in the forms of goods or services provided to the asset manager, or to a friend or a relative, or simply a third person who has an (implicit) account with the manager. Such an implicit trading relationship is called guan-xi in China, literally meaning "relationship." One obtains a "relationship" with a network of people with whom one can trade services and goods (or even jobs and other favors). Guan-xi had existed in China before the Communist rule began in 1949, because the market was not perfect and many assets were controlled by bureaucrats. Such trades became much more prevalent under Communist rule because the market became even more imperfect and more assets were controlled by bureaucrats.

As an interesting aspect of economic behavior in Chinese societies, including Hong Kong, Taiwan, as well as the Mainland, people are accustomed not to settle accounts immediately by money, because of the tradition of nonmarket nonspot and nonmonetary trading which existed partly as a result of market under-development. When a friend provides you with a service in a Chinese society, he or she accumulates a credit in the unwritten account with you and expects you to remember it in the future in case he needs something in return. Developing guan-xi is very useful. It is like having credits in many banks from which you can draw in case of need. Confucius canonized this practice by advising: "Do not expect returns when you provide a service to others. Do not forget when others provide a service to you." The practice will last as long as the Chinese follow Confucius' advice. For a popular account of guan-xi, the reader is referred to Butterfield (1982; and see Appendix at the end of this paper).

14.4. Managing Collections of Assets

14.4.1. *The responsibility system*

1. *In agriculture*

The success story of China's economic reform began in agriculture and was due to the initiative and ingenuity of local cadres managing the work teams in the communes rather than to the design of the central authorities in Beijing. Work teams under the Commune system were required to deliver assigned quotas of agricultural products to the government purchasing units at below market prices for redistribution. In 1977 some local managers of the work teams in Anhui Province, recalling experiences in the 1950s, realized that a better way to obtain the required output for delivery was to distribute the land under collective ownership of the commune to the farm households and to require each household to turn over a given quota of output to the team so that the latter can meet its own delivery quota (see Chow, 1985, p. 55).

Although the farm households do not have ownership rights to the land, they have the rights to use it for production. Any output above the assigned quota for delivery belongs to the farm household and can be used for consumption or for sale in the rural markets which were to be expanded rapidly in the late 1970s and early 1980s. The incentives are similar to those of the farmers in a market economy who lease a piece of land for a fixed rental. Since the marginal benefit of producing extra output belongs to the farm household, there are great incentives to produce. This illustrates the law of supply of asset service. Such an institutional arrangement was termed the responsibility system, with the farm household taking the responsibility of delivering the production quota and of using the land otherwise as it pleases. The success of this system led to its wide adoption and to the central authorities pronouncing it as official policy in 1978. Except for the uncertainty of holding the land for long periods and of limited rights of transfer, both of which were improved in the early 1980s by government policy, China began returning to private farming in 1978–1979 and abolished the Commune system in 1983.

2. *In small nonagricultural enterprises*

In the early 1980s, as the rural population developed small enterprises for handicraft and other nonagricultural production, trade and local transportation using the wealth accumulated from farming, the government tried to apply the idea of the responsibility system for urban economic reform. Many small public enterprises, including retail stores and small factories, were allowed and encouraged to adopt the responsibility system, with one manager leasing the enterprise, paying a fixed rental and distributing the profit. In a very small establishment the profit goes to the manager, who may pay higher wages or bonuses to the workers to increase their incentives. In larger enterprises there is social and ideological pressure for the manager not to take too large a payment himself from the profit of the enterprise. I will return to this point later when discussing medium and large public enterprises. In any case, success stories abound, some reported in newspapers, concerning the increases in outputs, services provided, and profits of these small enterprises.

3. *For parts of larger enterprises*

A significant landmark of economic reforms was the Decision of the Central Committee of the Communist Party of China on October 20, 1984 on Economic Reform. Among the major provisions of this Decision are reduction of the scope of central planning, development of a macroeconomic control system using the economic tools of fiscal and monetary policy, reform of the price system to arrive at a set of prices reflecting more the forces of demand and supply (with restrictions on price increases that would result in "abnormal" profits), reform of the management of state enterprises, encouraging the expansion of collective enterprises and the market sector, and the further strengthening of the open-door policy to encourage foreign trade and investment. As far as the management of state enterprises is concerned, an important component of the Decision is to encourage adoption of the responsibility system to parts of state enterprises. The responsibility is given by a state enterprise to the units within the enterprise to perform tasks with rewards for additional outputs or services. Workers and groups of workers within an enterprise can get paid by the quantities of their products, through piece rates and similar reward systems. Parts of an enterprise can keep or get paid for their outputs once a fixed quantity is delivered to the enterprise. The leasing arrangement is introduced to parts of state enterprises as much as possible, practicing the law of supply of asset services.

4. *For entire state enterprises*

1987 was the year when the "contract responsibility system" was introduced rapidly into Chinese state (central, provincial and local government) enterprises. By the end of that year, over 95 percent of public enterprises were placed under this system. The central idea is that the management of an enterprise signs an agreement with the government unit supervising it which specifies a fixed annual tax for several years, with the enterprise management retaining all the profits after the tax payment. This idea can be interpreted as an intended application of the law of supply of asset service, the asset being the enterprise. In practice, a number of problems arise concerning the effectiveness of the contract responsibility system.

The first problem is concerned with the compensation for the enterprise manager. Because of the possibly large profits of a state enterprise and the ideological and social objections to high compensation, the relation between additional profits and the manager's compensation is very limited. In practice, the management obtains consent from the staff and workers concerning his own compensation and the remuneration to the employees including wage, bonuses and other benefits. The link between marginal benefits to the manager and additional efforts is not satisfactorily established. One consequence of the law of rent seeking is that parts of the extra profits are used for distribution to the management, staff and workers in the form of bonuses. The bonuses may take the form of consumer goods such as color television sets and refrigerators. Funds of enterprises are often used to purchase consumer goods for distribution to staff and workers.

The second problem concerns the determination of an appropriate amount of the tax which an enterprise is required to pay. The collecting unit of the government would like to extract a large amount from the enterprise, leading to bargaining and negotiations not unlike those taking place during the period of central planning regarding output targets and material supplies assigned to the state enterprises. These is also uncertainty concerning the possible increase in the "fixed" tax when profit increases in the future, lessening the possible incentive from a truly fixed charge. The third, and related, problem is that profits do not necessarily reflect economic efficiency. State enterprises have monopoly power. Assets are assigned to state enterprises without appropriate rental charges; ideally the tax levied should reflect an appropriate rental for the capital under the enterprises' control. Finally, both output and input prices facing state enterprises might not reflect scarcity, invalidating the use of profits as a measure of enterprise efficiency.

Since the contract responsibility system is recognized by Chinese authorities and outside observers to be unsatisfactory for making state enterprises efficient, discussion inside and outside China continues on how to improve the functioning of state enterprises. To contribute to this discussion, I will provide below an economic analysis of the functioning of state enterprises before and after the economic reforms in the form of two models of management behavior. These models are very simple but, I believe, capture the most important features of Chinese state enterprises before and after urban economic reforms. As the rights to assets affect the cost-benefit calculations of people managing individual assets and thus their economic behavior, so will administrative arrangements provided for the managers of state enterprises affect managerial behavior.

14.4.2. *State enterprises before reform*

In model A for a state enterprise under central planning in China, I assume that for the short-run the enterprise is assigned given quantities k and n of capital and labor respectively. In reality, the enterprise was assigned a production target and sometimes targets for value of output and total wage, but no financial or cost targets (see Chow, 1985, p. 137). Since the main criterion for enterprise performance is output quantity, I assume for simplicity that the objective function of the manager is

$$u^A = u^A(y, m_1 + m_2) \tag{3}$$

where y denotes output of the enterprise, m_1 denotes management effort for coordinating production, and m_2 denote management effort for negotiating with planning authorities or ministries supervising the enterprise. The derivative u_1^A with respect to the first argument is positive, and the derivative u_2^A with respect to combined management effort $m_1 + m_2$ is negative.

The production function is

$$y = f[k, n, x(m_2), m_1] \tag{4}$$

where x denotes the quantity of material inputs, the supply of which can be increased by management effort m_2. The explicit use of the management effort m_1 in the production function captures one aspect of what Leibenstein (1966) termed X-efficiency. Management effort undoubtedly affects output, given the quantities of other inputs. The efficiency of labor input n is also affected by the rights to assets, as we have pointed out in Sec. 2.1 that the remuneration system for workers does not reward additional effort and hence discourages the workers from working hard. In the production function we choose to define n and other inputs as the quantities actually used and as recorded by statistics of the enterprises. Alternatively, one can choose to measure inputs by efficiency units, being the above quantities each multiplied by an efficiency factor which depends on institutional arrangements. We have subsumed this multiplicative factor in the production, yielding a larger quantity of labor input n required to produce a given output y, given the quantities of other inputs, than in the case of better labor incentives. The efficiencies of capital, labor and material inputs are all affected by management effort m_1 as the production function (4) implies.

The manager is assumed to maximize u^A subject to the constraint of this production function. This formulation also captures the idea of Kornai (1979, 1980) concerning a soft-budget constraint. First, financial items are not included in the objective function so that there is no reason to economize on the use of inputs. Second, insofar as an increase of output is desirable and can be achieved by an increase of the use of inputs, there is an incentive for the manager to negotiate for more material and other inputs, hence the soft-budget constraint. Much has been written on the soft-budget constraint. A notable example is the work of Goldfeld and Quandt (1988, 1990, 1991) which employs a stochastic rather than a deterministic model and uses profit rather than output in the objective function. Our formulation is deterministic and simple. Yet it captures some of the most important characteristics of the soft budget constraint.

For illustration and for possible econometric implementation, I will employ the following objective and production functions

$$u^A = y(1 - m_1 - m_2)^\theta \tag{5}$$

where 1 is the maximum effort possible, with $1 - m_1 - m_2$ corresponding to "leisure".

$$y = b(k, n)m_1^\alpha x^\beta = a(k, n)m_1^\alpha m_2^\gamma \tag{6}$$

where b is a function of capital k and labor n, which are treated as fixed, and where by assuming $x = cm_2^\delta$ we have substituted $c^\beta m_2^{\delta\beta}$ for x^β on the right-hand side, a for $c^\beta b$ and γ for $\delta\beta$. Substituting the right-hand side of (6) for y in (5) we have

$$u^A = am_1^\alpha m_2^\gamma (1 - m_1 - m_2)^\theta \tag{7}$$

which is to be maximized with respect to m_1 and m_2.

The first-order conditions for maximization are

$$\frac{\partial u^A}{\partial m_1} = \alpha m_1^{-1} y(1 - m_1 - m_2)^\theta - \theta y(1 - m_1 - m_2)^{\theta-1} = 0$$

$$\frac{\partial u^A}{\partial m_2} = \gamma m_2^{-1} y(1 - m_1 - m_2)^\theta - \theta y(1 - m_1 - m_2)^{\theta-1} = 0 \tag{8}$$

For an interior solution with $1 - m_1 - m_2 > 0$ these conditions become

$$\begin{array}{lll} \alpha m_1^{-1} - \theta(1 - m_1 - m_2)^{-1} = 0 & \text{or} & (\alpha + \theta)m_1 + \alpha m_2 = \alpha \\ \gamma m_2^{-1} - \theta(1 - m_1 - m_2)^{-1} = 0 & \text{or} & (\gamma + \theta)m_2 + \gamma m_1 = \gamma \end{array} \tag{9}$$

which can be solved for the management efforts m_1 and m_2. To illustrate, if $\theta = .5$, $\alpha = .7$ and $\gamma = .4$, the solution is $m_1 = .4375$ and $m_2 = .25$. Thus about 44% of management effort would be spent for management and 25% for negotiations with authorities for inputs, leaving about 31% for leisure. Reducing γ from .4 to .2 would produce a solution $m_1 = .5$ and $m_2 = 1/7$, increasing the effort for management and the leisure time while reducing the effort for negotiation as one would expect.

The above model captures three important aspects of the functioning of Chinese state enterprises under central planning. First, the laborers are inefficient as depicted by the functions $b(k, n)$ and $a(k, n)$ in (6). Second, management effort m_1 is limited by the desire to balance the possibly small benefits from increasing output with the disutility of additional effort. Third, the use of material and other inputs may be inefficient because of the lack of cost consideration in the objective function and of the desire to bargain for more inputs in order to achieve a higher output. One should also recall the discussion of Sec. 3.2.3 on delays in delivery of materials and physically defective or unsuitable items, a phenomenon described in Chow (1985). Given the poor quality of material delivery, the managers would need to order more materials to produce a given quantity of output. Such inefficiency in the use of material inputs can be incorporated in the specification of the production function (6) which, together with the utility function (5), forms the basis for the manager's decision to apply effort m_2 to increase the supply of inputs. One characteristic of China's industrial production is the large stock of inventories in relation to output (see Chow, 1985, p. 148). This phenomenon can be explained by our model if one uses the stock of inventory as an argument in the production function, or simply reinterprets the symbol x to mean the stock rather than the flow of materials, or supplies our production function (4) or (6) with the additional assumption of a constant ratio between the stock and the flow of material inputs.

For the analysis of production in the longer run, we can apply the above modeling of the manager's effort m_2 for increasing material supply x to the increase of capital stock k through negotiation with the supervising authorities. This is another aspect of the soft-budget constraint which existed in China under central planning.

14.4.3. *State enterprises after reform*

The main distribution between the assigned objective of a state enterprise before and after economic reforms is that the latter is asked to maximize profits rather than to achieve output targets and thus to include cost calculations in production decisions. For a discussion of the nature of the reform of state enterprises, see Chow (1987, pp. 235–236) and Perkins (1988, pp. 615–616). The purpose of the government in changing the objective is to increase economic efficiency. The limited success of enterprise reform is due to the loose connection between enterprise profits and additional benefits to the manager and to the inappropriate pricing of outputs and inputs. To analyze management behavior after the reforms, we assume the objective function of the manager in model B to be

$$u^B = u^B(py - qx, m_1) \tag{10}$$

where p and q are the prices for delivering marginal output and buying marginal inputs, respectively, and the production function to be

$$y = f(k, n, x, m_1) . \tag{11}$$

The argument m_2 is omitted from both the utility and the production functions because material inputs are assumed to be available for purchase at price q and not through bargaining. (One could study a more complicated model by assuming a part of the material input to be obtained by bargaining with authorities at below market prices.)

Again, to simplify exposition and for possible econometric implementation, I employ the following utility function

$$u^B = (py - qx)(1 - m_1)^\theta \tag{12}$$

and the production function (6), yielding the function

$$u^B = (pbm_1^\alpha x^\beta - qx)(1 - m_1)^\theta \qquad (13)$$

which is to be maximized with respect to m_1 and x. The first-order conditions are

$$\frac{\partial u^B}{\partial m_1} = \alpha pym_1^{-1}(1 - m_1)^\theta - \theta(py - qx)(1 - m_1)^{\theta-1} = 0$$

$$\frac{\partial u^B}{\partial x} = (\beta pyx^{-1} - q)(1 - m_1)^\theta = 0 . \qquad (14)$$

For an interior solution with $1 - m_1 > 0$, these conditions yield

$$m_1 = \alpha py/[\alpha py + \theta(py - qx)] = \alpha/[\alpha + \theta(1 - \beta)]$$

$$x = \beta py/q \qquad (15)$$

where the equation for x has been used to simplify the equation for m_1. By the equation for management effort m_1, the larger the relative elasticity θ of utility with respect to leisure as compared with marginal profit or the smaller the weight given to profit as compared with the disutility of management effort, the smaller will be the management effort. The larger the elasticity α of output with respect to management effort m_1, the larger will be the management effort. The larger the elasticity β of output with respect to input x, the larger will be the management effort because a larger β implies a larger marginal product of m_1. To illustrate, if $\theta = .5$, $\alpha = .7$ and $\beta = .3$ (which corresponds to $\gamma = .2 = \delta\beta$ in Model A, for $\delta = 2/3$), m_1 would be $2/3$. As compared with model A (for $\delta = 2/3$ and $\gamma = .2$), this solution for m_1 is larger than the sum $m_1 + m_2 = 4.5/7$, implying that managerial effort is larger than the combined managerial and negotiation efforts of the less productive model under central planning and that the output is larger also. The equation for the demand for input x is the familiar equation for a competitive firm in a market economy which is assumed to maximize profits subject to the constraint of a Cobb–Douglas production function, as it should be under our formulation.

The differences in behavior between model A under central planning and model B prevailing after urban economic reforms in 1980s are that in the latter case there is a tendency to maximize profits by increasing management effort, and that there is a tendency to economize on the use of material inputs because profits enter the objective function of the manager. Note, however, that these tendencies are weak if the relative elasticity parameter θ is large, reflecting the unimportance of marginal profits in the manager's utility function. This is the case for large and medium-size state enterprises, as compared with small state enterprises. In large state enterprises, marginal profits yield only small benefits to the manager, after an allowable amount of profit has been used for distribution as bonuses to management, staff and workers, both in cash and in the form of consumer durables. By contrast, the high profit incentive for the owner-manager of a private enterprise in a market economy is captured in model B, with θ set equal to zero. The appropriate link between marginal profits and the manager's marginal benefits remains a serious problem in enterprise reform in China.

If the stated differences between models A and B depict correctly the realities of China, one should observe higher efficiency in Chinese state industry and lower ratios of material inventories to output after urban economic reforms. In Chow (1993), I have presented the increases in total productivity of Chinese industry from 1981 to 1985 as percentage deviations of actual industrial output from the output computed from an aggregate Cobb–Douglas industrial production function estimated using annual data from the period 1952 to 1980 (excluding years 1961–1968). The fractional deviations from 1981 to 1985 are respectively — .006, .001, .042, .104 and .202. The corresponding increases in agricultural productivities are .077, .181, .269, .422 and .436 (see Table XI). Increases in industrial productivity occurred later (as industrial reforms also occurred later than agricultural reforms) and were smaller in magnitude (as the incentive system in terms of the rights to asset management was more problematic in industry). Concerning the ratio of material inventory to output, I present below the ratio of the value of circulating assets to net output (in 1980 prices) in Chinese industry using data from Chow (1993, Tables I and V). For the years 1970, 1975, 1980–1985) respectively, the ratios are .956, .950, .805, .851, .844, .821, 809 and .829, which show some decline after economic reforms. Concerning the ratio of capital stock to output there is evidence that it has declined after economic reforms. Using Chow (1993, Tables I and V) one finds the ratio of capital stock in industry to national income produced by industry (in 1980 prices) to be 3.88 in 1970, 4.13 in 1975, 3.95 in 1980, and to be 4.14, 4.14, 4.03, 3.83 and 3.58 respectively from 1981 to 1985. The declines in the ratios of circulating assets to industrial output and of total capital stock to industrial output are manifestations of the increase in total factor productivity cited above.

Current industrial reforms in China have to deal with the problems of (1) labor efficiency, (2) efficiency in the use of material and other inputs, (3) managerial incentives, all of which are discussed in this paper, as well as (4) the more market oriented pricing of outputs and material inputs for which our discussion provides only a part of its microeconomic foundation. Our discussion has incorporated two important reasons explaining the relative efficiencies of large and small state enterprises. First, for small enterprises, the weights given to profits in the utility function are larger in terms of the parameter θ. Second, for small enterprises, the prices p and q of outputs and inputs are more likely to reflect the market conditions of demand and supply under existing Chinese institutional arrangements. For both large and small state enterprises, besides providing sufficient incentives to management in the form of an appropriate system for distributing marginal profits, the Chinese reformers have yet to solve the problems of eating from a large rice pot by the workers and of extracting appropriate rental for the capital used in state enterprises.

Appendix

Butterfield (1982, pp. 94–95) has the following to say about guan-xi:

Ling's tickets to these movies were classic back-door deals. As Chinese friends described the working of the back door, these exchanges usually do not involve money. That would be considered bribery and therefore illegal. Instead they are based on traditional use of guan-xi, the cultivation of contacts and connections among friends, relatives, and colleagues. The longer I stayed in Peking, the more I sensed that almost anything that got done went through the back door. A nurse in Peking recalled that during the Cultural Revolution, when teenagers were shipped off to resettle in the countryside, she wanted her son to have a special skill that might help him avoid being rusticated. So she asked a neighbor, a famous pianist, to give him lessons. There were no private music schools or lessons, but the neighbor, out of long-standing friendship, consented. Later, when the pianist's mother fell ill, the nurse arranged for her admission to a good hospital. The piano lessons also did their trick — the nurse's son was kept in Peking and not sent to the countryside.

"No money changed hands, for that would have been condescending in China today," the nurse said. "It was just friendship. Even the Communists can't replace friendship with class struggle."

But I was puzzled why the pianist's mother couldn't get into the hospital on her own. The Communists have greatly expanded medical care in China since 1949 and much of it is free; it was one of their greatest accomplishments. The nurse shook her head at my naïvete. Yes, that was true, she admitted. But the hospitals were still terribly overcrowded—in part because medical care was so cheap— and doctors had to see an average of ten to fifteen patients an hour, like an assembly line. Western drugs were also in short supply because they were given low priority in the state plan.

"Patients in my hospital have to line up three times." said a balding, gregarious physician who had been trained by American missionaries. "First they have to queue at the registration desk, then at the doctor's office, and finally at the pharmacy counter for their prescriptions. You can spend the whole morning just waiting."

"Many doctors are so busy they just make a casual examination of the patient and then scribble something out. It's not good medicine and the patients know it."

"So many of the patients use the back door," the doctor added. "If you know a doctor, you don't have to line up for him but just walk right into his room. He will give you better attention."

"Patients who have an even closer relationship with a doctor will go see him at home, after working hours. That's where the best care is."

"Of course, in exchange, the patients must give presents to the doctors. And on New Year's holiday, they will bring around good cuts of meat, or a fish, or some fruits."

"That's why we say being a doctor in China is a 'fat job'," he continued. "There is a joke that doctors, drivers, and shop clerks are the 'three treasures', because they have more access to things that can be traded through the back door." He himself admitted that it was easier for him to get clothes made at one of the good tailor shops on Wangfujing Street, which often turn down customers, because the tailors knew him. And it was simple for him to get a table in the popular Mongolian hot-pot restaurant, where other diners had to buy tickets a day or more in advance, because the manager was his patient.

Drivers of trucks, buses, and cars are valued, I learned, because there is virtually no privately owned motor vehicle, and drivers therefore have an unusual ability to move around the country. Once in a noisy restaurant that stays open late and is frequented by drivers, I met a swarthy man in his late twenties who said he drove a truck for a farm machinery factory in Shandong province, east of Peking. After we exchanged a few toasts of beer and cheap white grain alcohol that stung my throat, he began recalling his adventures. It seemed that his factory often had slack periods, when there weren't enough raw materials or there was a shortage of electricity. When these occurred, he would take off in his truck to haul coal from another province. The scheme worked well, with him splitting the profits with the factory Party Secretary, until one evening he fell asleep at the wheel and crashed into another vehicle, wrecking his truck.

"It was too bad," the driver said wistfully, pouring both of us some more beer. "On Sundays I used to be able to use the truck to take my girlfriend and some of our other friends on picnics."

References

Butterfield, Fox, 1982, *China: Alive in the Bitter Sea*, New York: Bantam Books, Inc.

Chow G. C., 1985, *The Chinese Economy*, New York: Harper & Row; 2nd edn., 1987, Singapore: World Scientific.

———, 1987, " Development of a more market-oriented economy in China," *Science* **235**, 295–299.

———, 1993, *Quarterly Journal of Economics* **108**, 809–842. See chapter 16.

Goldfeld, S. M. and R. E. Quandt, 1988, "Budget constraints, bailouts, and the firm under central planning," *Journal of Comparative Economics* **12**, 502–520.

———, 1990, "Output targets, soft budget constraints and the firm under the central planning," *Journal of Economic Behavior and Optimization*.

———, 1991, *Effects of Bailouts, Taxes, and Risk-Aversion on the Enterprise*, Princeton University, Department of Economics, mimeo.

Kornai, János, 1979, "Resource-constrained versus demand-constrained systems," *Econometrica* **47**, 801–820.

———, 1980, *Economics of Shortage*, Amsterdam: North-Holland.

Leibenstein, Harvey, 1966, "Allocative efficiency vs. 'X-efficiency,' " *American Economic Review*, **LVI**, 392–415.

Lin, Justin Yifu, 1988, "The household responsibility system in China's agricultural reform: A theoretical and empirical study," *Economic Development and Cultural Change* **36** (no. 3, Supplement), S199–S234.

McMillan, John, Whalley, John, and Zhu, Lijing, 1989, "The impact of China's economic reforms on agricultural productivity growth," *Journal of Political Economy* **97**, 781-807.

Perkins, Dwight H., 1988, "Reforming China's economic system," *Journal of Economics Literature* **17**, 601–645.

Putterman, Louis, 1990, "Effort, productivity and incentives in a 1970s Chinese people's commune," *Journal of Comparative Economics* **14**, 88–104.

CHAPTER 15

OUTLINE OF AN ECONOMETRIC MODEL
FOR CHINESE ECONOMIC PLANNING*†

This paper outlines an econometric model for Chinese economic planning, consisting of four parts: (1) a dynamic input–output model, (2) final demand for products, (3) equations determining income and prices, and (4) government revenues and expenditures. It points out how optimal control techniques can be applied to economic planning using this model, in particular, to address the basic problems facing the PRC planners as cited in the introduction.

15.1. Introduction

The basic allocative problems facing the economic planners of the People's Republic of China are to determine what fractions of total national output are to be devoted to current consumption and investment, how total investment is to be distributed among different industries, and how much each industry is to produce in order to satisfy the needs of consumption and investment. These allocative problems can be solved by considering the productive capabilities of the economy and the preferences of the society for different categories of consumption goods and for present consumption as compared with future consumptions. An econometric model is an aid to economic planning as it describes quantitatively the production possibilities available and how different government decisions will affect the production and consumption of various commodities through time.

In the econometric model to be outlined in this paper, the production possibilities are described by a dynamic input–output table. For the production of each industry, the corresponding column of the table shows the input requirements from all industries, and the requirements of labor and capital goods. Service from skilled labor and the stocks of capital goods in different industries are considered to be

*Originally published in *Journal of Economic Dynamics and Control*, vol 4 (1982), pp. 171–190.
†The author would like to thank Li Chen of the Chinese Academy of Social Sciences and Princeton University, Cheng Hsiao of Princeton and Toronto Universities, John Taylor of Princeton University, and two referees for providing helpful comments on an earlier draft of this paper, without implying that they necessarily agree to the views expressed herein. Financial support from the National Science Foundation Grant No. SES80-12582, is gratefully acknowledged.

the limiting factors which restrict the quantities of final outputs. In any one year, the society has the option to allocate its final outputs for current consumption or for capital accumulation. The latter use will help increase the quantities of final outputs available in the future. The first part of our model, to be presented in Sec. 2, consists of a set of dynamic input–output relations, showing how the curtailment of current consumption can help augment the capital stocks for future production.

Besides describing the production possibilities, our model needs to explain how final outputs in different industries are determined. Basically, these products can be used for private consumption, public and government consumption, defense, investment, and exports. The second part of our model, to be presented in Sec. 3, consists of a set of equations explaining the components of final demand for the products. Some components of final demand are treated as control variables. Once the values of these control variables are given, the final demand equations and the production constraints given by the dynamic input–output relations will determine the outputs of different industries and their uses through time. Thus the time paths of all output, consumption, and capital stock variables can be determined by the first two parts of our model. Some important uses of these two parts of the model will be discussed in Sec. 3.

To insure that the consumption goods produced according to the first two parts of our model will be appropriately distributed to the consumers in rural and urban areas, the government exercises control over the total incomes of the rural and urban populations (by setting purchase prices and purchase quotas for farm products, and setting wage rates for workers), over the quantities of certain commodities to be consumed (by rationing), and over the prices of a large number of products. The third part of our model, to be presented in Sec. 4, is concerned with the determination of income and prices. Currently the government of the People's Republic of China is considering economic reforms, partly to allow the forces of the markets to function properly. We will indicate how part 3 of our model should be changed when these reforms are introduced.

The fourth and last part of our model deals with government revenues and expenditures. Not only is there a problem to insure that the consumption goods produced get distributed appropriately to the rural and urban consumers, as we discuss in part 3; there is also a problem for the government planners to balance the purchasing power available for private consumption, government consumption, defense, and investment. If prices of all consumer goods were fixed, then increasing the wage rates and the purchase prices of farm products would raise the incomes of urban workers and farmers, and thus tend to increase the quantities of goods demanded by private consumers. As the government increases urban wages and the purchase prices of farm products, provided that its budget is balanced, it will have less to spend on government consumption, defense, and investment. While the distribution of resources for different uses can be planned in physical terms according to parts 1 and 2 of our model, financial flows through the government budget serve to control the flows of physical resources.

Our model can help solve the allocative problems first posed in this paper. If the time paths of the important production, consumption and price variables are charted by the model, given the time paths of the policy variables, the policy makers will know the options available. Such knowledge would help them decide which options to choose. In addition, we will indicate how optimal control techniques can be used for the selection of good policies. If one is willing to assign weights to the target variables in an objective function, including consumption, defense, inflation, etc., one can apply the method of optimal control to find the best production and investment policies to achieve these objectives. A flexible way to use optimal control methods is to vary the weights in the objective function to trace out the highest consumption levels achievable given any defense requirements and the condition of price stability. Such control experiments will provide a more efficient way to obtain the options available to the government decision makers, and the optimal policies associated with these options.

15.2. A Dynamic Input–Output Model

One way to describe the production possibilities existing in the Chinese economy is by a dynamic input–output table in physical units. To facilitate discussion, we can refer to the static input–output table in 1952 prices constructed by Haruki Niwa (1969) for the Chinese economy in 1956.[1] This table includes 22 sectors. The gross output and the components of final demand for each industry, in billions of 1952 yuan, are given in table 1. Besides the 22 industries listed, we need an education industry which produces skilled labor. Note that our model would require an input–output table in physical units, whereas table 1 contains data in 1952 values.

Let z_t be a column vector of 23 elements denoting the gross outputs of these productive activities at time t, A be an input–output matrix whose jth column denotes the inputs of the 23 products used in producing one unit of the jth output, and y_t be a column vector denoting the final outputs. We have the familiar relation between the final outputs and gross outputs,

$$z_t = Az_t + y_t . \tag{1}$$

In addition to the intermediate products from the 23 industries, the production of each product may require using the stocks of two capital goods, machinery and construction, and skilled labor to be denoted by s_{1t}, s_{2t} and s_{3t}, respectively. Let B be a 3×23 matrix with each column specifying the input requirements from the stocks of two capital goods and skilled labor, to be denoted by the vector s_t. These resource requirements are given by

---

[1] An input–output table for the Chinese economy in 1979 has been constructed by the Institute of Industrial Economics of the Chinese Academy of Social Sciences in Peking under the direction of Professor Li Chen. The author hopes that this table will soon become available. The author is planning to estimate the parameters of the final demand equations by a combination of Chinese and international data, and the parameters concerning taxes and government revenues by institutional information.

Table 1

1956 output of PRC (billions of 1952 yuan).[a]

	z	Az	y	C	G	I	IN	VD	EX	IM
(1) Agriculture—food	39.9	13.0	26.8	26.4	0.0	0.0	−0.1		0.5	
(2) Agriculture—textile material	3.5	2.4	1.1	0.0	0.0	0.9			0.8	0.6
(3) Forestry	2.8	1.0	1.8	1.8	0.0					
(4) Coal & allied products	1.9	1.2	0.7	0.5	0.1		0.1			
(5) Petroleum	1.7	2.9	−1.2	0.0	0.1					1.3
(6) Iron ore	0.6	0.6	0.0	0.0	0.0					
(7) Non-ferrous metal	3.1	2.6	0.5	0.0	0.0				0.5	
(8) Processed food	13.7	3.1	10.5	8.2	0.0			0.1	2.4	0.1
(9) Textiles	17.5	8.8	8.7	8.2	0.0			0.1	0.5	0.2
(10) Construction materials	4.2	4.6	−0.4	0.2	0.0		−0.7		0.1	
(11) Chemicals	5.6	5.4	0.2	0.4	0.0				0.6	0.9
(12) Iron and steel	9.8	10.0	−0.2	0.0	0.0			0.1	0.2	0.5
(13) Metal working	4.0	3.5	0.5	0.5	0.0	0.2		0.1		0.2
(14) Machinery	8.9	2.5	6.3	0.6	0.0	4.7		3.0		2.0
(15) Other producer goods	3.1	2.5	0.5	0.2	0.0				0.5	0.3
(16) Industrial consumer goods	5.9	3.9	2.0	1.8	0.0				0.3	0.3
(17) Gas	0.1	0.0	0.1	0.1	0.0					
(18) Electric power	0.9	0.8	0.1	0.1	0.0					
(19) Transportation and communications	9.5	4.7	4.8	4.1	0.2	0.1		0.3	0.9	0.8
(20) Construction	15.3	1.4	13.9	0.0	0.0	13.8		0.1		
(21) Services	23.0	6.5	16.5	14.3	0.8	1.2		0.1	0.3	0.3
(22) Not classified	10.3	9.3	1.0	1.1	1.4		−1.5	0.1	0.5	0.5
Gross input	185.3	91.0	94.3	68.7	2.8	20.9	−2.3	3.9	8.2	8.0

[a]*Source*: Haruki Niwa (1969, table 1).

$$Bz_t \leqq s_{t-1} \,. \tag{2}$$

The vector s_{t-1} of capital stocks at the end of year $t-1$ is given for the production in each year t, but s_t will be affected by investment I_t in year t,

$$s_t = I_t + (I - \delta)s_{t-1} \,, \tag{3}$$

where δ is a diagonal matrix indicating the rates of depreciation of capital goods and human capital.

Let c be a row vector of requirements of unskilled labor in the production of the one unit of output in the 23 industries. The total demand for unskilled labor in producing gross output z_t is therefore cz_t. We assume for China that capital stocks and skilled labor but not unskilled labor are the limiting factors. Land itself is not treated here as a limiting factor for the production of agricultural products because the same piece of land can be made much more productive by suitable capital investments. From (1) and (2), it follows that the combination of net outputs y_t that can be produced by the available capital stocks s_{t-1} is given by

$$B(I-A)^{-1}y_t \leqq s_{t-1} . \tag{4}$$

Given any y_t, the total demand for unskilled labor is

$$cz_t = c(I-A)^{-1}y_t . \tag{5}$$

Once we can obtain projections of population and labor force, the difference between labor supply and labor demand given by (5) provides an estimate of unemployment which will require the attention of the government economic planners.

Of the 22 products listed in table 1, numbers 14 (machinery) and 20 (construction) are the two capital goods which, together with skilled labor, limit the productive capabilities of the economy. Numbers 6, 7, 10 and 12 are intermediate products. The outputs of these products constitute neither investment goods nor consumption goods, but the final demands may be positive if they are exported. The remaining 16 products are all consumption goods, except number 2, which, according to the table, mainly goes to investment. We will treat it as a consumer good when we come to explain the demand for final products in the next section because we do not consider the stock of this product as a limiting factor in the Chinese economy. Otherwise, s_t in Eqs. (2), (3) and (4) would be a vector consisting of four elements instead of three.

Let the vector y_t, including the production of skilled labor, be composed of subvector y_t^c (16 consumption goods), y_t^m (4 intermediate products), and y_t^i (3 investment goods, including investment in human capital). Accordingly, rewrite Eq. (4) as

$$B(I-A)^{-1}y_t = B_1 y_t^c + B_2 y_t^m + B_3 y_t^i = s_{t-1} . \tag{6}$$

Assuming B_3 to be non-singular, we can use (6) to determine the vector y_t^i of investment goods as a linear function of s_{t-1}, y_t^c and y_t^m,

$$y_t^i = B_3^{-1} s_{t-1} - B_3^{-1} B_1 y_t^c - B_3^{-1} B_2 y_t^m . \tag{7}$$

Equation (7) shows that, given the productive capabilities provided by the initial stock s_{t-1}, the more the resources are used to produce consumption goods y_t^c, the less will be available for the production of investment goods y_t^i. Investment goods will go either to I_t to increase the productive capacity of the economy or to the remaining uses which include defense and exports. If the government can decide on the quantities of consumption goods y_t^c to produce, the quantities of intermediate products y_t^m for net exports, and the quantities of investment goods used for defense and for exports, Eq. (7) will determine y_t^i and hence I_t, given s_{t-1}. Equation (3) will determine s_t. The dynamic evolution of the input–output model will thus be determined. It is to the explanation of y_t^c, y_t^m and the other uses of investment goods that we will turn in the next section.

15.3. Final Demand for Products

The government of a centrally planned economy can decide on the quantities of different consumption goods to produce, realizing that increasing the production of consumption goods y_t^c will mean the reduction of investment goods y_t^i at the rates given by the matrix $B_3^{-1}B_1$ in Eq. (7). In its decision on y_t^c, the government will consider the relative needs for the different consumer goods. Its perception of such needs may coincide, to various degrees, with the needs as expressed by the consumers themselves through their demand behavior. Our model will express these needs mathematically no matter whether they are based on the government's own perception or the demand behavior of the consumers.

According to table 1, each consumption good in y_t^c can be used for private consumption C, government consumption G, inventory accumulation INV, defense D or exports EX, while imports IM supplement the domestic production. We consider first the determination of the vector C for private consumption. Given the relative prices p_i of consumer goods, the expenditures p_iC_i on them are approximated by linear functions of total consumption expenditures $\sum_j p_jC_j$,

$$p_iC_i = a_i\left(\sum_j p_jC_j\right) + b_i ,\tag{8}$$

where $\sum_i a_i = 1$ and $\sum_i b_i = 0$. Such an expenditure system is only an approximation. These demand functions are not homogeneous of degree zero in prices unless b_i/p_i is. The constants b_i will be affected by the choice of units for p_i. Therefore, we assume a fixed numeraire consumer good for which the price is unity in order that the approximation (8) will be more accurate. The entire system of demand equations for m consumption goods can be written as

$$\begin{bmatrix} (1-a_1)p_1 & -a_1p_2 & \cdots & -a_1p_m \\ -a_2p_1 & (1-a_2)p_2 & \cdots & -a_2p_m \\ & & \ddots & \\ -a_mp_1 & -a_mp_2 & \cdots & (1-a_m)p_m \end{bmatrix}\begin{bmatrix} C_1 \\ C_2 \\ \vdots \\ C_m \end{bmatrix} = \begin{bmatrix} b_1 \\ b_2 \\ \vdots \\ b_m \end{bmatrix}.\tag{9}$$

The matrix on the left of (9) has rank $m-1$, since the sum of the m rows is a zero vector. If we let the first good be the numeraire good, for which $p_1 = 1$, the demand for all other goods can be expressed as a function of C_1 according to (9),

$$\begin{bmatrix} (1-a_2)p_2 & \cdots & -a_2p_m \\ & \ddots & \\ -a_mp_2 & \cdots & (1-a_m)p_m \end{bmatrix}\begin{bmatrix} C_2 \\ \vdots \\ C_m \end{bmatrix} = \begin{bmatrix} b_2 \\ \vdots \\ b_m \end{bmatrix} + \begin{bmatrix} a_2 \\ \vdots \\ a_m \end{bmatrix}C_1 .\tag{10}$$

C_1 can be used as a control variable in the model. Given C_1 the demand for the remaining consumer goods will be determined by (10).

To reflect the Chinese reality, it will be necessary to study the consumption patterns of the rural and urban populations separately. To do so, we simply decompose the vector C into its rural and urban components C^r and C^u. Each component will be explained by equations of the form (8) to (10), with superscripts 'r' and 'u' added to the parameters p_i, a_i and b_i. Both C_1^r and C_1^u will become control variables for the determination of the demands for the remaining consumer goods C_i^r and C_i^u ($i = 2, \ldots, m$) in the rural and urban areas.

Linear schemes of the same form can be used to determine the vectors G and D of government demand and defense demand respectively, the latter including both consumption goods and investment goods, as indicated in table 1. As a result, the vectors C^r, C^u, G and D can be expressed, respectively, as linear functions of the scalars C_1^r, C_1^u, G_1 and D_k, where D_k may be the defense use of machinery, for example. The vector IM of imports is assumed to be a linear function of the vector y_t of final outputs. So is the vector of planned inventory changes INV. The vector EX of exports is treated as exogenous to our model as it can be explained by a set of exports equations supplementary to our model; or some elements of it can be treated as control variables.

These assumptions permit us to write the vector y_t of final outputs as

$$
y_t = \begin{bmatrix} y_t^c \\ y_t^m \\ y_t^i \end{bmatrix} = \begin{bmatrix} 0 \\ 0 \\ I_t \end{bmatrix} + \begin{bmatrix} C_t^r \\ 0 \\ 0 \end{bmatrix} + \begin{bmatrix} C_t^u \\ 0 \\ 0 \end{bmatrix} + \begin{bmatrix} G_t \\ 0 \\ 0 \end{bmatrix}
$$
$$
+ D_t + INV_t - IM_t + EX_t
$$
$$
= \begin{bmatrix} 0 \\ 0 \\ I_t \end{bmatrix} + \Gamma_1 x_t + \Gamma_2 y_t + EX_t + \gamma_0 , \tag{11}
$$

where x_t denotes a vector of the four control variables C_1^r, C_1^u, G_1 and D_k which determine the demands C_t^r, C_t^u, G_t and D_t; Γ_2 is a matrix derived from the linear functions explaining planned inventory changes INV_t and imports IM_t; and γ_0 is a vector of constants collected from the above linear functions. Solving (11) for y_t, we obtain

$$
y_t = (1 - \Gamma_2)^{-1} \left(\begin{bmatrix} 0 \\ 0 \\ I_t \end{bmatrix} + \Gamma_1 x_t + EX_t + \gamma_0 \right)
$$
$$
= \Gamma_3 I_t + \Gamma_4 x_t + \Gamma_5 EX_t + \beta . \tag{12}
$$

The three components of y_t according to (12) can be written as

$$
\begin{bmatrix} y_t^c \\ y_t^m \\ y_t^i \end{bmatrix} = \begin{bmatrix} \Gamma_{31} \\ \Gamma_{32} \\ \Gamma_{33} \end{bmatrix} I_t + \begin{bmatrix} \Gamma_{41} \\ \Gamma_{42} \\ \Gamma_{43} \end{bmatrix} x_t + \begin{bmatrix} \Gamma_{51} \\ \Gamma_{52} \\ \Gamma_{53} \end{bmatrix} EX_t + \begin{bmatrix} \beta_1 \\ \beta_2 \\ \beta_3 \end{bmatrix} . \tag{13}
$$

The last equation of (13) can be solved for I_t,

$$I_t = \Gamma_{33}^{-1} y_t^i + \Gamma_{33}^{-1}\Gamma_{43}x_t - \Gamma_{33}^{-1}\Gamma_{53}EX_t - \Gamma_{33}^{-1}\beta_3 \ . \tag{14}$$

When the right-hand side of (7) is substituted for y_t^i in (14), I_t becomes a linear function of y_t^c, y_t^m, s_{t-1}, x_t and EX_t. When this linear function is substituted for I_t in the first two equations of (13), and the result is solved for y_t^c and y_t^m, we obtain

$$\begin{bmatrix} y_t^c \\ y_t^m \end{bmatrix} = \alpha_1 s_{t-1} + \alpha_2 x_t + \alpha_3 EX_t + \alpha_0 \ . \tag{15}$$

Equations (15) and (7) imply that y_t^i is also a linear function of s_{t-1}, x_t and EX_t. If y_t^i in (14) is replaced by this function, I_t also becomes a linear function of s_{t-1}, x_t and EX_t. By Eq. (3), s_t is a linear function of the same variables. These equations can be summarized by writing

$$\begin{bmatrix} y_t \\ I_t \\ s_t \end{bmatrix} = \begin{bmatrix} 0 & 0 & A_{13} \\ 0 & 0 & A_{23} \\ 0 & 0 & A_{33} \end{bmatrix} \begin{bmatrix} y_{t-1} \\ I_{t-1} \\ s_{t-1} \end{bmatrix} + Cx_t + BEX_t + b \ , \tag{16}$$

in the notation of Chow (1975). Equation (16) explains how the state variables y_t, I_t and s_t evolve through time, given the time paths of the control variables x_t and the exogenous variables EX_t. Thus the government planners need only to fix the four control variables C_1^r, C_1^u, G_1 and D_k in x_t and predict or plan the demand for exports exogenously. The productions, investments and capital stocks of the economy will be completely determined through time by the linear dynamic model (16).

There are several important uses of the model constructed so far. By keeping the time paths of the four components of demand C_{1t}^r, C_{1t}^u, G_{1t} and D_{kt} of the rural population, urban population, government consumption, and defense at a tolerable minimum, a government planner can use the model (16) to find out the time paths of investments I_t and capital stocks s_t that can be generated, subject to the constraints of the productive capacities of the economy and to the relative needs of the four major users for the different products. Such an exercise would help avoid planning a great leap forward that is economically not feasible. By raising the consumption paths C_{1t}^r and C_{1t}^u and observing the resulting decreases in the paths of investments I_t and capital stocks s_t, the planner can observe the trade-off relationship between consumption and capital formation and will be in a better position to decide on the fractions of total output to be allocated to consumption as compared with investment. Similarly, by raising the path D_{kt} of production for defense and observing the resulting changes in I_t and s_t, one is better able to decide on the allocation of resources for these uses. In the last section of this paper, we will point out how optimal control techniques can be applied to trace out such trade-off relationships more efficiently, and how to find out the quantities of consumption goods C_{1t}^r and C_{1t}^u which have to be sacrificed for hypothetical increases in defense expenditures, subject to the condition that the accumulation of capital stock should remain the same.

The byproducts of these calculations are the output vector y_t. Given y_t and the input–output relation (1), one can calculate the gross outputs z_t to be produced by different sectors. Using the matrices B and c in (2) and (5) respectively, one can also estimate the quantities of capital stock and investment to be allocated to each industry and the quantity of unskilled labor each industry will absorb. In sum, such a model can be used to answer the important questions often raised by the Chinese economic planners: What are the right proportions between consumption and investment, between agricultural output and industrial output, between outputs of heavy industry and light industry, and between investments in agriculture, light industry and heavy industry? How much labor can each industry absorb during a planning period and how much unemployment will be generated, given exogenous projections of the growths of population and the labor force?

While such a model is very useful in answering the above broad questions concerning the productive capabilities of an economy, it says nothing about how the planned production levels can actually be achieved — how to get the farmers, workers, and the managers to cooperate to produce the outputs which the economy is capable of producing. Furthermore, assuming that the outputs are actually produced according to plan, we need to know how they are appropriately distributed to the rural and urban consumers and to the government users. This topic will be discussed in the next two sections.

15.4. Income and Prices

There are two ways by which the government of PRC controls the distribution of outputs to the rural and urban populations. One is by controlling the incomes of these populations. Since the government fixes the prices of most commodities in China, it should not distribute much more incomes to the rural and urban populations than the total values of the consumer products available to them at these prices. Otherwise, shortages and/or inflation will result. The second way is by rationing. In China, urban housing, grain, vegetable oil, meat, sugar, and cotton cloth are rationed, among other commodities. We will first examine how rural and urban incomes are determined, and then try to explain the determination of prices.

The government exercises control over rural income mainly by setting the compulsory quota and the price of the output which it purchases from the farmers, and by a tax on agricultural output which was recently 9 percent for grain and 5 percent for other agricultural products. Let

q_{it} = government purchase quota of agricultural product i, $i \in A$,

   A being a set of agricultural products,

p_{it}^* = government purchase price of product i,

p_{it}^r = market price of product i in rural areas,

θ = fraction of agricultural income used for working capital,
equipment and welfare fund, and

t_i = tax rate on the ith agricultural output.

Then agricultural income is given by

$$Y_{At} = \sum_{i \in A} \{[y_{it}(1 - t_i) - q_{it}]p_{it}^r + q_{it}p_{it}^*\}(1 - \theta) . \tag{17}$$

Given the outputs y_{it}, the government controls agricultural income by controlling t_i, q_{it} and p_{it}^*. Rural income Y_{rt} includes both agricultural income and income from industrial sideline activities. To estimate the latter, let ψ_i denote the fraction of industrial output i produced by the rural sideline activities times the corresponding ratio of income to revenue and assume that the income obtained from these products will all accrue to the rural population. Total rural income will then be, with In denoting the set of industrial products,

$$Y_{rt} = Y_{At} + \sum_{i \in In} \psi_i y_{it} p_{it}^r . \tag{18}$$

To exercise control over urban income, the government sets the wage rates w_j for different categories of workers. If L_j denotes the number of urban workers in the jth category, urban income is essentially $\sum_j w_j L_j$, ignoring interest payments from bank deposits. If the prices p_{it}^r and p_{it}^u of consumer goods in rural and urban areas are to remain stable, the total incomes in these areas must not exceed significantly the values of the consumer goods available. Let γ_r and γ_u respectively be the fractions of income consumed by the rural and urban populations. The government planners must set the purchase prices and quotas for agricultural products and the wage rates for the workers in such a way that the following two equations hold

$$\gamma_r Y_{rt} = \sum_{i=1}^{m} C_{it}^r p_{it}^r , \tag{19}$$

$$\gamma_u Y_{ut} = \gamma_u \sum_j w_j L_j = \sum_{i=1}^{m} C_{it}^r p_{it}^r , \tag{20}$$

where Y_{rt} is explained by Eqs. (17) and (18); and C_{it}^r and C_{it}^u are explained by the model (16) in Sec. 3.

The reader should note that the purpose of setting up Eqs. (8) through (10) in Sec. 3 was to provide an approximate system of linear equations to determine the outputs of $m - 1$ consumer goods (in rural and urban areas) in terms of the output of one consumer good, C_1^r and C_1^u. We treated the *relative* prices p_j in (8) as given constraints, in order to obtain the coefficients in (10) for the calculation of $C_2, \ldots, C_m$ in terms of C_1 (superscript 'r' or 'u' omitted). Once the outputs $C_1, \ldots, C_m$ are determined, as discussed at the end of Sec. 3, one could see (8) as a system of equations to determine the relative prices $p_1, \ldots, p_m$ if it is an accurate system of demand equations. However, one can improve the scheme for determining the relative prices in the economy by using a possibly nonlinear system of demand equations.

Let the rural demand equations for consumption goods be

$$C_{it}^r = C_i^r (Y_{rt}/p_{rt}, p_{1t}^r/p_{rt}, \dots, p_{mt}^r/p_{rt}), \qquad i = 1, \dots, m , \qquad (21)$$

where $p_{rt} = \sum_{i=1} \delta_{ri} p_{it}^r$ is a price index of consumption goods in the rural areas. Let the urban demand equation be

$$C_{it}^u = C_i^u (Y_{ut}/p_{ut}, p_{1t}^u/p_{ut}, \dots, p_{mt}^u/p_{ut}), \qquad i = 1, \dots, m , \qquad (22)$$

where $p_{ut} = \sum_{i=1} \delta_{ui} p_{it}^u$ is a price index of consumption goods in the urban areas. There is a rich literature on systems of demand equations derived explicitly from the theory of consumer behavior, and several attractive functional forms are available. See Deaton and Muelbauer (1980) for a recent attempt and some important references. If the price indices p_{rt} and p_{ut} are known and if rural and urban incomes are given by (18) and $\sum_j w_j L_j$ respectively, we can solve Eqs. (21) and (22) to obtain the relative prices p_{it}^r/p_{rt} and p_{it}^u/p_{ut} of the rural and urban consumption goods which would prevail if the markets are free and the supplies C_{it}^r and C_{it}^u are determined by the model (16).

In China, however, a number of goods are rationed. Under this system, the quantities C_{it} and prices p_{it} of the rationed goods $(i = 1, \dots, m_1)$ are given. Assuming that rationing is effective, the income remaining for the purchases of non-rationed goods will be, for the rural and urban populations respectively,

$$Y_{rt}^* = Y_{rt} - \sum_{i=1}^{m_1} p_{it}^r C_{it}^r , \qquad (23)$$

$$Y_{ut}^* = Y_{ut} - \sum_{i=1}^{m_1} p_{it}^u C_{it}^u . \qquad (24)$$

A system of $m - m_1$ demand equations, analogous to (21) and (22) with Y_{rt}^* and Y_{ut}^* replacing Y_{rt} and Y_{ut} as income variables, can be used to find the relative prices of the remaining goods $(i = m_1 + 1, \dots, m)$.

Once the relative prices of consumption goods are determined, with or without rationing, the absolute prices of these goods will be determined if the price indices p_{rt} and p_{ut} are known. These price indices can be found by equating the purchasing power with the total value of consumption goods available in the rural and urban areas. That is to say, they are determined by

$$\gamma_r Y_{rt} = p_{rt} \sum_{i=1}^m C_{it}^r (p_{it}^r/p_{rt}) , \qquad (25)$$

$$\gamma_u Y_{ut} = p_{ut} \sum_{i=1}^m C_{it}^u (p_{it}^u/p_{ut}) , \qquad (26)$$

where, as we recall, Y_{rt} and Y_{ut} are subject to government control through fixing the purchase quotas and prices of farm products and the wage rates, C_{it}^r are determined by the model (16), and the relative prices (p_{it}^r/p_{rt}) and (p_{it}^u/p_{ut}) are determined by Eqs. (21) and (22), or a subset of $m - m_1$ of them determined by equations analogous to (21) and (22), leaving only the variables p_{rt} and p_{ut} to be determined. Even if the prices of the rationed goods are fixed, Eqs. (25) and (26) remain valid. The price indexes p_{rt} and p_{ut} will still go up when money incomes Y_{rt} and Y_{ut} go up as a result of government policies on purchase prices of farm products and on wage rates. The main difference is that the pressure on prices will fall mainly on the remaining goods whose prices are not fixed. For the prices that are fixed, there will be shortages and/or hidden inflation, with higher prices prevailing in the black markets. China has been experiencing some inflation in 1980–1981.

It should be remarked here that when rationing is introduced so that the purchases C_{it}^r and C_{it}^u are restricted by the numbers of ration coupons issued according to the limited supplies, there is really no need to control the prices of the rationed goods. Their relative prices can be determined by Eqs. (21) and (22). Their absolute prices will be determined by Eqs. (25) and (26), and inflation can be controlled by controlling Y_{rt} and Y_{ut}.

This may be the appropriate place to comment on two aspects of the current economic reform contemplated by some economic planners of the Chinese government. The first is the possible reduction of the number of rationed commodities and the decontrol of certain prices. As we have just pointed out, absolute prices p_{rt} and p_{ut} are determined by Eqs. (25) and (26), increasing as money incomes Y_{rt} and Y_{ut} increase. Once the purchasing power is restricted by controlling Y_{rt} and Y_{ut}, there is no need to control the individual prices in order to prevent inflation. Relative prices of commodities in short supply will go up so that consumers will economize on their use.

The second aspect of the current economic reform is to give the producers more discretion and incentives to produce their products, including private plots for the farmers and certain degrees of autonomy and percentage profit retention for the managers of enterprises. These reforms will have the effects of increasing productivity beyond the description of our input–output model. By working harder, the farmers can produce more without the input–output statistician noticing any changes in the recorded quantities of inputs. Any input–output relations estimated from current data are based on the current institutions governing production. If the institutions change significantly, the input–output table should be changed, Furthermore, the input–output model is well suited for a command economy where the central planners control the outputs of most industries by issuing production quotas or targets to the farmers and managers of enterprises, as it has been the case in China. We have assumed that the final outputs can be planned by the central planners, explicitly or implicitly, through a dynamic input–output model as described in Secs. 2 and 3, so that given any plan, the final outputs y_{it} can be so calculated. Such an analysis does not take into account the additional production incentives to be provided by the price mechanism. For example, the farmers in PRC operating their private plots will behave like the farmers in Taiwan; they will grow more of certain crops when the (relative) prices of those crops increase. In fact, the supply of pork in China did increase tremendously in 1980 as a result of the increase in purchase price. From the viewpoint of modeling, a set of supply functions showing the quantities supplied according to the relative prices of the outputs would replace the fixed supplies C_{it}. These supply functions, together with the demand functions (21) and (22) would determine the relative prices prevailing in the free markets, while the price indices of consumption goods remain to be determined by Eqs. (25) and (26).

15.5. Government Revenues and Expenditures

In setting the purchase prices of farm products and the wage rates, the government has to consider the restrictions of its budget. Increasing the purchase prices and wage rates will result in more government expenditures and less government revenues respectively, both requiring increasing receipts from other sources or reducing expenditures on other items, if the government budget is to be balanced. In this section, we discuss revenues and expenditures of the Chinese government.

Table 2 gives the estimates of government revenues and expenditures in 1980 as announced by the Chinese government in September 1980. It shows that 43.3 percent of total revenues are revenues of enterprises, to be denoted by R_E. Since government enterprises account for a large fraction ρ (over 80 percent) of industrial outputs, we have approximately

$$R_{Et} = \sum_{i \in In} \left(p_i Y_{it} - \sum_j w_j L_{jt} \right) \rho \,. \tag{27}$$

We subtract from the revenues of final products the total payment to labor to obtain the total revenues accrued to the government (part of which is remitted to the central government and the remaining part is left to the provincial and municipal governments, but all within the control of the national budget). A fraction ϕ_i can be inserted as a factor multiplying the gross revenue $p_i y_{it}$ to allow for other expenses than wage payments, if necessary. One point to note in (27) is that, by increasing the wage rates w_j, the government will have less revenues from enterprises. If the enterprises are allowed to retain parts of their revenues for reinvestment and other uses as suggested by recent reforms, a fraction λ_{it} should multiply the right side of (27). An equation explaining enterprise investment might be needed.[2]

The major category of revenues, some 51.2 percent in 1980, consists of taxes on production and sales of various commodities, such as the salt tax, tax on agricultural and industrial products. Total taxes T are explained by

---

[2] As more economic decisions are left to units other than the central government, more components of final demand in Eq. (11) will be explained endogenously by decentralized decisions. The economy may become more efficient and the input–output coefficients may have to be revised.

Table 2

Estimates of Chinese government revenues and expenditures in 1980.[a]

Revenues	Billion yuans	%
Revenues of enterprises	46.06	43.4
Taxes	54.40	51.2
Other revenues	0.24	0.2
Depreciation allowances of central enterprises	2.20	2.1
Foreign loans	3.39	3.2
Total	106.29	100.00

Expenditures	Billion yuans	%
Construction	37.35	32.7
Enterprise renovations + innovations	6.98	6.1
Enterprise working capital + bank loans	3.72	3.3
Farm subsidies + other expenditures	7.74	6.8
Education, Health and Science	14.83	13.0
Defence	19.33	16.9
Administration	5.78	5.1
Development of backward areas	0.50	0.4
Reserve funds	1.88	1.6
Interest + repayment of foreign loans	2.17	1.9
Total	114.29	100.00

[a]*Source*: People's Daily, 13 Sept. 1980.

$$T_t = \sum_i t_i y_{it} p_{it} \tag{28}$$

as a crude approximation, where the tax rates t_i are treated as given. We treat total revenue R_t as the sum of four items,

$$R_t = R_{Et} + T_t + DA_t + FL_t \,, \tag{29}$$

where depreciation allowances DA_t of centrally administered enterprises and foreign loans FL_t are exogenous variables.

On the expenditure side, the first three items given in table 2 include construction and other investment expenditures. These items, in physical units, are explained by our model (16) in the vector I_t. Money expenditures for them can be estimated simply by multiplying I_t by the corresponding prices. Note that our model is concerned only with total investment expenditures, leaving unanswered the question as to who (the central government, provincial or local governments or the individual enterprises themselves) should carry out what proportions of the total investment. Whether the central planning authority (the Planning Commission of the State Council in China) decides to execute the investment projects itself or leave them to the initiative of the individual enterprises it should have an overall picture of the total national resource available for consumption and investment, as not to make plans which are beyond the productivity capabilities of the national economy. The next item, farm subsidies and other expenditures, is dependent on the purchase prices (as compared with the ration prices or the market prices) and purchase quotas of farm products. Given the ration prices or the market prices of the farm products, increasing the purchase prices paid to farmers will increase government farm subsidies which equal

$$\sum_{i \in A} q_{it}(p_{it}^* - p_{it}^u) \ .$$

Expenditures (in real terms) on Education, Health and Scientific Research and on government administration are also explained by the model (16). Money expenditures are obtained by conversion with the appropriate price indices. Defense is explained likewise, once the control variables of model (16) are given. The last three items in the list of expenditures on table 2 are treated as exogenous. Thus all items of expenditures are determined by our model.

Given the tax rates and wage rates, our model also determines the total revenues of the government by determining the outputs y_{it}. While the expenditure items are subject to the control of the government as we have explained in Sec. 3, the resulting expenditures need not produce a balanced budget. For example, in 1980, the estimated deficit according to Table 2 amounted to 8 billion yuans. Using the econometric model, the government should be able to predict the likely consequences of its policies. Anticipating a deficit if expenditures remain the same (and the rising prices associated with it because of the excesses of money demands by consumers and government over the available supply of goods at existing prices), the government planning authority may decide to reduce its expenditures.

It is interesting to note that Deputy Prime Minister Yao Yilin, Chairman of the State Planning Commission, in a speech before the Standing Committee of the National People's Congress on February 25, 1981 (summarized in *New York Times*, March 1, 1981, p. 1; *Wall Street Journal*, March 9, 1981, p. 27; with full text appearing in *Ta Kung Pao*, March 8, 1981, p. 2), reported a government deficit of 12.1 billion yuan, 4.1 billion over the estimate made in September 1980, and announced his plan to achieve a balanced budget at 97.6 billion in 1981 by reducing basic construction and investment expenditures from the original 55 billion to 30 billion. The 4.1 billion figure resulted partly from excesses of the actual over the planned figures in construction and investment (2 billion), farm subsidies (0.6 billion), administration (1.0 billion), and education, health and science (0.9 billion). If the Chinese government intends to run a balanced budget, deficit DF is zero in an equation equating total revenues and expenditures. This would provide an additional equation to our model which would restrict the government choices of its control variables G_1 and D_k given the farm purchase prices p_i^*, the wage rates w_i, and the tax rates t_i,

$$R_t + DF_t = \sum_i I_{it}p_{it} + \sum_{i \in A} q_{it}(p_{it}^* - p_{it}^u) + \sum_i G_{it}p_{it} + \sum_i D_{it}p_{it} . \qquad (30)$$

15.6. Uses of the Model for Planning

Our model consists of three sets of equations. The first, summarized by (16), determines the physical quantities of production and investment in various industries. The second, consisting of (17), (18), (21), (22), or the analogue of (21) and (22) under rationing, (25) and (26), determines total incomes of the rural and urban populations and the prices of consumption goods. The third, consisting of Eqs. (27) to (30), determines government revenues and expenditures and, assuming a balanced budget, restricts the government's choice of the values for the control variables. The control variables include C_{1t}^r, C_{1t}^u, G_{1t} and D_{kt} which control the resources devoted to rural consumption, urban consumption, government consumption and defense. Although the government can control the purchase quotas q_{it}, the purchase prices p_{it}^*, the wage rates w_{it}, the tax rates t_i, as well as the prices of many producer and consumer goods, it will be preferable to treat them as parameters rather than control variables when we study the dynamic properties of the model under control since they should not be changed frequently, and for the quotas q_{it}, smooth trends should be assumed.

At the end of Sec. 3, we have discussed the applications of the physical part of our model. With the addition of the last two parts to the model, we can trace out the paths of incomes, prices and government revenues and expenditures through time. This would provide the economic planners with additional information on the likely economic consequences of their policies.

There are two ways to use the model outlined in this paper in the formulation of economic policies. One is to try out certain hypothetical policies, such as increasing the control variables C_{1t}^r, C_{1t}^u, G_{1t} and D_{kt} by one percent per year, and calculate the paths of investments, capital stocks, unemployment, and the price indices through time using the econometric model. The planner can choose that policy which, according to the model, will generate the most desirable economic consequences. This method is unsystematic. One may miss trying out some better policies. Even for the policies actually tried, the economic consequences involving the time paths of many economic variables are complicated and difficult to compare. Therefore, we recommend a second and more systematic approach to the selection of economic policies by the use of optimal control methods.

To apply optimal control, one first defines an objective function which includes the time paths of the important economic variables as arguments. For example, one may wish to specify that the above four control variables should ideally increase by 4 percent per year, that the paths of capital stocks should increase by 5 percent per year, while the two price indices should remain constant. These ideal objectives may not be achievable simultaneously; if they were, the planner should raise his aspirations and aim at better targets. According to the relative importance of meeting the targets, one assigns penalty weights to the squared deviations of these variables from their targets, and obtains a measure of welfare loss which is to be minimized by choosing the time paths of the control variables. Optimal control methods are used to find the time paths of the control variables which will minimize the value of a given loss function, subject to the constraint of the econometric model. These methods and their economic applications are discussed in Chow (1975 and 1981).[3]

One interesting application to the economic planning of PRC is to find out how much consumption has to be sacrificed in order to strengthen defense, assuming the growth of capital stocks and the price indices remain the same. We start by using a loss function which penalizes the deviations of consumption, defense, capital stocks and the price levels from their respective target paths, and solving an optimal control problem to obtain the paths of these four variables that can be achieved.[4] If the solution paths of these variables are satisfactory, we solve a second optimal control problem. In this problem, the target paths of defense, capital stocks and the price levels are set equal to the solution paths of the first problem but the target path for consumption is set higher. We assign very heavy penalty weights to all variables except defense. The solution of the second optimal control problem will yield higher consumption levels and approximately the same capital stock growths and the same price levels because of the high penalties, but will result in smaller outputs for defense. Thus the trade-off relation between consumption and defense can be traced out by using optimal control methods. Similar methods have been applied in Chapter 7 of Chow (1981) to trace out the trade-off relations between unemployment and inflation in the United States using two econometric models of the United States economy. These methods can be applied to find the trade-off between any two important variables for Chinese economic planning.

Until recently, when linear input–output models were used for economic planning, the optimization technique employed was linear programming which

---

[3]When the inequality in (4) was converted into an equality in (6), we assumed that the constraints of all capital goods are binding . This assumption may produce unstable trajectories in dynamic Leontief systems. To allow for the possibility of disposing of excess capital goods, we can introduce a vector of excess capital goods x_t^a as additional control variables in (16),

$$s_t = A_{33}s_{t-1} + C_3 x_t - x_t^a + B_3(EX)_t + b_3 .$$

To solve the optimal control problem, the dynamic programming algorithm of Chow (1975, pp. 176–179) will have to be modified. To find the optimal policy $(\hat{x}_t, \hat{x}_t^a)$ for each period t backward in time $(t = T, T-1, \ldots, 1)$, we minimize the total expected loss V_t from period t on with respect to (x_t, x_t^a) subject to $\hat{x}_t^a \geq 0$. If some elements of $\hat{x}_t^a$ are zero, the optimal feedback control equation $\hat{x}_t = G_t y_{t-1} + g_t$ (where $\hat{x}_t$ includes both $\hat{x}_t$ and $\hat{x}_t^a$) will have zeroes for the corresponding coefficients and intercepts, i.e., corresponding rows of G_t and g_t.

[4]The balance of trade can be an additional target variable, in which case we need as equation explaining trade deficit as the excess of the values of imports over exports. Our model explains imports endogenously and treats exports as exogenous variables, but some components of exports can be treated as control variables as well. These changes can easily be incorporated in the methodological discussion that follows.

assumes a linear objective function. As reported by Taylor (1975, pp. 88–89), and certainly expected from the nature of the optimization problem, the linear programming solutions of a multiperiod planning problem led to the concentration of consumption in one year. A quadratic objective function is more suitable for this problem, and linear-quadratic control theory provides the necessary tools for optimization. Furthermore, parts of the model may be nonlinear, as the demand Eqs. (21) and (22) of Sec. 4. Random disturbances will affect the economy as weather conditions will affect agricultural output beyond the description of a deterministic input–output model. To deal with optimal planning over time using a nonlinear stochastic model, the method of stochastic control will be useful. The solution to such optimization problem takes the form of feedback control equations which recommend an optimal strategy in period t based on the random events occurring up to period $t-1$. Although a five-year plan announced in year 1 contains projections of all economic variables including the control variables for five years, the policies to be actually implemented in years 2, 3, 4 and 5 will depend on what shall have occurred up to that time in order to compensate for the effects of unforseen events. Hence stochastic control methods appear to be the natural tools to use for economic planning.

References

Chow, G. C., 1975, *Analysis and Control of Dynamic Economic System*, New York: Wiley.

———, 1981, *Econometric Analysis by Control Methods*, New York: Wiley.

Deaton, Angus and Muellbauer, John, 1980, An almost ideal demand system, *American Economic Review* **70**, 312–326.

Howe, Christopher, 1978, *China's Economy: A Basic Guide*, New York: Basic Books.

Niwa, Haruki, 1969, An outline of the compilation work on the input–output table for Mainland China (1956), *Kwansei Gakuin University Annual Studies* **18**, 119-126.

Taylor, Lance, 1975, Theoretical foundations and technical implications, in Charles R. Blitzer, Peter B. Clark and Lance Taylor, eds., *Economy-wide Models and Development Planning*, London: Oxford University Press for the World Bank, 33–109.

Part V

Modeling Growth and Fluctuations

CHAPTER 16

CAPITAL FORMATION AND
ECONOMIC GROWTH IN CHINA*†

First, production functions are estimated for China's aggregate economy and for the five sectors — agriculture, industry, construction, transportation, and commerce — using annual data (some constructed by the author) from 1952 to 1980. Then, this paper measures the contribution of capital formation to the growth of these sectors, the effects of the Great Leap Forward of 1958–1962 and of the Cultural Revolution of 1966–1976 on outputs, the impact of economic reforms since 1979 on growth, the rates of return to capital, and the effects of sectorial growths on relative prices.

16.1. Introduction

The economic development strategy of the People's Republic of China during the three decades beginning in the early 1950s is characterized by a high rate of capital accumulation at the expense of consumption and the promotion of industry at the expense of agriculture. This paper describes the growth, fluctuations, and the allocation of resources among sectors of the Chinese economy guided by such a development strategy. To what extent has capital formation in the economy and in the five productive sectors of agriculture, industry, construction, transportation, and commerce contributed to economic growth? To what extent have outputs in the economy and in the five sectors been affected by the political disturbances of the Great Leap Forward of 1958–1962 and the Cultural Revolution of 1966–1976? What are the impacts of the economic reforms beginning in 1979 on national income and

*Originally published in *The Quarterly Journal of Economics*, August 1993, pp. 809–842.

†The author would like to thank President Huang Da of the People's University and China Statistical Information and Consultancy Service Centre, Beijing, for supplying unpublished official data, Jianping Mei, Gordon Rausser, two anonymous referees, and Oliver Jean Blanchard for helpful comments, and Princeton University's John M. Olin Program for the study of Economic Organization and Public Policy, and the National Science Foundation for financial support. This paper was presented before the Conference on Investment, Trade, and Economic Development sponsored by the Institute for the Study of Free Enterprise Systems of the State University of New York at Buffalo on May 26, 1990, and before the International Conference on Quantitative Economics and Its Applications to Chinese Economic Development and Reform in the 1990s organized by the Institute of Quantitative & Technical Economics of the Chinese Academy of Social Sciences in Beijing on June 26, 1990. Comments from the participants at these conferences are gratefully acknowledged.

income originating in the five sectors? What have been the rates of return to capital in the economy and in the five sectors? What have been the marginal products of labor? How have the relative growths of the five sectors affected the relative prices of their outputs? How was the high rate of capital formation financed? These are the major questions to be discussed.

To answer these questions, I rely on official data provided by the State Statistical Bureau. Most of the data used can be found in *Statistical Yearbook of China 1989*, Chinese edition (to be abbreviated as *SYC89*), and the remainder are obtained by private communications with the State Statistical Bureau. I have discussed the quality of official Chinese Statistics in Chow [1986, pp. 193–94], where supporting evidence is provided for my judgement that official statistical reporting in China is by and large honest.

Several factors in the collection of statistics affect their quality: the limited training of the officials, the limited financial resources of the State Statistical Bureau which is responsible for directing all activities in the collection, processing, storage, and distribution of statistics, possible political pressures to falsify statistics by the reporting units (e.g., rural communes eager to fulfil production targets during the Great Leap of 1958–1962), and on the positive side the ability of the government to reach its population at the level of city blocks and families. I have found Chinese statistics, by and large, to be internally consistent and accurate enough for empirical work after using them to study the Chinese economy in general in Chow [1985a], and to estimate a simple multiplier–accelerator model of the macroeconomy in Chow [1985b] and an econometric model of inflation in Chow [1987]. In this paper further cross-checks will be provided to ensure that the data are internally consistent and reasonable from our understanding of the economy.

In Sec. 2 some important facts concerning the growth of China's national income will be stated. Section 3 explains how data on capital stock are estimated. By using a one-sector model, Sec. 4 discusses the role of capital formation on economic growth, the effects of major political disturbances and of economic reform on national output, the degree of technological change, and the marginal productivity of capital in the economy. By estimating production functions of five sectors, Sec. 5 discusses the above issues for each sector as well as the allocation of resources and pricing among the sectors. Section 6 shows briefly how consumption expenditures are controlled and funds are made available for capital accumulation. A summary of findings will be provided in Sec. 7.

16.2. Growth of National Income and its Components

Chinese national income consists of net material output from the five productive sectors mentioned above. National income in constant prices is computed as the weighted sum of the real outputs of the five sectors using base-period prices as weights. Needless to say, prices are subject to government control. Base-period prices for real national income from 1949 to 1957 are 1952 prices; 1957 prices serve from 1957 to 1970; 1970 prices serve from 1970 to 1980; and 1980 prices serve from 1980 to 1988. From 1952 to 1980 the index of real national income increased from 100 to 516.3, or at an average annual of 0.060. Much of this growth can be attributed to the rapid growth of industry starting from a small base and the large price weights given to it.

The growth rates of the five sectors are uneven, as shown by the indices of real output given in Table I [*SYC89*, p. 30]. The industry sector grew the most rapidly, followed by construction and transportation. The agriculture sector grew the most slowly. Since prices of industrial products declined relative to prices of agricultural products, and industrial output grew much more rapidly, national income estimated by using end-of-period prices instead of beginning-of-period prices would give smaller weights to industrial products and show a smaller rate of annual growth than 0.06. For example, by using 1980 prices (as revealed by the current-value national incomes in the five sectors) to weigh the real output indices for the period 1970–1980, 1970 prices for the period 1957–1970, and 1957 prices for the period 1952-1957, one finds the resulting real national income index to have grown at an annual rate of growth of 0.054 instead of 0.060. Liu and Yeh [1963, pp. 32–33] point out that prices of agricultural products were depressed in 1952 as compared with industrial products by government policy. This would lead to a high rate of growth of estimated real national income beginning in 1952.

A second measure of economic growth is "national income available" consisting of its two components: Consumption and accumulation. It equals national income plus imports minus exports plus statistical discrepancies. During the period 1952–1980 the fraction of national income available devoted to accumulation averaged to about 0.30. The official index of real consumption, exhibited in Table II, shows an increase from 100 in 1952 to 380.8 in 1980, or an average annual rate of increase of 0.049. This rate of increase slower than the 0.060 rate for real national income reflects the government policy of restricting consumption to achieve accumulation. The fraction of real national income available devoted to consumption has declined. In 1952 consumption was 477 (100,000 RMB), or 0.786 of national income available. If one estimates real national income available in 1952 prices, for which there are no official data, by using the implicit price deflator for national income, one obtains an estimate of 3047.6 for 1980 (implying an average annual growth rate of 0.0593) and a ratio 0.596 of real consumption to real income available. In current 1980 prices, consumption equals 0.685 of national income available, reflecting the larger increases in the prices of consumer goods relative to the prices of capital goods.

Concerning the prices of capital goods, it has been assumed by Jefferson, Rawski, and Zheng [1989, p. 42] that "prior to 1980 changes in investment goods prices were negligible." To check this assumption and the consistency of real national income available as the sum of consumption and accumulation, I have used the implicit price deflator for national income (comparing Tables I and II) to estimate real national income available in 1952 prices. Subtracting consumption in 1952 prices from this series yields a hypothetical series of real accumulation. The ratio of accumulation in current prices to this hypothetical series gives a price index for accumulation, as shown in Table III. This index up to 1983 is not far from unity

TABLE I
INDICES OF REAL NATIONAL INCOME

Year	National income	Agri-culture	Indus-try	Construc-tion	Transpor-tation	Commerce
1952	100.0	100.0	100.0	100.0	100.0	100.0
1953	114.0	101.6	133.6	138.1	120.0	133.0
1954	120.6	103.3	159.1	133.3	136.0	136.4
1955	128.3	111.5	169.1	152.4	140.0	137.5
1956	146.4	116.5	219.1	261.9	164.0	146.6
1957	153.0	120.1	244.5	242.9	176.0	146.6
1958	186.7	120.3	383.5	367.0	270.8	155.9
1959	202.0	100.6	501.5	388.6	356.5	170.3
1960	199.1	83.6	541.4	394.0	383.6	164.1
1961	140.0	84.7	315.9	129.5	221.1	130.1
1962	130.9	88.7	267.4	161.9	171.5	117.7
1963	144.9	98.9	300.7	205.1	176.0	120.8
1964	168.8	111.9	374.9	259.0	198.6	123.9
1965	197.4	122.9	477.7	286.0	261.7	128.0
1966	231.0	131.9	598.5	313.0	297.8	155.9
1967	214.3	134.2	504.3	296.8	239.2	164.1
1968	200.3	131.6	458.6	237.5	225.6	151.8
1969	239.0	132.2	622.3	323.8	284.3	179.6
1970	294.6	139.8	863.0	421.0	343.0	199.2
1971	315.3	142.0	979.0	468.3	370.8	201.2
1972	324.3	140.5	1043.5	452.5	389.3	208.0
1973	351.2	153.1	1134.3	457.8	412.5	224.5
1974	355.2	159.2	1128.9	484.1	394.0	220.6
1975	384.7	162.3	1297.3	542.0	444.9	220.6
1976	374.5	159.1	1249.2	568.3	426.4	214.8
1977	403.7	155.1	1434.0	578.8	491.3	242.0
1978	453.4	161.2	1679.1	573.5	546.9	296.4
1979	485.1	171.5	1814.7	584.1	560.8	316.8
1980	516.3	168.4	2012.7	757.7	584.0	318.8
1981	541.5	180.4	2046.8	770.0	607.2	379.4
1982	585.8	201.6	2170.1	806.9	681.3	397.5
1983	644.2	218.7	2383.7	954.3	755.5	449.1
1984	731.9	247.0	2738.8	1056.7	852.8	499.5
1985	830.6	253.7	3275.2	1310.6	1024.3	593.7
1986	894.5	261.4	3590.6	1540.0	1140.2	636.3
1987	985.7	273.2	4058.8	1744.8	1269.9	715.0
1988	1095.1	279.4	4765.0	1884.0	1413.6	760.8

except for the years 1961–1963. The abnormally low values for 1961–1963 may be partly the result of our overestimating real accumulation during these years of economic collapse as the difference between real national income available and real consumption. Real national income available would be overestimated if its deflator did not move up sufficiently. The above index justifies the assumption to be adopted

TABLE II
NATIONAL INCOME IN CURRENT PRICES

Year	National income	Agri-culture	Indus-try	Con-struction	Transpor-tation	Com-merce	Per capita national income
1952	589	340	115	21	25	88	104
1953	709	374	156	28	29	122	122
1954	748	388	174	26	32	128	126
1955	788	417	179	30	33	120	129
1956	882	439	212	55	37	139	142
1957	908	425	257	45	39	142	142
1958	1118	440	401	68	59	150	171
1959	1222	376	527	76	78	165	183
1960	1220	332	565	79	84	160	183
1961	996	432	345	25	48	146	151
1962	924	444	303	32	38	107	139
1963	1000	488	337	40	39	96	147
1964	1166	549	422	50	44	101	167
1965	1387	641	505	53	58	130	194
1966	1596	692	606	58	66	164	216
1967	1467	703	505	55	52	172	197
1968	1415	714	449	44	49	159	183
1969	1617	722	587	60	62	186	203
1970	1926	778	789	80	74	205	235
1971	2077	808	891	91	80	207	247
1972	2136	808	942	88	84	214	248
1973	2318	886	1020	92	89	231	263
1974	2348	922	1015	99	85	227	261
1975	2503	946	1152	113	96	196	273
1976	2427	940	1106	120	92	169	261
1977	2644	913	1263	124	106	238	280
1978	3010	986	1487	125	118	294	315
1979	3350	1226	1628	130	121	245	346
1980	3688	1326	1804	185	126	247	376
1981	3941	1509	1840	193	131	268	397
1982	4258	1723	1948	209	147	231	422
1983	4736	1021	2136	259	166	254	464
1984	5652	2251	2516	303	205	377	547
1985	7040	2492	3163	409	259	717	674
1986	7899	2720	3573	514	320	772	747
1987	9361	3154	4262	637	365	943	872
1988	11770	3818	5432	783	438	1299	1081

TABLE III
CONSUMPTION, ACCUMULATION, AND ESTIMATED PRICE INDEX FOR ACCUMULATION

Year	National income available (100 million)	Consumption (100 million)	Accumulation (100 million)	Index of real consumption	Estimated price of accumulation
1952	607	477	130	100.0	1.000
1953	727	559	168	111.0	1.056
1954	765	570	195	112.5	1.027
1955	807	622	185	122.7	0.981
1956	888	671	217	132.1	0.912
1957	935	702	233	137.2	0.852
1958	1117	738	379	142.6	0.906
1959	1274	716	558	135.9	0.942
1960	1264	763	501	129.6	0.839
1961	1013	818	195	117.6	0.702
1962	948	849	99	124.1	0.497
1963	1047	864	183	138.8	0.791
1964	1184	921	263	151.8	0.921
1965	1347	982	365	169.5	1.138
1966	1535	1065	470	182.0	1.047
1967	1428	1124	304	192.2	1.029
1968	1409	1111	298	189.4	1.098
1969	1537	1180	357	203.0	0.966
1970	1876	1258	618	216.0	0.937
1971	2008	1324	684	226.5	0.957
1972	2052	1404	648	239.6	0.936
1973	2252	1511	741	257.1	0.946
1974	2291	1550	741	262.8	0.941
1975	2451	1621	830	274.3	0.912
1976	2424	1676	748	283.1	0.877
1977	2573	1741	832	291.5	0.901
1978	2975	1888	1087	312.9	0.948
1979	3356	2195	1161	346.7	0.961
1980	3696	2531	1165	380.8	0.946
1981	3905	2799	1106	411.0	0.922
1982	4290	3054	1236	441.4	0.902
1983	4779	3358	1421	479.2	0.921
1984	5701	3905	1796	547.4	1.034
1985	7507	4879	2628	633.8	1.198
1986	8492	5548	2944	682.3	1.222
1987	9638	6340	3298	732.1	1.327
1988	12099	7971	4128	791.8	1.447

in this paper that the price index for accumulation goods between 1952 and 1983 remained constant. From 1984 on, the index is assumed to increase at the same rate as the implicit deflator for the construction sector, being 1.057, 1.150, 1.230, 1.345, and 1.531 for 1984–1988, respectively. When the accumulation data are summed over time to form capital stock in the next section, they are deflated only after 1984 as here indicated. Jefferson, Rawski, and Zheng [p. 36] start deflating capital stocks from 1981 on. The difference does not affect the production functions estimated in this paper which use data up to 1980. Using somewhat higher values for the deflator of capital goods would slightly reduce the estimated stocks of capital from 1981 on and increase the estimates of efficiency improvement following the economic reforms.

16.3. Data on Accumulation and Estimates of Capital Stock

Since the analysis in this paper is based on the official data on accumulation and the data on capital stock that I have estimated from them, it is important to set forth the nature of these data and the method of estimation. Four sets of official data concerning capital formation will be used in this paper. The first is "accumulation," defined [*SYC87*, p. 798] as

that part of the national income used for expanded reproduction, nonproductive construction and increase of production and nonproductive stock of the society. Its material form is the newly added fixed assets of material and non-material sectors (less depreciation of the fixed assets) during a given period, and circulating funds .... Productive accumulation includes newly added fixed assets of productive use (deducted by the wear of these assets) in material production sectors and the increase in circulating assets held by enterprises, such as stock of materials, fuels, semifinished goods, means of production (finished), stock by commercial departments, reserve of materials and so on. Nonproductive accumulation covers newly added fixed assets of nonproductive use and residential buildings (all deducted by wear and tear), as well as the increase in stock of consumer goods held by industrial enterprises or commercial departments.

I will treat accumulation as a net increase in capital stock.

The second is "newly increased fixed assets," which [*SYC87*, p. 815] "refers to the value of projects completed and put into operation or turned over to use, the purchase of equipment, tools and instruments which meet standards for fixed assets, and other costs. This is a comprehensive indicator, in value terms, of the result of investment in fixed assets ...." Note that "newly increased fixed assets" are only fractions of "investments in fixed assets" by Chinese official usage because work performed in investment may not produce results that meet standards for fixed assets, the factions being called "rates of fixed assets turned over to use" and varying for different periods between 60 to 87 percent [*SYC87*, p. 419]. The third and fourth are "net value of fixed assets" and "quota circulating funds" of state-owned enterprises "under the state budget" [*SYC89*, pp. 25–26]. These enterprises are state-owned "enterprises under the management of the financial budget of all levels of government" and "exclude state-owned enterprises outside the state budget as well as non-independent accounting industrial enterprises" [*SYC87*, p. 799]. "Original value of fixed assets refers to the original value of all the fixed assets owned by industrial enterprises, calculated as the cost paid at the time of purchase or construction.... Net value of fixed assets is obtained by deducting depreciation over the years from the original value of fixed assets" [*SYC87*, p. 907]. Circulating funds has been defined above in connection with accumulation.

Accumulation data consisting of fixed assets and circulating funds can be found in *SYC89* [p. 42]. From communications with the State Statistical Bureau, I have obtained annual data from 1952 to 1985 on accumulation of fixed assets and of circulating funds by state enterprises, urban collective enterprises, rural collective enterprises, and individuals, as shown in Table IV. My task is to distribute the accumulation of the two kinds of assets by the three types of enterprises (excluding individuals) to the five economic sectors, and to sum these accumulations over time, with appropriate initial values for 1952, to form capital stocks in the five sectors. For fixed assets of state enterprises, I rely on Table 10-28 [*SYC89*, p. 509], which gives "newly increased fixed assets through capital construction" of all state enterprises in the five sectors and other nonmaterial-producing sectors. Annual data from 1953 to 1979 (except 1966–1974) have been obtained from the State Statistical Bureau to supplement the five-year totals given in Table 10-28. Accumulations of fixed assets by state enterprises are divided among five sectors proportionally according to the supplemented table.

For circulating assets of state enterprises, I rely on Table 2-7 [*SYC89*, p. 26], which gives data only for selected years before 1975, annually after 1975, and only for state enterprises "under the management of the financial budget." The ratios in this table are used to distribute the sums, over time, of accumulations of circulating assets of state enterprises among the five sectors. The same method could be applied to estimate fixed assets of state enterprises in the five sectors by using Table 2-5 [*SYC89*, p. 26], on "net value of fixed assets." Table 10-28 is used instead because its coverage of state enterprises is broader than that of Table 2-5 and because annual data are available (except for 1966–1974). A difference between these two tables is that in Table 10-28 "agriculture, forestry, water conservancy and meteorology" are treated as one sector, while in Table 2-5 (and Table 2-7) "agriculture" constitutes a sector. My judgement is that the former sector corresponds more closely to the recorded output of the "agricultural" sector. Table IV shows that state enterprises dominate the two types of collective enterprises in accumulation.

Accumulations of fixed assets by urban collective enterprises are distributed 0.77 to industry, 0.03 to construction, 0.045 to transportation, 0.020 to commerce, and 0.045 to agriculture from 1952 to 1977, and from 1978 on by using a table on sectorial investments by urban collectives obtained from the State Statistical Bureau. The above stated fractions before 1977 are averages for 1978 and 1979. Accumulations of fixed assets by rural collectives are distributed 0.6 to industry, 0.12 to agriculture, 0.04 to construction, 0.04 to transportation, and none to commerce according to fragmentary data for the eighties given in *SYC81* [p. 193], *SYC83* [p. 206], *SYC85* [pp. 297–98], *SYC86* [p. 124], and *SYC89* [p. 559]. Initial values of fixed assets of state, urban-collective, and rural-collective enterprises combined are obtained by expanding the initial values given in Table 2-5 [*SYC89, p. 25*], for state

TABLE IV

ACCUMULATION BY THREE TYPES OF ENTERPRISES AND INDIVIDUALS

Year	State enterprises		Urban collectives		Rural collectives		Individuals
	Total	Fixed assets	Total	Fixed assets	Total	Fixed assets	Total
1952	103	43	10	1	15	11	2
1953	142	71	12	3	12	9	2
1954	153	87	25	8	13	10	4
1955	148	91	24	7	11	9	2
1956	145	137	33	7	35	31	4
1957	203	126	3	2	25	10	2
1958	359	259	3	2	13	15	4
1959	523	338	4	2	28	29	3
1960	492	384	5	4	2	9	2
1961	176	135	7	4	10	7	2
1962	62	73	6	4	27	15	4
1963	127	93	6	4	44	30	6
1964	195	149	7	5	51	39	10
1965	291	191	9	6	53	44	12
1966	377	233	15	9	63	50	15
1967	231	136	10	7	48	44	15
1968	229	98	7	5	47	48	15
1969	284	210	10	7	48	46	15
1970	508	331	13	8	79	62	18
1971	564	373	15	10	85	65	20
1972	521	366	21	14	84	77	22
1973	602	375	22	15	94	89	23
1974	570	399	25	18	118	108	28
1975	630	473	27	20	142	124	31
1976	554	443	29	22	134	127	31
1977	616	446	32	24	152	143	32
1978	847	572	36	26	169	150	35
1979	874	590	40	28	178	151	69
1980	863	613	44	30	141	133	117
1981	791	496	48	32	144	127	123
1982	848	650	55	35	197	148	136
1983	961	731	58	38	226	180	176
1984	1162	934	98	53	330	265	206
1985	1920	1335	138	92	325	314	245

enterprises by the ratios of total accumulations from 1953 to 1957 for the estimated series and the series given in the above table except for agriculture for which no initial value is recorded.

Accumulations of circulating funds by urban and rural collectives are distributed to the five sectors by using as ratios of circulating funds to fixed assets

0.41 for industry; 1.0 in 1952–1975, and 0.8 in 1976–1985 for construction; 0.08 for transportation; 9.0 in 1952–1970, 7.0 in 1971–1979, and 5.0 in 1980–1985 for commerce; and 0.8 for agriculture. These ratios are based on comparison of Table 2-7 and Table 2-5 [*SYC89*, pp. 25–26]. The products of these ratios and the fractions stated in the last paragraph for distributing the accumulations of fixed assets in urban collectives and rural collective are used as proportions to divide circulating funds in the five sectors. Initial 1952 values of circulating funds of state, urban-collective, and rural-collective enterprises combined are obtained by expanding the initial values given in Table 2-7 [*SYC89*, p. 26] for state enterprises by the ratios of total accumulation from 1953 to 1957 for the estimated series and the series given in the above table, except for agriculture for which no initial value is recorded. The initial capital stock for agriculture in 1952 will be discussed in Subsec. 5.1 below. Our estimates of components of capital stock are given in Table V, with zero initial value for agriculture.

16.4. One-Sector Analysis of Growth, Fluctuations, and Reform

Using the capital stock data of the last section, and the national income (in 1952 prices), and labor force data from *SYC89* [pp. 29–30, 101], presented, respectively, in Tables II, I, and X, one can estimate an aggregate production function to study economic growth, fluctuations, and the effects of economic reform since 1980. For this purpose, land is combined with capital stock. Tentatively let the initial capital in agriculture in 1952 be 450 (100 million yuan), which will be justified in Subsec. 5.1 below, and let the initial value of land be 720. This value of land is estimated by attributing 0.40 of the agricultural output 340 to land and assuming an annual yield of 0.19 (the yield is also to be justified in Subsec. 5.1). The total value of capital and land, including 582.67 for nonagriculture as given in Table V, would be about 1750 in 1952, when national income equals 589. The capital output ratio of 1750/589 or 2.97 appears to be a reasonable figure. The sensitivities of our results to the initial capital stock will be examined below.

Figure I plots log (national income/labor) against log (capital/labor) for the years 1952–1985. If the years from 1958 (when the Great Leap began and agricultural output might have been overestimated) to 1969 are omitted, the points from 1952 to 1980 are fairly close to a straight line, as shown in Fig. II. Figure I also shows the tremendous economic losses of the Great Leap and the improved productivity from 1981 to 1985 which might be attributed to economic reforms. The estimation of production functions presented below is based on the *assumption* that the years from 1958 to 1969 are abnormal because of the great upheavals of the Great Leap Forward Movement and the Cultural Revolution. In 1958 Chairman Mao Zedong launched the Great Leap, reorganized agricultural production into communes, and demanded unrealistic production targets. The economic failures afterwards are well-recognized historical facts and are demonstrated by Fig. I. Figure I shows the agreement of official data with well-established historical evidence. Thus, to

TABLE V

ESTIMATES OF CAPITAL STOCK IN FIVE SECTORS

Year	Agriculture		Industry		Construction		Transportation		Commerce	
	Total	Fixed	Total	Fixed	Total	Fixed	Total	Fixed	Total	Fixed
1952	0.0	0.0	248.0	158.8	9.0	3.1	152.3	141.9	173.3	11.8
1953	8.2	6.9	299.1	191.9	18.2	6.8	162.6	151.4	228.7	14.4
1954	15.5	12.3	366.3	237.4	27.8	10.8	179.7	167.7	285.3	19.0
1955	24.6	19.9	436.8	288.2	36.9	15.0	198.0	185.4	334.7	22.9
1956	44.5	37.1	539.2	372.3	47.5	23.2	219.3	206.3	356.8	31.0
1957	59.1	47.9	632.0	443.0	59.2	28.2	243.4	229.6	415.1	34.9
1958	85.7	74.9	844.4	614.1	61.6	31.9	287.4	268.4	452.8	41.0
1959	113.9	103.3	1147.8	839.3	67.4	39.8	350.4	321.6	520.0	50.0
1960	152.2	143.2	1436.6	1086.5	73.9	48.2	406.3	371.8	563.7	58.6
1961	170.5	160.2	1545.4	1174.5	76.1	50.4	427.9	391.2	582.4	61.4
1962	189.2	176.2	1600.0	1224.9	79.0	51.7	437.2	400.9	585.0	62.7
1963	220.4	203.8	1682.0	1292.6	83.8	54.6	445.1	410.0	614.0	65.0
1964	254.5	234.7	1805.5	1401.7	91.1	60.0	460.5	426.8	655.2	68.9
1965	287.3	265.2	1957.2	1533.6	100.0	66.5	494.2	463.8	727.8	74.0
1966	319.0	293.2	2198.5	1697.6	108.8	74.2	537.3	502.9	810.2	79.6
1967	338.4	311.4	2352.1	1803.7	114.2	79.4	563.4	526.4	966.1	83.0
1968	353.3	326.5	2496.4	1889.8	118.1	83.8	584.5	544.0	938.5	85.4
1969	379.3	351.8	2682.7	2037.5	125.2	90.8	621.7	579.2	990.6	90.5
1970	422.4	390.3	3001.0	2261.6	137.1	101.2	681.6	634.2	1096.4	98.5
1971	479.0	430.4	3335.8	2511.9	153.8	112.0	759.9	706.0	1202.6	110.3
1972	531.5	471.6	3657.0	2768.7	169.0	123.3	836.2	777.1	1297.1	122.0
1973	590.0	515.0	4015.7	3038.4	186.1	135.3	917.1	850.5	1423.6	134.0
1974	650.8	563.0	4384.2	3334.9	204.0	148.6	1001.5	929.1	1530.2	146.9
1975	722.2	619.7	4805.3	3700.9	225.4	164.8	1092.7	1018.4	1622.3	163.2
1976	804.5	684.2	5239.1	4037.7	246.2	179.7	1185.3	1103.9	1661.8	178.3
1977	870.3	744.1	5661.4	4408.5	261.9	194.2	1263.3	1179.0	1819.8	194.3
1978	1007.9	812.78	6158.5	4826.2	284.6	212.0	1383.6	1299.0	2007.7	213.6
1979	1101.1	887.5	6680.1	5273.3	311.6	232.9	1464.9	1374.6	2200.3	236.8
1980	1165.4	953.3	7126.0	5674.2	351.0	251.2	1551.1	1466.7	2434.2	268.5
1981	1210.9	998.7	7587.3	6025.4	383.2	267.1	1597.5	1515.7	2706.3	299.6
1982	1279.7	1054.0	8060.4	6418.4	414.4	287.1	1686.8	1609.1	2970.1	346.7
1983	1367.0	1134.9	8614.4	6860.3	451.7	309.5	1796.1	1714.1	3193.5	390.8
1984	1435.1	1210.3	9391.4	7406.8	520.5	350.3	1957.4	1867.1	3257.9	444.6
1985	1578.6	1291.6	10514.0	8079.4	606.9	385.1	2205.7	2085.4	3053.5	524.3

exclude the years 1958 to 1969 in estimating an aggregate production function is a reasonable and rewarding procedure. However, if a reader still wishes to question the exclusion of these years, my answer is that it is *interesting* to find out how abnormal the excluded years are *if* the remaining years up to 1980 are *assumed* normal years, as most readers familiar with this period of Chinese history would agree. Data are provided in this paper for any reader who wishes to select some other years as abnormal to draw her own conclusions.

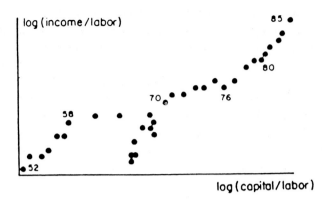

Fig. I

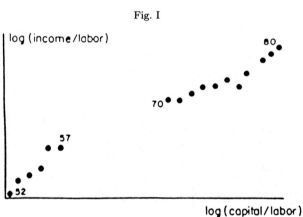

Fig. II

TABLE VI
AGGREGATE PRODUCTION FUNCTIONS

1952 capital	Intercept	Coefficient ln capital	Coefficient ln labor	R^2/s
1550	1.331 (1.007)	0.6952 (0.1939)	0.0232 (0.5755)	0.9953/0.0418
1650	1.428 (1.032)	0.6624 (0.1945)	0.1694 (0.5630)	0.9951/0.0428
1750	1.517 (1.052)	0.6332 (0.1945)	0.2981 (0.5495)	0.9949/0.0436
1850	1.596 (1.069)	0.6074 (0.1941)	0.4108 (0.5357)	0.9947/0.0444
1950	1.666 (1.084)	0.5848 (0.1934)	0.5093 (0.5219)	0.9946/0.0450
2213	1.307 (1.065)	0.6353 (0.1862)	0.3584 (0.5067)	0.9951/0.0427

Realizing the possible inaccuracy of the initial stock estimate, I have regressed log income on log capital and log labor from 1952 to 1980, omitting 1958 to 1969, using initial capital stocks ranging from 1550 to 1950 and obtained the results of Table VI. The standard errors (in parentheses) of the coefficients, except for log capital, are very large. The estimates of the coefficient of log labor are unreliable. However, the failure to estimate accurately the relative effects of capital and labor does not prevent the data from throwing light on the existence of technological change from 1952 to 1980, the economic losses due to the Great Leap and the Cultural Revolution, the effects of economic reform, and the rates of return to capital. These questions are studied by using 1550, 1750, and 1950 as initial stocks.

The absence of technological change is apparent from Fig. Ib. By adding a linear trend to the regressions of log (income/labor) on log (capital/labor) using 1550, 1750, and 1950 as initial capital stock one obtains the results of Table VII. Thus, the absence of technological change is confirmed.

TABLE VII
AGGREGATE PRODUCTION FUNCTIONS

1952 capital	Intercept	Coefficient ln (cap/labor)	Coefficient trend	R^2/s
1550	2.065 (0.142)	0.5530 (0.0191)		0.9825/0.0411
	2.729 (3.492)	1.2820 (0.5309)	−0.0375 (0.0273)	0.9846/0.0400
1750	1.718 (0.158)	0.5958 (0.0211)		0.9815/0.0422
	0.270 (3.236)	0.8123 (0.4838)	−0.0103 (0.0231)	0.9818/0.0434
1950	1.361 (0.177)	0.6396 (0.0234)		0.9803/0.0436
	2.051 (2.875)	0.5379 (0.4234)	0.0045 (0.0188)	0.9804/0.0450
2213	1.328 (0.168)	0.6317 (0.0219)		0.9823/0.0413
	0.336 (2.878)	0.7749 (0.4155)	−0.0065 (0.0187)	0.9825/0.0426

The regressions of Table VII using the logs of ratios to labor impose the constraint that the exponents of capital and labor in the Cobb–Douglas production function sum to one, and yield much smaller standard errors for the capital (and labor, by implication) coefficient, reductions from about 0.19 to about 0.02. While the imposition of this linear restriction reduces the originally large standard errors of the regression coefficients, it hardly affects the goodness of fit of the regression, as measured by the standard deviation s of its residuals. For those who are curious about the effects of omitted observations, I can report, using 1750 as initial 1952 capital stock, that unconstrained estimates of the (log) capital and labor coefficients are −0.233 (0.231) and 2.740 (0.684), respectively, for the sample period 1952–1980, and −0.277 (0.228) and 2.990 (0.626) for the sample period 1952–1985. Constrained to sum to one, the capital coefficient is estimated to be 0.587 (0.067) from the sample of 1952–1980 and 0.682 (0.055) from the sample of 1952–1985. I do not regard these results as very interesting. More interesting are the results reported below when one *assumes* the years 1958–1969 to be abnormal and ends the sample period in 1980 in order to see what the data for the unfitted years would look like.

Table VIII presents the deviations of observed real incomes from the estimates by the regression equations of Table VI as fractions of the latter, using 1550, 1750, and 1950 as initial capital stock. Estimates of the loss of national income range

TABLE VIII
PERCENTAGE DEVIATIONS OF NATIONAL INCOME AND
MARGINAL VALUE PRODUCT OF CAPITAL

1952 capital	Deviations of national income			Marginal value product of capital		
	1550	1750	1950	1550	1750	1950
1952	−0.074	−0.061	−0.085	0.285	0.232	0.193
1953	−0.004	−0.009	−0.018	0.278	0.228	0.191
1954	−0.010	−0.010	−0.010	0.271	0.223	0.187
1955	−0.006	−0.002	0.001	0.264	0.218	0.184
1956	0.070	0.075	0.075	0.258	0.214	0.181
1957	0.050	0.057	0.062	0.251	0.210	0.179
1958	0.169	0.157	0.148	0.242	0.208	0.181
1959	0.139	0.145	0.153	0.231	0.195	0.169
1960	0.021	0.048	0.069	0.222	0.186	0.160
1961	−0.304	−0.280	−0.262	0.219	0.183	0.157
1962	−0.360	−0.339	−0.323	0.217	0.182	0.156
1963	−0.311	−0.291	−0.276	0.815	0.181	0.156
1964	−0.228	−0.210	−0.197	0.211	0.180	0.156
1965	−0.139	−0.123	−0.110	0.207	0.177	0.155
1966	−0.522	−0.037	−0.026	0.202	0.174	0.153
1967	−0.152	−0.143	−0.136	0.199	0.173	0.152
1968	−0.234	−0.230	−0.227	0.196	0.171	0.152
1969	−0.121	−0.122	−0.123	0.193	0.170	0.152
1970	0.017	0.014	0.011	0.188	0.167	0.150
1971	0.022	0.016	0.012	0.183	0.163	0.147
1972	−0.005	−0.006	−0.007	0.179	0.159	0.143
1973	0.017	0.017	0.016	0.175	0.155	0.140
1974	−0.025	−0.025	−0.025	0.171	0.152	0.137
1975	0.001	0.001	0.001	0.167	0.149	0.135
1976	−0.071	−0.071	−0.070	0.163	0.146	0.132
1977	−0.047	−0.046	−0.044	0.160	0.143	0.129
1978	0.006	0.011	0.013	0.156	0.139	0.126
1979	0.024	0.026	0.028	0.152	0.136	0.124
1980	0.040	0.038	0.037	0.150	0.135	0.123
1981	0.044	0.038	0.033	0.147	0.133	0.121
1982	0.081	0.068	0.060	0.144	0.131	0.121
1983	0.137	0.121	0.110	0.142	0.129	0.119
1984	0.231	0.207	0.190	0.139	0.128	0.118
1985	0.324	0.293	0.271	0.136	0.125	0.116

from 0.30 to 0.26 in 1961, from 0.36 to 0.32 in 1962, from 0.31 to 0.28 in 1963, are significantly small in 1966, increase to approximately 0.14, 0.23, and 0.12 in 1967–1969, and decrease to zero in 1970. The effect of economic reforms on total productivity is about 0.04 in 1981, 0.07 in 1982, 0.12 in 1983, 0.20 in 1984, and 0.30 in 1985. The marginal product of one yuan of capital ranges from 0.19 to 0.28 in

1952 and from 0.12 to 0.15 in 1980. In 1985 it rises to about 0.125×1.293 or 0.16, when the effect 0.293 due to economic reforms is incorporated.

The results of regressions using 1750 as initial capital remain almost identical if, instead, the capital stock is estimated simply by summing the accumulation data of Table III, with 2213 as the initial capital in 1952 (2213 being 1750 times 1.26457, the ratio of total accumulations of the two series from 1953 to 1985). The last of aggregate production functions in Tables VI and VII marked with 2213 initial capital employs this alternative capital series. When this series is linked in 1985 with the original series (with 1740 initial capital), the percentage deviations of national income from the regression (with 1750 initial capital) for 1985 to 1988 are, respectively, 0.293, 0.301, 0.344, and 0.400.

The aggregate production function obtained by using a capital stock series that is simply the sum of official data on accumulation (meaning "net" addition to capital) yields the important conclusion that technological progress was absent in 1952–1980, as seen in the bottom row of Table VII. This conclusion may be questioned because official data on accumulation may be overestimated due to the low depreciation rates employed. Overestimation of capital stock growth would lead to underestimation of technical progress, as illustrated by the three regressions with trend in Table VII using three different initial values of capital that correspond to three (decreasing) sets of rates of capital accumulation. There are two responses to this question. First, plausible magnitudes of official underestimation of the depreciation rate, or overestimation of capital stock growth, is unlikely to change this conclusion as a comparison of the above three regressions suggests. Second, the conclusion that there was no technical progress according to official statistics is itself interesting. The Chinese government has reported a great deal of capital accumulation. To find out that such accumulated capital does not lead to improved total productivity in the period 1952–1980 is an interesting result. This result is consistent with the official data cited in Chow [1985a, p. 123], where a plot of log of output per worker against log of recorded capital per worker for state industrial enterprises in seven selected years from 1952 to 1981 is very close to a straight line, with a slope of 0.602 (0.207). The seven years 1952, 1957, 1965, 1975, and 1979–1981 were selected because data for other years were not published in 1983 when Chow [1985a] was written.

Since the absence of technological progress in China from 1952 to 1980 is a major conclusion of this paper, and the conclusion is reached by regression analysis using a Cobb–Douglas production function with an exponential trend included, one should look at the data differently and examine the robustness of this conclusion. Because of the high correlation between the capital stock and the trend variables, it might be difficult to assess accurately their relative importance in explaining the growth of output in time-series analysis. Note, however, that in spite of the high correlation, our time-series data did eliminate the trend variable as insignificant while maintaining the significance of the capital stock variable. Before providing additional evidence, consider some basic facts concerning the growth accounting for the aggregate Chinese economy. The exponential rates of growth of output, capital (1750 in 1952) and labor according to the data used to estimate the aggregate production functions of Table VII are, respectively, 0.05863, 0.07374, and 0.02553, implying annual growth rates of 6.04, 7.65, and 2.59 percent. Weighting the exponential rates of capital and labor by 0.6 and 0.4, respectively, would generate an exponential growth rate of output of 0.0545, almost sufficient to explain the observed rate of 0.0586. The above are growth rates computed from endpoints of the data. If we regress log output minus 0.6 log capital minus 0.4 log labor on trend using data from 1952 to 1980 (omitting 1958–1969), the coefficient of the trend variable is −0.00022 with a standard error of 0.00101. Changing the coefficient of log capital to 0.5, 0.4, and 0.3, with the coefficient of log labor being 0.5, 0.6, and 0.7 would yield trend coefficients of 0.0045 (0.0010), 0.0093 (0.0010), and 0.0141 (0.0010). The standard errors of the regressions for capital exponent of 0.6, 0.5, 0.4, and 0.3 are, respectively, 0.04220, 0.04253, 0.04293, and 0.04356. Thus, the goodness of fit becomes worse as the capital exponent decreases from 0.6.

To provide cross-sectional evidence for using a capital exponent of 0.6, which would imply the absence of technical progress, I first cite the study of Mankiw, Romer, and Weil [1990, Table 1], where, using the framework of a Solow model and cross-country data for 98 nonoil countries and 75 OECD countries, the authors found a capital coefficient of 0.60 (0.02) and 0.59 (0.02), respectively. Second, using the share of labor income to total income in China, one may consider a year 1953 when the economy was still mostly a market economy. In 1953 the wage income of the nonagricultural labor force was 179 (see Table XVI and the discussion of Sec. 6 below), while the total national income from the four nonagricultural sectors was 335 (see Table II), implying a labor share of 0.53. Similar calculations for 1967 and 1970 give labor shares of 0.44 and 0.32, respectively. One might argue that these low labor shares are the result of deliberate government policy to restrict labor income in order to finance a high rate of capital formation, but even a 0.5 coefficient for labor would imply less than one half of 1 percent annual growth contributed by technological progress.

Third, a cross-section estimate of the labor share in Chinese agriculture for the period 1921–1924 can be obtained from the classic study of Buck [1930]; who surveyed 2866 farms in seventeen localities and seven provinces in China. Total farm receipts (including value of products from the farm used by the family) averaged 376.24 yuan [p. 86]. Value added per farm is obtained by subtracting cash expenditures 40.11 other than expenditures on labor [p. 86], yielding 336.13 yuan. Expenditures on hired labor plus imputed value of family labor equals 24.87 plus 64.22 or 89.09 [p. 86], which does not include the value of the labor of the farm operator [p. 75]. To include the latter, note that there were 2.29 man-equivalent workers per farm [p. 50], which I translate to 3.29 working persons including the farm operator. Multiplying labor cost 89.09 by 3.29/2.29 gives 127.99. The labor share is 127.77/336.13 or 0.38, close to the 0.40 figure used in our analysis.

16.5. Analysis of Five Sectors

Estimates of capital stocks presented in Table V, net output data in Table I, and labor force data in *SYC89* [pp. 102, 105], supplemented by communication with the State Statistical Bureau as presented in Table IX, have been used to estimate production functions for five sectors. For agriculture I have considered different values for the initial capital stock in 1952 and employed an additional input variable "sown area" [*SYCV89*, p. 192; *SYC84*, p. 137]. The reported sown area did not increase much in the sample period, being 2.12 billion mu in 1952 and 2.20 billion mu in 1980.

TABLE IX
AGRICULTURE PRODUCTION FUNCTIONS

1952 capital	Intercept	Capital	Labor	Land	Trend	R^2/s
250	−7.682	0.2102	0.2305	0.9959		0.9830
	(2.193)	(0.0376)	(0.1102)	(0.2372)		0.02750
	−8.879	0.2964	0.3007	1.054	−0.0069	0.9830
	(7.453)	(0.4847)	(0.4095)	(0.407)	(0.3085)	0.02859
450	−8.563	0.2501	0.3167	1.034		0.9832
	(2.888)	(0.0443)	(0.0946)	(0.235)		0.02732
	−11.255	0.4246	0.4980	1.160	−0.0117	0.9833
	(8.798)	(0.5384)	(0.5657)	(0.456)	(0.0361)	(0.02830)
650	−9.090	0.2906	0.3589	1.046		0.9834
	(2.876)	(0.0512)	(0.0870)	(0.234)		0.02719
	−13.232	0.5646	0.6449	1.228	−0.0159	0.9836
	(9.783)	(0.6190)	(0.6499)	(0.475)	(0.0358)	(0.02807)

16.5.1. *Production function for agriculture*

To find reasonable estimates of the stock of capital in agriculture in 1952, I first referred to Tang [1981] and found an estimate of 112.9 (100 million RMB) in 1952, an increase by 17.95 from 1952 to 1957, and an increase by 205.40 (100 million 1952 RMB) from 1952 to 1980. The large discrepancies between these increases and the corresponding increases in my series for agriculture presented in Table V are very puzzling. Our series of capital stock increases by 59.10 from 1952 to 1957 and by 1165.48 from 1952 to 1980, three to five times Tang's. The coverages of the two series must be different, with ours including circulating assets and covering "agriculture, forestry, water conservancy and meteorology." Without being able to resolve the difference, I had to find an independent estimate of 1952 capital in agriculture.

In 1985 the "original value of fixed assets for production" per peasant household is reported to be 792.53 [*SYC86*, p. 109]. Multiplied by approximately 161 million farm households [*SYC86*, pp. 73, 84], this gives an estimate of about 1276 (100,000 RMB). This estimate, plus circulating assets and public goods but subtracting depreciation, is broadly consistent with our estimate of 1579 for the increase of capital in the agriculture sector from 1952 to 1985, and equals four times Tang's estimate of 318.3 for capital in 1980. Our estimates of increases from 1952 to 1957 and from 1952 to 1980 are, respectively, 59.10/17.95 or 3.29 and 1165.48/205.40 or 5.67 times Tang's. Quadrupling Tang's initial estimate would give 450 as 1952 capital stock. To estimate capital stock independently, one may attribute 0.25 of the 1952 agricultural output of 340 to capital and use a rate of return for capital of 0.19. The resulting estimate happens to be 450 also. When I use 450 as initial capital to estimate a production function reported in Table IX, I have found 0.25 as the share of output contributed by capital and 0.19 as the annual rate of return to capital in 1952 in Table X. Thus, the 450 estimate is reasonable and consistent with the regression results. After the above was written, I discovered an estimate by Liu [1968, p. 171], "Total farm capital was therefore 40.95 billion yuan in 1952." This estimate excludes rural residential housing and is close to our 45.0 billion figure for capital in the agricultural sector. To examine the sensitivities of the results to initial estimates of capital, I have used 250, 450, and 650 as initial estimates and report three sets of results from Cobb–Douglas production functions below covering the sample period 1952–1980, omitting 1958–1969.

The regression coefficients are not very sensitive to variations of the initial capital stock from 250 to 650. The coefficient of log land is high perhaps because the variations in land use through time are not properly reported. When a linear trend is added, its coefficient is very small as compared with the standard error, suggesting no technical change through time. Because of multicollinearity, the standard errors of the other coefficients greatly increase when trend is added, but the results stand up in spite of the presence of trend. Omitting the trend variable, I present in Table XI the percentage deviations of actual output from the regressions with three different initial capital stocks as fractions of the latter, and the associated marginal value products of capital estimated from the regression equations. The deviations show the enormous losses (of about one-quarter) in the years 1960–1963 due to the Great Leap but smaller losses than for aggregate output in the 1967–1969 period due to the Cultural Revolution. The improvement in productivity from 1981 on has been greater in agriculture than in the economy as a whole, as is generally recognized. These results are not sensitive to the values of the initial capital stock in 1952. Our estimates of percentage deviations of agricultural output, being 0.77, 0.181, 0.269, and 0.422 for 1981–1984, respectively, are close to the estimates of total productivity increases of 0.105, 0.203, 0.270, and 0.406 for these years given by McMillan, Whalley, and Zhu [1989, p. 794], although these authors did not estimate an aggregate production function for Chinese agriculture using regression analysis. The estimates of the rates of return to capital in agriculture are reasonable. Even these estimates are not very sensitive to the large variations in the values of initial capital stock, except for the early years before 1963 when the three estimates are, respectively, 0.18, 0.15, and 0.13, with a large initial stock associated with a low value of the rate of return to capital.

TABLE X
LABOR FORCE IN FIVE SECTORS (10,000)

Year	Total	Agriculture	Industry	Construction	Transportation	Commerce
1952	20729	17317	1246	285	235	579
1953	21364	17747	1373	342	257	940
1954	21832	18151	1501	381	259	833
1955	22328	18592	1400	513	272	809
1956	23018	18544	1375	1093	275	828
1957	23771	19309	1401	741	442	846
1958	26600	15490	4416	2660	852	1751
1959	26173	16271	2881	2521	684	1865
1960	25880	17016	2979	1133	730	2047
1961	25590	19747	2224	632	546	629
1962	25910	21276	1705	354	455	828
1963	26640	21966	1632	406	468	831
1964	27736	22801	1695	488	479	841
1965	28670	23396	1828	580	491	861
1966	29805	24297	1974	626	502	880
1967	30814	25165	2032	629	516	918
1968	31915	26063	2092	651	576	940
1969	33225	27117	2365	665	571	921
1970	34432	27811	2809	709	584	945
1971	35620	28397	3233	757	605	998
1972	35854	28283	3496	780	605	1003
1973	36652	28857	3704	788	603	991
1974	37369	29218	3900	812	632	1032
1975	38168	29456	4284	868	666	1098
1976	38834	29443	4692	919	694	1172
1977	39377	29340	4809	1022	742	1224
1978	40152	28373	6091	1065	749	1155
1979	41024	28692	6298	1155	789	1248
1980	42361	29181	6714	1221	846	1381
1981	43725	29836	6975	1274	833	1511
1982	45295	30917	7204	1340	850	1604
1983	46436	31209	7397	1481	906	1762
1984	48197	30927	7930	1858	1080	2036
1985	49873	31187	8349	2175	1222	2363
1986	51282	31311	8980	2376	1305	2485
1987	52783	31720	9343	2526	1373	2655
1988	54334	32308	9661	2634	1434	2829

TABLE XI

PERCENTAGE DEVIATIONS OF AGRICULTURE OUTPUTS FROM REGRESSION AND
MARGINAL VALUE PRODUCT OF CAPITAL

	Percentage deviations of output			Marginal value products of capital		
	Initial 1952 capital			Initial 1952 capital		
Year	250	450	650	250	450	650
1952	0.010	0.011	0.012	0.283	0.187	0.150
1953	−0.006	−0.006	−0.005	0.283	0.190	0.153
1954	−0.026	−0.027	−0.027	0.286	0.194	0.158
1955	0.016	0.014	0.014	0.286	0.197	0.161
1956	−0.006	−0.005	−0.004	0.284	0.201	0.166
1957	0.017	0.018	0.019	0.273	0.197	0.164
1958	0.090	0.118	0.132	0.235	0.171	0.143
1959	−0.055	−0.028	−0.015	0.209	0.156	0.132
1960	−0.280	−0.260	−0.251	0.206	0.160	0.137
1961	−0.266	−0.253	−0.246	0.196	0.155	0.135
1962	−0.235	−0.225	−0.220	0.189	0.152	0.134
1963	−0.166	−0.154	−0.149	0.180	0.148	0.132
1964	−0.099	−0.088	−0.083	0.176	0.148	0.133
1965	−0.028	−0.016	−0.011	0.168	0.134	0.127
1966	−0.002	−0.006	−0.011	0.166	0.145	0.133
1967	0.013	0.020	0.024	0.161	0.142	0.131
1968	0.016	0.022	0.025	0.153	0.136	0.126
1969	−0.006	−0.003	−0.001	0.151	0.136	0.127
1970	0.013	0.014	0.015	0.147	0.134	0.127
1971	−0.009	−0.008	−0.007	0.140	0.131	0.125
1972	−0.047	−0.046	−0.046	0.135	0.128	0.123
1973	0.014	0.014	0.014	0.129	0.123	0.120
1974	0.035	0.034	0.034	0.122	0.119	0.117
1975	0.030	0.029	0.029	0.116	0.114	0.114
1976	−0.008	−0.009	−0.009	0.109	0.109	0.109
1977	−0.042	−0.043	−0.042	0.103	0.104	0.105
1978	−0.026	−0.024	−0.023	0.094	0.096	0.098
1979	0.029	0.030	0.031	0.088	0.091	0.094
1980	0.011	0.010	0.010	0.084	0.088	0.091
1981	0.080	0.077	0.075	0.082	0.086	0.089
1982	0.188	0.181	0.178	0.079	0.084	0.088
1983	0.278	0.269	0.264	0.077	0.081	0.085
1984	0.432	0.422	0.416	0.073	0.078	0.083
1985	0.449	0.436	0.428	0.068	0.074	0.079

16.5.2. *Production functions for four nonagricultural sectors*

By using the net output data of Table I, capital stock data of Table V, and labor force data of Table X, Cobb–Douglas production functions have been estimated for the four nonagricultural sectors as shown in Table XII. When in doubt, CES production functions have also been estimated, but they show no appreciable improvement. The sample period covers 1952–1980, but the omitted years vary somewhat among the four sectors, as chosen partly by the goodness of fit.

TABLE XII

PRODUCTION FUNCTIONS OF NONAGRICULTURE SECTORS

Sector	Sample period	Intercept	Capital	Labor	Trend	R^2/s
Industry	1952–1980 excluding 1961–1968	1.787 (0.356)	0.6824 (0.0361)	0.3179 (0.0742)		0.9936 0.0800
		0.605 (0.575)	0.8846 (0.0882)	0.3021 (0.0659)	−0.0229 (0.0093)	0.9953 0.0707
Con-strained		1.785 (0.222)	0.6826 (0.0253)			0.9745 0.0779
		1.295 (0.528)	0.7473 (0.0681)		−0.0048 (0.0047)	0.9759 0.0778
Construc-tion	1954–1980 excluding 1961, 1962, 1968	2.776 (0.183)	0.5170 (0.0276)	0.3660 (0.0405)		0.9616 0.0901
		2.672 (.910)	0.5450 (0.2408)	0.3624 (0.0516)	−0.0023 (0.0200)	0.9619 0.0923
Con-strained		2.836 (0.205)	0.5489 (0.0280)			0.9457 0.1017
		2.297 (0.275)	0.6475 (0.0453)		−0.0108 (0.0041)	0.9590 0.0905
Transpor-tation	1952–1980 excluding 1959–1969	2.579 (0.418)	0.4689 (0.0362)	0.4221 (0.0683)		0.9897 0.0637
		2.085 (4.016)	0.5609 (0.7446)	0.4118 (0.1091)	−0.0073 (0.0590)	0.9898 0.0659
Con-strained		3.419 (0.325)	0.4132 (0.0349)			0.8975 0.0749
		1.921 (0.623)	0.5915 (0.0728)		−0.0097 (0.0036)	0.9307 0.0636
Commerce	1953–1980 excluding 1958–1968	5.692 (0.620)	0.2199 (0.0343)	0.8755 (0.1778)		0.9737 0.0548
	1975–1977	4.922 (1.484)	0.4060 (0.3256)	0.9701 (0.2464)	−0.0166 (0.0289)	0.9746 0.0566
Con-strained		5.318 (0.194)	0.2367 (0.0213)			0.9110 0.0535
		5.724 (0.983)	0.1855 (0.1232)		0.0036 (0.0085)	0.9125 0.0554

TABLE XIII

PERCENTAGE DEVIATIONS OF OUTPUT OF NONAGRICULTURE SECTORS

Year	Industry	Construction	Transportation	Commerce
1952	−0.133	0.542	−0.125	−0.269
1953	−0.012	0.384	−0.019	−0.053
1954	−0.004	0.321	0.057	0.027
1955	−0.040	−0.086	0.019	0.027
1956	0.083	0.046	0.132	0.058
1957	0.078	−0.002	−0.053	0.004
1958	−0.036	−0.075	0.022	−0.446
1959	0.171	−0.046	0.345	−0.444
1960	0.073	0.235	0.314	−0.515
1961	−0.346	−0.505	−0.165	−0.158
1962	−0.412	−0.249	−0.307	−0.238
1963	−0.352	−0.123	−0.303	−0.229
1964	−0.240	−0.008	−0.234	−0.228
1965	−0.105	−0.020	−0.033	−0.237
1966	0.011	−0.002	0.048	−0.109
1967	−0.194	−0.078	−0.186	−0.110
1968	−0.303	−0.284	−0.280	−0.207
1969	−0.134	−0.061	−0.115	−0.057
1970	0.054	0.138	0.013	0.000
1971	0.064	0.165	0.025	−0.056
1972	0.039	0.060	0.029	−0.045
1973	0.040	0.017	0.045	0.021
1974	−0.041	0.014	−0.061	−0.047
1975	0.005	0.053	−0.004	−0.109
1976	−0.114	0.033	−0.097	−0.185
1977	−0.043	−0.020	−0.018	−0.133
1978	−0.018	−0.084	0.043	0.093
1979	−0.007	−0.136	0.019	0.070
1980	0.033	0.033	0.003	−0.036
1981	−0.006	−0.012	0.035	0.036
1982	0.001	−0.024	0.122	0.009
1983	0.042	0.064	0.176	0.033
1984	0.104	0.008	0.184	0.008
1985	0.202	0.090	0.277	0.067

For industry only the years 1961–1968 are omitted, as a plot of log (output/labor) against log (capital/labor) for the remaining years shows the points to be close to a straight line. A part of Chinese history, confirmed by our data, is that in the beginning of the Great Leap and during much of the Cultural Revolution, industrial production was less affected than agriculture, reflecting a government policy to maintain the growth of industry in years of political disturbance. For construction the sample begins in 1954 as the recorded initial capital in 1952 is very small, and only years 1961–1962 and 1968 among the remaining years appear to show abnormally low outputs, perhaps reflecting the same government policy as industry. The results are very similar when the entire period 1961–1968 is excluded. For transportation the excluded years are 1959–1969. For commerce they are 1958–1968 and 1975–1977, the latter possibly reflecting the disruptive effects of the Cultural Revolution. In each case, a linear trend is added to test the presence of technological change. None is found, except for industry which shows a negative trend.

If we impose the restriction that the coefficients of log labor and log capital sum to one by regressing log (output/labor) on log (capital/labor), the results for each sector are given in the last two regressions in Table XII; the first without a trend; and the second with a trend. The coefficients for log capital do not change much but have smaller standard errors. The negative trend for industry becomes insignificant, while the negative trends for construction and transportation become significant. All results support the conclusion of no positive technological change in these four sectors of the Chinese economy.

Table XIII shows the percentage deviations of actual outputs in the five sectors from their regression equations (imposing no restrictions and omitting the trend variable). The negative effects of the Great Leap on industry and construction outputs did not occur until 1961 and were more severe than in agriculture. 1968 was a bad year for both, with negative deviations of approximately 30 percent. The positive effects of economic reform after 1980 are slower to occur and smaller in industry than in agriculture; they are hardly detectable in construction. Transportation output was abnormally high in 1959–1960, only to experience large negative effects of the Great Leap in 1961–1964 and of the Cultural Revolution in 1968. The positive effects of reform for transportation are larger than in industry but smaller than in agriculture. For commerce the effects of the Great Leap began in 1958 and were very severe, being over 40 percent during 1958–1960 and continuing to 1968. No improvement in total factor productivity after 1980 can be discerned.

16.5.3. *Resource allocation in five sectors*

Did supply and demand affect the prices of products of the five sectors? Price indices in 1980 (with 1952 = 100) obtained by taking the ratios of current to real outputs in Tables I and II are 231.6 for agriculture, 77.94 for industry, 116.3 for construction, 86.3 for transportation, and 88.04 for commerce. Divided by the implicit deflator of national income, the relative price indices of the five sectors are, respectively, 191.0, 64.27, 95.90, 71.16, and 72.59. On the supply side, indices of per capita output in 1980 (with 1952 = 100) obtained by dividing the output indices of Table I by a population index of 1.7171 for 1980 [*SYC89*, p. 87] are 98.07 for agriculture, 1172.15 for industry, 441.26 for construction, 340.11 for transportation, and 185.66 for commerce. On the demand side, per capital real national income (with 1952 = 100) is 300.7 in 1980, while per capita consumption is 221.8 (see Table III).

Changes in supply and demand clearly affected the prices of agricultural and industrial products. For agriculture, output per capita in 1980 remained about the same as in 1952, while per capita total consumption more than doubled. For industry, output per capita was about twelve times in 1980, while per capita real national income was only three times, national income being used to measure the force of demand, since before 1980 more than half of industrial products consisted of producer goods of "heavy industry." There is no question that in 1980, demand exceeded supply at 1952 prices for agriculture, and supply exceeded demand at 1952 prices for industry, at least partly causing the price changes to 191.0 and 64.27. Assume per capita demand functions with constant total consumption (or income) and own-price elasticities. If total consumption elasticity is 0.79 for agricultural products (see Chow [1985a, p. 165]), the total consumption effect on demand would be $2.218^{.79}$ or 1.876. A price elasticity of -1.00 would restrict demand to 0.9807 of the 1952 level, assuming equilibrium in 1952 and 1980. For industrial products an income elasticity of 2 applied to 3.007 would be consistent with a price elasticity of -0.59 to explain the price reduction to 0.6427 in 1980.

The explanations by supply and demand for the remaining three sectors with smaller price changes are less clearcut, but still plausible. For construction, since relative price remained almost the same, an income elasticity of 1.35 could explain the increase in per capita demand to 4.41. For transportation, income and price elasticities of 1 and -0.36 could explain the price reduction to 0.7716. For commerce, total consumption and price elasticities of 0.6 and -0.44, respectively, could explain the price reduction to 0.7259.

The rates of return (in 1952 output value) to capital accumulated in the five sectors have been computed from production functions reported in Tables IX and XII and are presented in Tables XI and XIV. Adjusted by prices in 1980, the rates in 1980 (with standard errors in parentheses) are 0.20 (0.077) in agriculture, 0.17 (0.029) in industry, 0.26 (0.041) in construction, 0.038 (0.018) in transportation, and 0.023 (0.026) in commerce. The very low rate of return for transportation may reflect the fact that much of transportation facilities, including highways and waterways, is a public good of which the marginal value product of capital is not explicitly included in the measured output. The rates of return to investment and pricing in railroads deserve to be further examined. The very low rate of return in commerce is accounted for by the very large quantity of circulating assets (being five to nine times fixed assets according to Table V and *SYC89* [pp. 25–26]). These circulating assets are recorded officially as a part of accumulation. The presence of large quantities in commerce with a very low rate of return might suggest the inefficient use of these assets.

Marginal value products of labor estimated from production functions of Table IX and XII are presented in Table XV. In 1980 prices they are 142 (67) in agriculture, 827 (370) in industry, 537 (152) in construction, 627 (414) in transportation, and 1632 (2335) in commerce. For reference the 1980 average annual wage is 784 in industry, 857 in construction, 842 in transportation, and 694 in

TABLE XIV
RATES OF RETURN TO CAPITAL
(IN 1952 OUTPUT VALUE)

Year	Industry	Construction	Transportation	Commerce
1952	0.365	0.781	0.088	0.153
1953	0.355	0.594	0.088	0.119
1954	0.342	0.504	0.084	0.090
1955	0.316	0.490	0.081	0.077
1956	0.294	0.573	0.077	0.075
1957	0.282	0.446	0.090	0.068
1958	0.370	0.699	0.108	0.120
1959	0.293	0.656	0.089	0.114
1960	0.276	0.468	0.084	0.116
1961	0.245	0.373	0.073	0.051
1962	0.223	0.296	0.066	0.051
1963	0.217	0.303	0.067	0.049
1964	0.214	0.311	0.066	0.047
1965	0.214	0.317	0.064	0.045
1966	0.211	0.313	0.062	0.042
1967	0.209	0.306	0.061	0.041
1968	0.207	0.305	0.063	0.040
1969	0.210	0.299	0.061	0.037
1970	0.214	0.293	0.058	0.035
1971	0.217	0.284	0.056	0.034
1972	0.216	0.274	0.053	0.032
1973	0.213	0.263	0.050	0.030
1974	0.211	0.254	0.049	0.029
1975	0.211	0.248	0.048	0.030
1976	0.211	0.243	0.047	0.031
1977	0.208	0.245	0.046	0.030
1978	0.218	0.239	0.044	0.026
1979	0.215	0.235	0.044	0.026
1980	0.215	0.227	0.044	0.025
1981	0.213	0.221	0.043	0.026
1982	0.211	0.217	0.042	0.026
1983	0.208	0.216	0.042	0.026
1984	0.207	0.219	0.043	0.030
1985	0.203	0.215	0.043	0.035

commerce [*SYC89*, p. 139]. Note the large standard errors in our estimates of the marginal value products of labor, especially for commerce. Not much inference can be drawn from them, except perhaps to note the low value for agriculture, a fact recognized to be associated with high population density.

TABLE XV
MARGINAL VALUE PRODUCT OF LABOR
(IN 1952 OUTPUT VALUE)

Year	Agriculture*	Industry	Construction	Transportation	Commerce
1952	62	338	175	513	1077
1953	62	360	224	502	1151
1954	63	389	261	524	1226
1955	64	460	250	533	1275
1956	68	538	176	556	1289
1957	66	592	253	444	1329
1958	75	329	115	328	1238
1959	68	544	124	409	1266
1960	72	619	216	422	1274
1961	62	795	318	512	1436
1962	58	975	468	574	1437
1963	57	1040	443	570	1452
1964	58	1063	411	571	1471
1965	58	1067	387	582	1501
1966	58	1096	385	597	1532
1967	56	1126	394	601	1547
1968	53	1150	392	574	1570
1969	53	1110	398	594	1593
1970	53	1066	401	612	1623
1971	54	1041	408	631	1646
1972	56	1051	420	660	1672
1973	56	1077	439	691	1709
1974	57	1104	452	700	1728
1975	58	1102	456	708	1737
1976	59	1099	460	718	1732
1977	59	1139	444	712	1757
1978	63	1027	452	739	1809
1979	62	1061	450	736	1828
1980	62	1061	462	727	1846
1981	60	1079	470	743	1868
1982	59	1100	474	754	1893
1983	59	1131	465	748	1901
1984	60	1144	434	704	1875
1985	62	1193	425	693	1814

*Initial capital in 1952 is 450.

16.6. Financing Capital Accumulation

The financing for capital accumulation has been achieved mainly through keeping the consumption of peasants roughly equal to the income of the agricultural sector and the consumption of nonagricultural residents roughly equal to total wage. This observation is evident from the data on Table XVI (see *SYC89* [pp. 38, 138]).

TABLE XVI

CONSUMPTION OF PEASANTS AND NONAGRICULTURAL RESIDENTS AND
RELATED VARIABLES

Year	Consumption of peasants	Consumption of non-agricultural residents	Estimated income of non-agricultural residents	Ratio of column 1 to agriculture income	Ratio of column 2 to column 3
1952	298	136	152	0.876	0.896
1953	332	176	179	0.888	0.983
1954	348	179	190	0.897	0.941
1955	389	186	197	0.933	0.945
1956	397	216	269	0.904	0.803
1957	412	237	278	0.969	0.851
1958	435	248	595	0.989	0.416
1959	339	302	507	0.902	0.596
1960	346	337	453	1.042	0.744
1961	418	337	298	0.968	1.131
1962	459	322	255	1.034	1.261
1963	487	306	269	0.998	1.137
1964	539	302	289	0.982	1.044
1965	581	314	311	0.906	1.009
1966	637	332	321	0.921	1.034
1967	679	347	332	0.966	1.046
1968	670	350	338	0.938	1.037
1969	705	363	351	0.976	1.034
1970	770	375	371	0.990	1.010
1971	804	391	404	0.995	0.967
1972	824	439	445	1.020	0.986
1973	898	466	458	1.014	1.018
1974	915	481	476	0.992	1.010
1975	946	504	505	1.000	0.997
1976	965	537	540	1.027	0.994
1977	974	579	578	1.067	1.002
1978	1043	630	724	1.058	0.870
1979	1212	698	824	0.989	0.847
1980	1384	839	1004	1.044	0.835
1981	1572	901	1072	1.042	0.840
1982	1737	951	1147	1.008	0.829
1983	1941	1016	1258	1.010	0.808
1984	2232	1163	1682	0.992	0.691
1985	2728	1512	2145	1.095	0.705
1986	2994	1779	2654	1.101	0.670
1987	3381	2096	3073	1.072	0.682
1988	4166	2792	3848	1.091	0.726

Comparing consumption (in current prices) of peasants in Table XVI with income of the agricultural sector in Table II, one finds the ratio of the former to the latter to fall between 0.90 and 1.07 in all years from 1954 to 1984. Government exercises some control over the money income of peasants by setting purchasing prices of farm and sideline products. The index of these prices [*SYC89*, p. 688] is almost identical to the implicit price deflator for the agricultural sector obtained from comparing Tables I and II. Comparing consumption of nonagricultural residents in Table XVI with estimated wage income, which equals average annual wage of staff and workers [*SYC89*, p. 138] times nonagricultural labor force (Table X), one finds the ratio of the former to the latter to fall between 0.84 and 1.05 in the years 1952 to 1980, excluding 1956 and 1958–1963. By controlling the wage rate, the government can limit the consumption of nonagricultural residents.

16.7. Summary

Using official information on "newly increased fixed assets through capital construction" of all state-owned enterprises and on circulating funds of state-owned enterprises "under the state budget," I have estimated capital stock annually from 1952 to 1985 in the five income-producing sectors of the Chinese economy by distributing official data on net capital accumulation of fixed and circulating assets in three types of enterprises to the five sectors. These estimates, together with official data on net income, labor force, and agricultural land, are used to estimate production functions for the aggregate economy and the five production sectors.

The production functions estimated are used to assess the economic losses in the aggregate economy and in the five sectors due to the Great Leap and the Cultural Revolution, and to measure the improvement of productivity in the 1980s after the economic reforms. The percentage losses in 1962 are about 0.34 for the aggregate economy, 0.22 for agriculture, 0.41 for industry, 0.25 for construction, 0.31 for transportation, and 0.24 for commerce. The percentage gains in 1985 are about 0.30 for the aggregate economy, 0.44 for agriculture, 0.20 for industry, none for construction, 0.28 for transportation, and none for commerce.

The capital coefficients of Cobb–Douglas production functions are about 0.60 for the aggregate economy, 0.25 for agriculture, 0.68 for industry, 0.52 for construction, 0.47 for transportation, and 0.22 for commerce, with the rate of return to capital in 1980 being, respectively, 0.16, 0.20, 0.17, 0.26, 0.04 (not including social return to transportation capital), and 0.02 (including much circulating assets in commerce). From 1952 to 1985 aggregate income grew by an average rate of 0.06 of which 0.045 is attributed to the 0.076 growth rate of capital (including land). The average annual growth rates of the five sectors are, respectively, 0.019, 0.113, 0.075, 0.065, and 0.042, of which 0.015, 0.085, 0.052, 0.040, and 0.021 are attributable to capital growth rates of 0.064, 0.127, 0.102, 0.086, and 0.099 in these sectors (beginning date being 1954 for construction). The marginal value products of labor have not been accurately estimated. Changes in prices in the five sectors appear to be broadly consistent with the changes in supply relative to demand.

A major theme in the study of economic growth since Solow's classic paper [1956] has been the explanation of technological progress without which any theory on the growth of western economies is deficient. Romer [1990] is a recent example of this theme. A major finding of this paper is that technological change was absent in the growth of the Chinese economy from 1952 to 1980. Solow's classic paper, absent technical progress, would do well explaining China's growth during this period, with capital formation playing an important role as the Chinese economic planners and Solow's theory intended.

If one accepts the empirical finding of no technological change in China from 1952 to 1980, one may try to explain why it happened. It is an accepted fact that the Chinese economic planners tried to introduce industrial technology and the method of planning from the Soviet Union in the 1950s and began the First Five-Year Plan in 1953. The Chinese planners also tried to increase output by investing a large fraction of national output in industry, especially heavy industry. This paper has described the increases in outputs in five sectors and in total through capital formation in these sectors by using sectorial and aggregate production functions. These is no reason to assume that technological progress occurred during the period up to 1980. Economic cooperation with the Soviet Union ended in the 1960s. Without incentives from private enterprises to innovate, where could technological progress have come? I have found no theory to support the assertion that central planning will produce technological progress. It might happen, as suggested by Young [1992] for the case of Singapore, that much government direction in industrial investment does not lead to an increase in total factor productivity. Although technological progress defined in the context of Solow's [1956] growth model is an important phenomenon to explain for a market economy like the United States, one cannot presume its existence in a country like China during a period when private initiatives for innovations or adopting new technology from abroad appeared to be absent. For such an economy one does not need to find explanations for the varying rates of productivity changes as Romer [1987] attempted to do for the United States. However, after the reforms in the 1980s when profit-seeking enterprises began to grow, the study of technological progress in China is an important and interesting topic for further research.

References

Buck, John L., 1930, *Chinese Farm Economy*, Chicago, IL: The University of Chicago Press.

Chow, G. C., 1985a, *The Chinese Economy*, New York, NY: Harper and Row; 2nd edn., 1987, Singapore: World Scientific.

———, 1985b, A model of Chinese national income determination, *Journal of Political Economy* **93**, 782–792.

————, 1986, Chinese statistics, *The American Statistician* **40**, 191–196.

————, 1987, Money and price level determination in China, *Journal of Comparative Economics* **11**, 319–333.

Jefferson, Gary H., Rawski, Thomas G., and Zheng, Yuxin, 1989, Growth efficiency and convergence in Chinese industry: A comparative evaluation of the state and collective sectors, University of Pittsburgh, Department of Economics, Working Paper no. 251.

Liu, Ta-chung, 1968, Quantitative trends in the economy, in Alexander Eckstein, Walter Galenson, and Ta-chung Liu, eds., *Economics Trends in Communist China* Chicago, IL: Aldine Publishing Company, pp. 87–182.

Liu Ta-chung and Yeh, Kung-chia, 1963, *The Economy of the Chinese Mainland: National Income and Economic Development, 1933–1959*, Santa Monica, CA: The Rand Corporation.

Mankiw, N. Gregory, Romer, David, and Weil, David N., 1992, A contribution to the empirics of economic growth, *Quarterly Journal of Economics* **107**, 407–438.

McMillan, John, Whalley, John, and Zhu, Lijing, 1989, The impact of China' s economic reforms on agricultural productivity growth, *Journal of Political Economy* **97**, 781–807.

Romer, Paul M., 1987, Crazy explanation for the productivity slowdown, *NBER Macroeconomic Annual 1987*, Stanley Fisher, ed., Cambridge, MA: The MIT Press.

————, 1990, Endogenous technological change, *Journal of Political Economy* **98**, S71–S102.

Solow, Robert M., 1956, A contribution to the theory of economic growth, *Quarterly Journal of Economics* **70**, 65–94.

Statistical Yearbook of China, Beijing: State Statistical Bureau.

Tang, Anthony, 1981, Chinese agriculture: Its problems and prospects, Vanderbilt University, Department of Economics, Working Paper No. 82-W09.

Young, Alwyn, 1992, A tale of two cities: Factor accumulation and technical change in Hong Kong and Singapore, Massachusetts Institute of Technology, Sloan School of Management, mimeo.

CHAPTER 17

A MODEL OF CHINESE NATIONAL INCOME
DETERMINATION*

A model consisting of a consumption function and an investment function is used to explain Chinese annual data in constant prices from 1953 to 1982. The data confirm Robert Hall's version of the permanent income hypothesis and the accelerations principle. Deviations of the observations from predictions of this model are attributed to political factors, including the Great Leap Forward in 1959–62, the Cultural Revolution in 1967–68, and the special government policies in 1978 and 1981.

Since the establishment of the People's Republic of China in 1949, the national income of China was subject to two downswings, The first occurred in 1960–62 as a result of the economic failure of the Great Leap Forward Movement, which began in 1958. The second occurred in 1967–68 and may be attributed to the economic disruptions of the Cultural Revolution. Most observers, including me, agree that political factors have contributed to the explanation of national income and output in China. However, political forces operate not by themselves but in an environment governed by economic factors. To assess the influence of political forces, it is necessary to determine how the economy would evolve without them. One way to achieve this goal is to build an econometric model of national income in China and attribute to political forces the deviations of the historical observations from the predictions of the model. This is the main objective of the present article.

Because of data limitations and my desire to start with a simple model, I have chosen to explain only the two major components of national income, namely, consumption and investment or capital accumulation. There are two approaches to formulating such a model. One is to specify structural equations based on economic hypotheses to explain consumption and investment. The second is to ascertain purely statistical relationships for the two time series as generated by a vector autoregressive (VAR) process. I have adopted the first approach and selected a multiplier–accelerator model to guide my statistical analysis. In analyzing aggregate consumption and investment data, one realizes that any structural interpretations are colored by the prior notions of the econometrician and are subject to questions.

*I would like to thank Orley Ashenfelter and two referees for helpful comments, Loretta Mester and Xiaokai Yang for research assistance, and the National Science Foundation for financial support.

Some readers will find such interpretations useful. Others may simply take the reduced-form equations as representing a VAR process.

17.1. A Multiplier–Accelerator Model

Economists are familiar with multiplier–accelerator models as their significance was pointed out by Samuelson (1939). The particular version used in this article has been estimated empirically using U.S. data and studied analytically by Chow (1967, 1968). It can be derived from a discrete version of the Harrod–Domar model of economic growth by introducing simple distributed lags (see Harrod 1948; Domar 1957). Let Y_t, C_t, and I_t denote, respectively, national income, consumption, and investment in year t, all in constant prices. The Harrod–Domar model consists of two equations. First, the savings function explains aggregate savings $S_t = Y_t - C_t$ as a fraction σ of national income,

$$S_t = Y_t - C_t = \sigma Y_t , \tag{1}$$

implying the consumption function

$$C_t = (1 - \sigma)Y_t = \gamma Y_t . \tag{2}$$

Second, the ratio of capital stock K_t to output Y_t is assumed to be a constant,

$$K_t = \alpha Y_t . \tag{3}$$

When simple distributed lags are introduced, Eqs. (2) and (3) become

$$C_t = \gamma_0 + \gamma_1 Y_t + \gamma_2 C_{t-1} , \tag{4}$$
$$K_t = \alpha_0 + \alpha_1 Y_t + \alpha_2 K_{t-1} . \tag{5}$$

Equation (5) is converted to an investment function by using the identity $I_t = \Delta K_t = (K_t - K_{t-1})$, where I_t stands for net investment, and by first differencing

$$I_t = \alpha_1 \Delta Y_t + \alpha_2 I_{t-1} . \tag{6}$$

The multiplier–accelerator model consists of Eqs. (4) and (6) and the identity

$$Y_t = C_t + I_t . \tag{7}$$

It is the purpose of this article to examine the empirical validity of this model using Chinese data.

17.2. Chinese National Income Data

Official Chinese national income data are provided by the State Statistical Bureau of the State Council of the Chinese government in its publications *Almanac of China's Economy* and *Statistical Yearbook of China* beginning in 1981. The data given in Table 1 are found in *Statistical Yearbook of China 1983*, Chinese edition. The English edition of *Statistical Yearbook of China 1981* defines national income, consumption, and capital accumulation as follows:

Table 1
Consumption, capital accumulation, and price indices in China

Year	Consumption (Billion Yuan)	Accumulation (Billion Yuan)	Implicit National Income Deflator	Consumption Deflated by National Income Deflator	Accumulation Deflated by National Income Deflator	Retail Price Index (1950 = 100)
1952	47.7	13.0	1.00000	47.700	13.0000	1.118
1953	55.9	16.8	1.05591	52.940	15.9105	1.156
1954	57.0	19.5	1.05303	54.130	18.5181	1.183
1955	62.2	18.5	1.04276	59.649	17.7414	1.195
1956	67.1	21.7	1.02285	65.601	21.2152	1.195
1957	70.2	23.3	1.00758	69.672	23.1247	1.213
1958	73.8	37.9	1.01668	72.590	37.2784	1.216
1959	71.6	55.8	1.02657	69.747	54.3556	1.227
1960	76.3	50.1	1.03981	73.379	48.1817	1.265
1961	81.8	19.5	1.20786	67.723	16.1443	1.470
1962	84.9	9.9	1.19844	70.842	8.2607	1.526
1963	86.4	18.3	1.17170	73.739	15.6183	1.436
1964	92.1	26.3	1.17276	78.532	22.4256	1.383
1965	98.2	36.5	1.19232	82.360	30.6125	1.346
1966	106.2	47.0	1.16567	91.364	40.3201	1.342
1967	112.4	30.4	1.17808	95.410	25.8048	1.332
1968	111.1	29.8	1.19879	92.677	24.8584	1.333
1969	118.0	35.7	1.14819	102.770	31.0923	1.318
1970	125.8	61.8	1.10959	113.376	55.6965	1.315
1971	132.4	68.4	1.11840	118.383	61.1588	1.305
1972	140.4	64.8	1.11756	125.631	57.9834	1.302
1973	151.1	74.1	1.11994	134.917	66.1640	1.310
1974	155.0	74.1	1.12230	138.109	66.0250	1.317
1975	162.1	83.0	1.10465	146.744	75.1372	1.319
1976	167.6	74.8	1.10057	152.284	67.9646	1.323
1977	174.1	83.2	1.11223	156.532	74.8046	1.350
1978	188.8	108.7	1.12762	167.433	96.3980	1.359
1979	219.5	116.1	1.17294	187.136	98.9817	1.386
1980	252.1	116.5	1.21700	207.149	95.7273	1.469
1981	278.1	110.6	1.24060	224.166	89.1506	1.504
1982	302.1	123.3	1.24513	242.626	99.0261	1.533

Source — Consumption and accumulation in billion yuan are from *Statistical Yearbook of China 1983*, Chinese ed. (p. 25). Implicit national income deflator is the ratio of national income in current prices (p. 22) to national income in 1952 comprable prices (p. 23). Retail price index is from p. 455.

The term national income used in the *Yearbook* refers to the sum total of net output, in value terms created during a year in the following material production sectors: industry, agriculture, construction, transportation and commerce (the catering trades and material supplies and marketing enterprises included) ....

Excluded are non-material production sectors such as the service trades, educational, scientific research, cultural, and public health departments, as well as military and government administrations. These sectors are an indispensable part of social development as a whole, because they, too, render services that are useful to the people's livelihood and society's material production. But since they are not directly involved in the material production of society, they are not taken into account in the calculation of national income.

Through the process of distribution and redistribution, the available portion of the national income is further broken down into two parts: The consumption fund and the accumulation fund.

Consumption fund is that part of the national income represented by expenditure by individuals as private consumption and that by the public as public consumption. Its material formation is the total expenditure on consumer goods by individuals and the public plus the wear and tear of non-productive fixed assets, including residential houses, during a year.

Accumulation is the part of the national income which is used for expanded reproduction and non-productive construction and increase of productive and non-productive stock. Its material formation is the newly added fixed assets of material and non-material sectors (less depreciation of the total fixed assets) and the newly acquired circulating fund in kind by the material sectors during the year. [p. 509]

Data on consumption and capital accumulation in billions of yuan are given in the first two columns of Table 1. To convert these data to real figures two deflators can be used. The first is an implicit national income deflator obtained as the ratio of national income in current prices to a real national income index with 1952 = 100. All these data are provided by the *Statistical Yearbook of China 1983*. Note that consumption plus capital accumulation is equal to national income available, which differs from national income by including the excess of imports over exports and a statistical discrepancy. The real national income index has been constructed by linking real national income figures of various years with real national incomes in 1949–57 expressed in 1952 prices, in 1957–71 expressed in 1957 prices, in 1971–80 expressed in 1970 prices, and after 1980 in 1980 prices (see *Statistical Yearbook of China 1981*, English ed., p. 510). The deflator so obtained is used to convert the consumption and capital accumulation figures into real terms, as shown in the fourth and fifth columns of Table 1. The second deflator is a retail price index provided in *Statistical Yearbook of China 1983* and exhibited in the last column of Table 1. Presumably, the implicit national income deflator is more comprehensive and should be preferred. On the other hand, the retail price index might be more flexible and reflect market prices better. I proceeded with the calculations using both deflators and found the results to be almost identical. The results based on the first deflator will be presented in the text, those based on the second in the Appendix.

It is interesting to note that national income available in 1952 prices (the sum of deflated consumption and capital accumulation in Table 1) decreased from a peak of 124.102 billion yuan in 1959 to a trough of 79.103 billion in 1962 following the Great Leap Forward Movement, which began in 1958. Real national income available also decreased from a peak of 131.684 billion in 1966 to a trough of 117.535 billion in 1968 following the Cultural Revolution, which began in 1966. Using the model of Sec. 1, we can trace the shocks of these two political movements as they worked through the consumption and investment relations.

17.3. Statistical Analysis

The method of two-stage least squares is applied to estimate Eqs. (4) and (6) using the 30 annual observations from 1953 to 1982 given in Table 1. In the first stage, Y_t is regressed on C_{t-1} and I_{t-1} to obtain the estimated $\hat{Y}_t$. The regressions obtained in the second stage are

$$C_t = -5.0456 - 0.0935\hat{Y}_t + 1.2502C_{t-1}, \qquad R^2 = 0.9933 \qquad (8)$$
$$ (2.7645) \quad (0.1358) \quad (0.2251) \qquad s^2 = 18.489$$

$$I_t = 1.5643 + 0.6656(\hat{Y}_t - Y_{t-1}) + 0.8920I_{t-1}, \qquad R^2 = 0.8787$$
$$ (3.7992) \quad (0.2729) \qquad\qquad (0.0722) \qquad s^2 = 103.027 . \qquad (9)$$

Originally, I formulated a consumption function (4) with income and lagged consumption as explanatory variables. This consumption function is consistent with the permanent income hypothesis as expounded by Friedman (1957). When this consumption function was estimated in Eq. (8), we find estimated current income insignificant. Equation (8) is consistent with the stochastic version of the permanent income hypothesis suggested by Hall (1978). According to Hall, as a first approximation, consumption evolves according to a random walk; no variable apart from C_{t-1} should be of any value in predicting C_t, as Eq. (8) suggests. Indeed, C_{t-2}, I_{t-1}, and I_{t-2} are all insignificant in predicting C_t given C_{t-1}. Equation (9) is consistent with the acceleration principle, showing the importance of $(\hat{Y}_t - Y_{t-1})$ in explaining current investment, apart from I_{t-1}. Thus it is possible to interpret Eqs. (8) and (9) as structural equations based on the permanent income hypothesis and the acceleration principle.

By substituting $C_t + I_t$ for Y_t on the right-hand sides of (8) and (9) and solving the resulting equations for C_t and I_t, we obtain the reduced-form equations. These reduced-form equations are identical with those obtained by regressing C_t and I_t on C_{t-1} and I_{t-1} because each of the structural equations (8) and (9) is just identified. (See Chow [1983] on identification.) We can consider (8) and (9) as two simultaneous structural equations determining the two endogenous variables

C_t and I_t by the predetermined variables C_{t-1} and I_{t-1}. Equation (8) is just identified because exactly one predetermined variable I_{t-1} is absent. Equation (9) is just identified because there is exactly one linear restriction on the coefficients, the coefficient of $C_t + I_t$ being the negative of the coefficient of $C_{t-1} + I_{t-1}$. Applying least squares to estimate the reduced-form equations for C_t and I_t, we obtain

$$C_t = -4.2852 + 1.1225C_{t-1} - 0.0495I_{t-1}, \quad \begin{aligned} R^2 &= 0.9933 \\ s^2 &= 18.489 \\ DW &= 1.826; \end{aligned} \quad (10)$$
$$ (2.1247) \quad (0.0424) \quad (0.0719)$$

$$I_t = -3.8511 + 0.2439C_{t-1} + 0.5787I_{t-1}, \quad \begin{aligned} R^2 &= 0.8787 \\ s^2 &= 103.027 \\ DW &= 1.421. \end{aligned} \quad (11)$$
$$ (5.0154) \quad (0.1000) \quad (0.1696)$$

Note that the estimated values of C_t and I_t from these reduced-form equations are the same as those of the structural equations (8) and (9) because both equations are just identified. Accordingly R^2, s^2, and the Durbin–Watson statistic (DW) are the same as in (8) and (9).

It is interesting to examine the residuals of Eqs. (10) and (11) to see how well these equations fit the data for 1959–62 and 1967–68. The residuals, defined as the actual minus the predicted values, are shown in the first two columns of Table 2. For consumption, the standard error of regression (10) is 4.30 billion. For investment, the standard error of regression (11) is 10.15 billion. In 1959, we found a large investment that is about 19 billion above the predicted values as the investment drive of the Great Leap Forward began. In the same year , consumption was reduced to 5.6 billion below the predicted value. As the downward movement of national income continued, consumption and investment in 1961 were, respectively, 8.0 billion and 25.8 billion below their predicted values. In the downturn associated with the Cultural Revolution, we found investment to be about 16 billion below the predicted figure for 1967 and consumption and investment in 1968 to be below their respective predicted values by 8.9 and 9.5 billion. In 1978 actual investment was about 18.5 billion higher than predicted. That year was marked by very ambitious investment plans, which had to be scaled down in 1979. In 1981, investment was drastically curtailed to achieve a balanced budget and to slow down inflation (see Chow 1985, p. 234). Almost identical comments can be made for the residuals obtained by using the retail price index to deflate the consumption and investment data, as shown in the last two columns of Table 2.

The data for real consumption that show a small decline from 72.590 billion in 1958 to 67.723 billion in 1961 are questionable. We know that millions of people in China were starving during 1959–62. Coale (1984, pp. 7, 70) estimates that in the years 1958–63 there were about 27 millions deaths in excess of a linear trend of deaths derived from the death rates in the adjacent years. *Statistical Yearbook of China 1983* (Chinese ed., p. 105) shows a death rate of 25.43 per 1,000 for 1960, as compared with 10.80 for 1957. The difference, 14.63, multiplied by a population of 662 million implies 9.7 million extra deaths in 1960 alone. Both price indices used in this article show a large increase from 1960 to 1961, but possibly not large enough to reflect the actual increases in the prices of consumer goods. Furthermore, the consumption data in current prices for 1960–61 may be inaccurate. The year 1963 is known to be one of improved consumption, and the recorded consumption did increase according to Table 1. It is recognized by economists in China that in the years 1960–62, when there was strong political pressure to fulfill unreasonable production targets, false statistical reporting was not uncommon. If true (deflated) consumption in 1960 were lower than 73.379 billion, as recorded in Table 1, the estimated consumption in 1961 by Eq. (10) would be lower, leading to a small residual (in absolute value) than is shown in Table 2.

TABLE 2

RESIDUALS OF CONSUMPTION AND INVESTMENT
(Billions of Yuan)

Year	$C_t - \hat{C}_t$	$I_t - \hat{I}_t$	$C_t - \tilde{C}_t$	$I_t - \tilde{I}_t$
1953	4.3234	.606	5.1023	.746
1954	−.2255	.251	−2.0051	−.480
1955	4.0879	−2.325	2.6004	−2.837
1956	3.8050	.253	2.3837	−.203
1957	1.3669	−1.300	−.6515	−1.868
1958	−.1909	10.756	.4123	10.359
1959	−5.6089	18.932	−5.2604	17.755
1960	2.0589	3.569	.3076	2.401
1961	−7.9789	−25.782	−7.5346	−23.704
1962	−.0961	−13.747	−2.7002	−12.741
1963	−1.0899	−2.588	2.1452	−1.289
1964	.8153	−.745	3.9623	.419
1965	−.4010	2.334	3.3713	3.662
1966	4.7106	6.371	2.9675	5.501
1967	−.8700	−15.958	.9685	−15.018
1968	−8.8628	−9.492	−6.8065	−8.845
1969	4.2517	−2.043	1.3707	−2.976
1970	3.8354	16.492	.7731	14.546
1971	−1.8452	5.130	.3723	5.903
1972	.0509	−2.428	.5539	−2.137
1973	1.0452	5.823	.9979	5.519
1974	−5.7834	−1.315	−5.3967	−1.260
1975	−.7380	7.099	−2.4824	5.768
1976	−4.4396	−7.452	−4.4340	−7.122
1977	−6.7661	2.187	−6.7694	1.773
1978	−.2955	18.787	1.7334	18.348
1979	8.2391	6.216	11.8271	7.889
1980	6.2624	−3.338	2.8023	−4.700
1981	.6534	−12.913	1.1891	−11.703
1982	−.3144	−3.381	−1.8003	−3.704

NOTE.—The first two cols. are residuals using the implicit national income deflator. The last two cols. are residuals using the official retail price index as deflator.

A significant conclusion of this article is that a model based on the permanent income hypothesis of consumption and the acceleration hypothesis of investment, which can explain national income of developed market economies, is also applicable to a less developed planned economy like the Chinese economy. Although Eqs. (8) and (9) are consistent with the permanent income and the acceleration hypotheses, skeptics might not be convinced of such structural interpretation. Even for the skeptics, these equations would provide a crude model of Chinese national income determination and serve as a yardstick to measure the improvement of future models. The residuals from the equations have provided us with a basis to assess the influences of political forces on Chinese national income in 1959–62, 1967–68, 1978, and 1981. As a by-product, this study casts doubt on Chinese official consumption data for the years 1960–62.

Appendix

When the retail price index, converted to $1952 = 1.00$, is used to deflate consumption and investment, the results are

$$C_t = -3.5834 - 0.0554\hat{Y}_t + 1.1764C_{t-1}, \quad R^2 = 0.9922 \quad (8')$$
$$ (2.6391) \quad (0.1352) \quad (0.2226) \quad\quad s^2 = 17.879 \; ;$$

$$I_t = 1.2229 + 0.6971(\hat{Y}_t - Y_{t-1}) + 0.8967I_{t-1}, \quad R^2 = 0.8732 \quad (9')$$
$$ (3.7145) \quad (0.2992) \quad\quad\quad (0.719) \quad\quad s^2 = 91.292 \; ;$$

$$C_t = 3.2184 - 1.1023C_{t-1} - 0.0309I_{t-1}, \quad R^2 = 0.9922 \quad (10')$$
$$ (2.1452) \quad (0.0447) \quad (0.0753) \quad\quad s^2 = 17.879$$
$$ \mathrm{DW} = 1.566 ;$$

$$I_t = -3.3688 + 0.2354C_{t-1} + 0.5879I_{t-1}, \quad R^2 = 0.8732 \quad (11')$$
$$ (4.8473) \quad (0.1010) \quad (0.1702) \quad\quad s^2 = 91.292$$
$$ \mathrm{DW} = 1.380 .$$

References

Chow, G. C., 1967, Multiplier, accelerator and liquidity preference in the determination of national income in the United States, *Rev. Econ. and Statis.* **49**, 1–15.

———, 1968, The acceleration principle and the nature of business cycles, *Quarterly J. Econ.* **82**, 403–418.

———, 1983, *Econometrics*, New York: McGraw–Hill.

———, 1985, *The Chinese Economy*, New York: Harper & Row; 2nd edn. 1987, Singapore: World Scientific.

Coale, A. J., 1984, *Rapid Population Change in China, 1952–1982*, Washington: National Academy Press.

Domar, E. D., 1957, *Essays in the Theory of Economic Growth*, New York: Oxford University Press.

Friedman, M., 1957, *A Theory of the Consumption Function*, Princeton, N.J.: Princeton University Press.

Hall, R. E., 1978, Stochastic implications of the life cycle–permanent income hypothesis: Theory and evidence, *J. Pol. Econ.* **86**, 971–987.

Harrod, R. F., 1948, *Towards a Dynamic Economy: Some Recent Developments of Economic Theory and Their Application to Policy*, London: MacMillan.

Samuelson, P. A., 1939, Interactions between the multiplier analysis and the principle of acceleration, *Rev. Econ. and Statis.* **21**, 75–78.

Statistical Yearbook of China, 1981, 1983, Beijing: State Statistics Bureau.

CHAPTER 18

MONEY AND PRICE LEVEL DETERMINATION IN CHINA*†

The quantity theory of money provides a useful starting point in explaining the price level in China. The ratio of money supply to real output is an important variable in explaining the price level, but the elasticity is below unity, suggesting that velocity is not constant. A short-run model for changes in the price level explains the Chinese annual data from 1952 to 1983 better than the United States data from 1922 to 1953. This model is stable after 1979 and forecasts well in 1984. *J. Comp. Econ.* September 1987, **11**(3), pp. 319–333. Princeton University, Princeton, New Jersey 08544, ©1987 Academic Press, Inc.

Journal of Economic Literature Classification Numbers: 123, 134, 311.

18.1. Introduction

The possible effect of an increase in money supply on inflation became an important issue for the Chinese economic reform officials in 1985 when currency in circulation had actually increased by about 50% from the end of 1983 to the end of 1984, mainly as a result of the policy to allow individual banks the discretion to extend credit without having established a mechanism of monetary control by the central bank. The main purpose of this paper is to study the effect of money supply on the price level in China. This topic is not only of theoretical interest in economics, but is of relevance to the choice of different options in carrying out price reforms. To the extent that inflation is found to be a monetary phenomenon, there should be less concern over possible inflationary effects of decontrolling or adjusting prices of selected individual commodities. At the same time, to the extent that upward movements of prices of selected consumer goods require, for political reasons, and assuming downward price rigidity, certain adjustments in money wages which may lead to an increase in money supply, the inflationary effect of the policy can be quantitatively evaluated.

In Sec. 2, I discuss the theoretical issues in applying the quantity theory of money to explaining the price level in the Chinese institutional setting. In Sec. 3,

---

*Originally published in *Journal of Comparative Economics*, vol. 11, (1987), pp. 319–333.
†The author thanks Josef Brada, John Fei, Dwight Jaffee, and Bruce Reynolds for helpful comments, The Garfield Foundation and the National Science Foundation for financial support.

long-run relations based on the quantity theory will be empirically established using Chinese annual data from 1952 to 1983. In Sec. 4, equations explaining short-run price changes from year to year will be estimated and tested. In Sec. 5, for comparison purposes, analogous equations for the long run and the short run will be estimated using data from the United States from 1922 to 1953. The similarities of results between the two countries are noteworthy. In Sec. 6, additional issues concerning short-run price determination will be addressed, including the possible direct effect of aggregate wage on the price level, a possible structural change after the economic reform began in 1979, and the use of the short-run model for forecasting inflation.

18.2. Theoretical and Institutional Issues

Economists have suggested that the quantity theory of money may provide a crude explanation of the price level. It is of interest to ascertain how well this theory can explain the price level in China from 1952 to 1983, and to compare the results with those obtained for the United States using similar data three decades earlier. To do so, it is necessary to specify the theory more precisely and discuss its relevance in the Chinese setting.

The quantity theory of money is based on the quantity equation

$$Mv = Py ,\qquad(1)$$

where M is the stock of money, P is the price level, y is national income in real terms, and v is income velocity. The quantity Eq. (1) can be interpreted merely as an identity which defines the velocity v as the ratio of national income Py in money terms to the stock of money M. If so interpreted, it cannot serve as an explanation of P. However, if v is nearly constant through time and if changes in y are largely independent of changes in M, and these are big ifs, then a change in M will lead to a proportional change in P. The quantity theory of money is derived from Eq. (1) on the condition that these two presuppositions are roughly valid. Under this condition, the theory provides an explanation for the price level P.

There are many reasons the constancy of v is at best a rough approximation to reality. A well-known one is the Keynesian argument that when prices are rigid an increase in M will lead to a downward movement in the rate of interest and a reduction in v, rather than a rise in P. How good is the assumption of the constancy of v? This question has been answered both theoretically and empirically mainly by reinterpreting (1) as a demand equation for money,

$$\frac{M}{P} = ky ,\qquad(2)$$

where $k = v^{-1}$. If the demand for real money balances, M/P is approximately proportional to real income y, or if (2) is a good approximation to reality, k or its inverse v can be treated approximately as a constant. Theoretically, it is known that the demand for M/P depends also on the rate of interest, and that the income elasticity of demand for money does not have to be unity as (2) implies. These two considerations aside, it is still worthwhile to observe how well Eq. (2) fits the data.

However, assuming that Eq. (2) fits the data reasonably well by some standard, one cannot thereby conclude that an increase in M, given y, will lead to a proportional increase in P. To demonstrate this point, suppose hypothetically that the data for M and y satisfy the relation $M = ky$, or

$$\log M = \log k + \log y \ .$$

Suppose also that $\log P$ is generated as an independent, identically distributed random variable ϵ. Under these two hypothetical assumptions, the data will satisfy

$$\log(M/P) = \log k + \log y - \epsilon \ .$$

A regression of $\log(M/P)$ on $\log y$ may yield a coefficient of unity and possibly a high R^2, supporting the hypothesis (2). Yet, by the way the data on P are constructed, changes in M do not affect changes in P. Hence by studying the demand for real money balance through Eq. (2), one learns little about how well money supply explains the price level. Nevertheless, the demand for money is itself a subject of interest.

To apply the quantity theory of money to explain the price level P, we rewrite (1) as

$$P = v(M/y) \ . \tag{3}$$

If v were close to being constant, regressing $\log P$ on $\log(M/P)$ would yield a coefficient of unity and a good fit. If v itself is negatively associated with (M/y), changes in P will be less than proportional to changes in (M/y). As long as an increase in (M/y) is not completely offset by a proportional reduction in v, it will have a positive effect on P. The question of how good the assumption of a constant v is should be answered differently depending on the variable one wishes to explain. A constant k may be satisfactory when Eq. (2) is used to explain M/P. A constant v may be more or less satisfactory when Eq. (3) is used to explain P. A more relevant question for the purpose of this paper is how well the theoretical framework suggested by (3) can explain the price level P in China. We will try to answer this question in Sec. 3, and study the short-run dynamics of changes in P in Sec. 4. Before proceeding, let us consider briefly the institutional setting of China and examine whether the theoretical framework above is applicable.

Three sets of issues have to be addressed when the quantity theory is applied to explain a general price index in China. First, prices of many producer and consumer goods have been controlled. Therefore these prices may not adjust to monetary forces as they would in a market economy. However, the theory could still provide a good explanation of the general price level if the remaining, uncontrolled prices were able to adjust sufficiently. Second, the quantity theory assumes that all income flows are associated with money payments. As in a less developed economy, some agricultural products in China are a part of national income but do not go through market transactions. Furthermore, as in a centrally planned economy, many producer goods are paid for by transfers of funds to and from bank accounts held by state enterprises. Bank deposits of state enterprises are often earmarked for specific purposes and cannot be used to finance general purchases. If these deposits are excluded from our definition of money supply, certain flows of producer goods will be excluded from both sides of the quantity equation. The theory may be applicable if we confine ourselves to expenditure flows paid by consumers provided that the variables M, P, and y are defined accordingly. Third, related to the choice of variables is the accuracy of Chinese official statistics which will be used to test the theory. The quality of these data has been subject to question by scholars. I have discussed this issue in Chow (1986). It suffices to point out here that these data have been found reasonable when used to estimate simple economic relationships, including those reported in Chow (1985b, pp. 123, 129, 165–166, and 263; and 1985a). By using these data to test economic hypotheses as in this paper, one learns more about their quality.

Bearing in mind that the stock of money M has to be defined consistently with the output y being purchased at an average price level P, I have decided to confine my attention to retail purchases by consumers. The main price index to be explained is a general index of retail price. The relevant stock of money is currency in circulation. In China consumers do not use checks and demand deposits by consumers are nonexistent. However, saving deposits exist and could be included in the definition of money. Concerning the output variable y, one may choose to include only those products that are related to final purchases by consumers and to exclude producer goods purchased by state enterprises. I have decided to use a more comprehensive measure of output, namely, national income available as reported in Chinese official statistics. This measure will be appropriate if it is highly correlated with final purchases by consumers. It is interesting to find out how well such a measure which is usually employed in testing the quantity theory can perform in the Chinese context, realizing that the measures of P and M are more narrowly defined. To employ a more narrowly defined measure of y would make the theory less powerful because such a measure itself has to be explained.

18.3. Long-Run Explanations of the Price Level

The general index of retail prices is one of the five price indices regularly published in the *Statistical Yearbook of China*. In the 1981 edition of the *Yearbook* (pp. 519–520), the following explanations are given:

> In China there are several ways in pricing commodities, including list prices of the state-owned commercial departments and the free markets (fair trade), the negotiated price and the purchasing price of the surplus farm and sideline products. Therefore, apart from the indexes of the list price, it is important to compile the general retail price index and the general index of the cost of living of the workers and staff members, both of which include the list retail price and the negotiated retail price and the retail price in free market, as well as general purchasing price indexes for farm and sideline products that include the list purchasing price, negotiated purchasing price and the purchasing

price of surplus farm and sideline products. The actual value of sales and purchases based on different prices is taken as the weights for calculating the general indexes.

(1) The index of the list retail price is calculated by the formula of weighted arithmetic mean. The weights used are adjusted annually based on the data on actual retail sales. The markets and items of commodities selected for calculation have been on the increase. At present more than 140 cities and 230 county towns are selected as the basic units for data collection; 450 items of commodities in the cities and 400 in the county towns are included in the calculation. The price of a standard commodity from each item of products is adopted in the calculation.

Almost identical explanations are found in the 1984 edition (pp. 569–579) and the 1985 edition (p. 672). This is the main price index to be studied. Annual data are available, presumably referring to the middle of the year or to an average within the year.

The stock of money is measured by currency in circulation reported in a table on "bank credit receipts and payments" of the *Statistical Yearbook*. The data are for the end of each year, although for our purpose the unavailable mid-year figures would be more appropriate. The chosen measure of output is national income available. In Chinese official statistics, it is the sum of consumption and capital accumulation, government expenditures being included in either of the two. Some service items are excluded from Chinese national income figures, "National income available" differs from "national income" by including imports minus exports and a statistical discrepancy. To obtain a measure of national income available in real terms, I have deflated it by an implicit deflator which is the ratio of national income in current prices to national income in constant prices (the last two series being found on pp. 29 and 30, respectively, of *Statistical Yearbook of China, 1984*).

Annual data from 1952 to 1983 on the general index of retail price P, currency in circulation M, national income available in real terms y and in nominal terms Y are given in Table 1. In this section, we will examine how well the quantity theory of money can provide a framework for explaining the demand for money and the level of retail prices in China, without regard to the short-run dynamics of annual changes. To get some preliminary idea about the possible constancy of income velocity v in the context of the demand for money, I have exhibited the ratio $k = v^{-1}$ of M to Y in the last column of Table 1. Observe that the ratio k changes somewhat from year to year, with large increases occurring in 1960 and 1961 and falling to about normal levels in 1964, smaller but still significant increases in 1967 and 1968, and taking higher values in the 1980s than before. The large increases in k during the political-economic crises of 1960–1961 and 1967–1968 may be attributed to the reductions in national income in the denominator. The higher values in the 1980s may signify the effect of economic reforms leading to an increase in the demand for money. In spite of these changes in velocity, can the quantity theory provide a crude explanation of the demand for money and of the price level?

To investigate the demand for money, we take natural logarithms of both sides of Eq. (2) and explain $\ln(M/P)$ by $\ln y$ in the following regression using annual data from 1952 to 1983,

TABLE 1

PRICE LEVEL AND ITS DETERMINANTS

Year	Index of retail price (P)	Currency in circulation (100,000 yuan) (M)	Real national income available (100,000 1952-yuan) (y)	Nominal national income available (100,000 yuan) (Y)	Ratio M/Y (k)	Total wage (100,000 yuan) (W)
1952	1.118	38.55	607.0	607.0	0.0635	68.78
1953	1.156	39.60	688.5	727.0	0.0545	90.15
1954	1.183	41.19	726.5	765.0	0.0538	99.79
1955	1.195	40.13	773.9	807.0	0.0497	110.44
1956	1.195	57.03	868.2	888.0	0.0642	161.56
1957	1.213	52.80	928.0	935.0	0.0565	188.44
1958	1.216	67.59	1098.7	1117.0	0.0605	200.62
1959	1.227	74.98	1241.0	1274.0	0.0589	262.73
1960	1.265	96.10	1215.6	1264.0	0.0760	300.82
1961	1.470	125.67	838.7	1013.0	0.1241	289.87
1962	1.526	106.66	791.0	948.0	0.1125	265.32
1963	1.436	89.76	893.6	1047.0	0.0857	265.22
1964	1.383	80.26	1009.6	1184.0	0.0678	281.59
1965	1.346	90.82	1129.7	1347.0	0.0674	295.49
1966	1.342	108.25	1316.8	1535.0	0.0705	305.48
1967	1.332	121.97	1212.2	1428.0	0.0854	313.57
1968	1.333	134.12	1175.4	1409.0	0.0952	317.72
1969	1.318	137.29	1338.6	1537.0	0.0893	328.61
1970	1.315	123.56	1690.7	1876.0	0.0659	342.78
1971	1.305	136.23	1795.4	2008.0	0.0678	367.42
1972	1.302	151.02	1836.1	2052.0	0.0736	412.43
1973	1.310	166.33	2010.8	2252.0	0.0739	428.91
1974	1.317	176.36	2041.3	2291.0	0.0770	450.62
1975	1.319	182.70	2218.8	2451.0	0.0745	469.47
1976	1.323	203.82	2202.5	2424.0	0.0841	490.14
1977	1.350	195.37	2313.4	2573.0	0.0759	514.95
1978	1.359	212.27	2638.3	2975.0	0.0714	570.09
1979	1.386	267.71	2861.2	3356.0	0.0798	651.62
1980	1.469	346.20	3037.0	3686.0	0.0939	776.93
1981	1.504	396.34	3144.8	3887.0	0.1020	818.76
1982	1.533	439.12	3448.1	4256.0	0.1032	879.79
1983	1.556	529.78	3812.8	4731.0	0.1120	931.51

$$\ln(M/P) = -3.927 + 1.162 \ln y, \qquad R^2 = 0.9083 \qquad (4)$$
$$(0.492) \quad (0.067) \qquad s = 0.1971$$
$$\mathrm{DW} = 0.7847 \, ,$$

where the standard errors of the regression coefficients are put in parentheses, s stands for the standard error of the regression, and DW for the Durbin–Watson statistic. This demand for money equation appears reasonably good except for the facts that the coefficient of $\ln y$, or the income elasticity of demand for money, is larger than unity, contradicting the quantity theory, and that the Durbin–Watson statistic is low, signifying positive serial correlation in the residuals. Both of these characteristics have been found in demand for money equations estimated using data for the United States (see Eq. (4A) of Sec. 5). A simple way to account for the positive serial correlation in the residuals is to assume that $\ln y$ explains only the equilibrium level of $\ln(M/P)$, and that the actual change in $\ln(M/P)$ is only a fraction of the difference between this equilibrium level and the actual level, leading to the equation, for 1953–1983,

$$\ln(M/P) = -1.322 + 0.3504 \ \ln y + 0.7409 \ \ln(M/P)_{t-1}, \quad R^2 = 0.9749 \quad (5)$$
$$\qquad\quad (0.394) \quad (0.0966) \qquad\quad (0.0813) \qquad\qquad\quad s \quad = 0.1024$$
$$\qquad\qquad\qquad\qquad\qquad\qquad\qquad\qquad\qquad\qquad\qquad\qquad DW = 2.101 \ .$$

The positive serial correlation in the residuals is eliminated in Eq. (5) as seen from the Durbin–Watson statistic. For our purpose, it is important to note that the quantity theory as formulated in Eq. (2) provides a reasonable first approximation in explaining the demand for money in China.

To find out how well the price level can be explained, we take logarithms of both sides of (3) and regress $\ln P$ on $\ln(M/y)$ using annual data from 1952 to 1983, obtaining

$$\ln P = 0.9445 + 0.2687 \ \ln(M/y), \quad R^2 = 0.8217 \quad (6)$$
$$\qquad\quad (0.0567) \quad (0.0229) \qquad\qquad s \quad = 0.0363$$
$$\qquad\qquad\qquad\qquad\qquad\qquad\qquad DW = 1.003 \ .$$

Equation (6) shows that the ratio M/y does provide a good explanation of the price level P, as the quantity theory predicts. The t statistic for the coefficient of $\ln(M/y)$ is $0.2687/0.0229$ or 11.76, and the R^2 is fairly high. However, the coefficient of $\ln(M/y)$ is only 0.2687 and very much below unity, contradicting the quantity theory. The conclusion is that although the ratio M/y can explain the price level P fairly well, changes in M/y lead to less than proportional changes in P. This can happen if v is negatively associated with M/y so that when M/y increases, its effect is partly absorbed by the reduction in v and only partly reflected in an increase in P. A second shortcoming of Eq. (6) is the low Durbin–Watson statistic, a subject to studied in Sec. 3. Before concluding this section, we will check whether the variables M and y should enter Eq. (6) separately or as a ratio as implied by the quantity theory. Regressing $\ln P$ on $\ln M$ and $\ln y$ separately yields

$$\ln P = 0.6219 + 0.2388 \ \ln M - 0.2046 \ \ln y, \quad R^2 = 0.8566 \quad (7)$$
$$\qquad\quad (0.1320) \quad (0.0237) \qquad\quad (0.0319) \qquad\quad s \quad = 0.0331$$
$$\qquad\qquad\qquad\qquad\qquad\qquad\qquad\qquad\qquad\qquad DW = 0.9546 \ .$$

The coefficient of $\ln y$ turns out to be approximately equal to the negative of the coefficient of $\ln M$. To test the null hypothesis that the coefficient of $\ln y$ indeed equals the negative of the coefficient of $\ln M$, we compare the sum of squared residuals of the restricted regression (6), or 0.039577, with the corresponding sum of the unrestricted regression (7), or 0.031834. The ratio of their difference 0.007743 to the latter sum is only 0.2432, far from being significant as a statistic from the $F(1, 29)$ distribution and supporting the hypothesis that $\ln(M/y)$ is an appropriate variable to use in explaining $\ln P$.

18.4. Short-Run Dynamics of Price Changes

In Eqs. (6) and (7) we have found that the price level P can be reasonably explained by the ratio M/y as suggested by the quantity theory, although velocity is not constant, resulting in less than proportional changes in P. It is often easier to explain the levels of economic variables than their changes. How well can the theoretical framework of Eq. (6) explain annual changes in $\ln P$? To answer this question two common approaches are taken. The first is to introduce the lagged dependent variable $\ln P_{t-1}$ in Eq. (7), as we did in Eq. (5), and the resulting equation to explain $\Delta \ln P$ by subtracting $\ln P_{t-1}$ on both sides. The second is to take the first difference of Eq. (6) and try to explain $\Delta \ln P$ by $\Delta \ln(M/y)$, allowing for more complicated lag structures.

Pursuing the first approach we find

$$\Delta \ln P = \underset{(0.0656)}{0.5167} + \underset{(0.0201)}{0.1491} \ \ln(M/y) - \underset{(0.0708)}{0.5054} \ \ln P_{t-1}, \qquad \begin{aligned} R^2 &= 0.6824 \quad (8) \\ s &= 0.0199 \\ DW &= 1.341 \ . \end{aligned}$$

The coefficient of $\ln P_{t-1}$ is significant. To use Eq. (8) for explaining the level $\ln P$ rather than the difference $\Delta \ln P$, the coefficient of $\ln P_{t-1}$ would be $(1 - 0.5054)$ or 0.4946, and R^2 would be higher. Although (8) is an improvement over (7), it still leaves a positive serial correlation in the residuals as seen in the Durbin–Watson statistic.

To pursue the second approach, we attempt to explain $\Delta \ln P$ by $\Delta \ln(M/y)$. Using the simplest lag structure, we find

$$\Delta \ln P = \underset{(0.00461)}{0.00747} + \underset{(0.0252)}{0.1266} \ \Delta \ln(M/y), \qquad \begin{aligned} R^2 &= 0.4647 \quad (9) \\ s &= 0.0254 \\ DW &= 1.723 \ . \end{aligned}$$

The result shows that $\Delta \ln(M/y)$ is a significant variable in explaining $\Delta \ln P$. R^2 is lower in Eq. (9) than in Eq. (8), but the Durbin–Watson statistic shows less positive serial correlation in the residuals. To establish a more satisfactory lag structure, we employ the modeling techniques of error correction and cointegration. Engle and Granger (1987) provide an exposition of these techniques. I will review briefly the essential ideas before applying them to the Chinese data.

Suppose that one is interested in establishing a dynamic relationship between the first differences Δy_t and Δx_t of two economic variables and that the levels y_t and x_t of these variables are believed to satisfy certain stable relationships in the long run. In our problem, we may believe that the levels of the variables $\ln P$ and $\ln(M/y)$ satisfy certain long-run equilibrium relationships as estimated by Eq. (6), and we are interested in constructing a dynamic model for $\Delta \ln P$ and $\Delta \ln(M/y)$. If one were not concerned with the long-run relationship, one might choose the model

$$\Delta y_t = \beta \Delta x_t + \epsilon_t . \tag{10}$$

However, if the ϵ_t are independent and identically distributed, Model (10) implies a nonstationary relationship between the levels y_t and x_t. To convert (10) to a relation between the levels, we use the identity

$$y_t = \sum_{s=1}^{t} \Delta y_s + y_0 \tag{11}$$

and substitute the right-hand side of (10) for Δy_s in (11), yielding,

$$y_t = \sum_{s=1}^{t}(\beta \Delta x_s + \epsilon_s) + y_0 = \beta \sum_{s=1}^{t} \Delta x_s + \sum_{s=1}^{t} \epsilon_s + y_0$$

$$= \beta x_t + y_0 - \beta x_0 + \sum_{s=1}^{t} \epsilon_s . \tag{12}$$

The residual $\sum_{s=1}^{t} \epsilon_s$ in the regression of y_t on x_t is not only serially correlated but has a variance increasing linearly with time.

To allow for a stable long-run relationship $y_t = \alpha x_t$ between y_t and x_t in a model explaining Δy_t by Δx_t, one may introduce an error correction mechanism by using the lagged deviation $(y_{t-1} - \alpha x_{t-1})$ from the long-run relationship as an additional variable in (10). The model becomes

$$\Delta y_t = \beta \Delta x_t - \gamma(y_{t-1} - \alpha x_{t-1}) + \epsilon_t . \tag{13}$$

The rationale is that if in the last period y_{t-1} is above its long-run equilibrium level αx_{t-1}, the change in y_t during the current period should be smaller, and vice versa. The error correction model (13) has two desirable characteristics. It is stationary. The long-run change in y_t associated with a permanent unit change in x_t is α. Both can be easily shown by converting (13) into an equation in the levels of the variables:

$$y_t = (1 - \gamma)y_{t-1} + \beta x_t - (\beta - \alpha\gamma)x_{t-1} + \epsilon_t . \tag{14}$$

When $0 < \gamma < 1$, the coefficient $(1 - \gamma)$ is smaller than one, giving a stationary model for y_t. The long-run relation between y and x is given by

$$[1 - (1 - \gamma)]y = [\beta - (\beta - \alpha\gamma)]x , \tag{15}$$

which is obtained by collecting all the coefficients of the y and x variables while ignoring the time subscripts. From (15), we have $y = \alpha x$, which is the long-run relationship.

These two desirable characteristics remain when the error correction term $\gamma(y_{t-1} - \alpha x_{t-1})$ is added to a more complicated distributed lag relation between Δy_t and Δx_t than (10), such as

$$\Delta y_t = \beta_1 \Delta x_t + \beta_2 \Delta x_{t-1} + \beta_3 \Delta y_{t-1} + \epsilon_t \ . \tag{16}$$

An error correction model is a special case of a dynamic model for the first differences of variables in which the variables are "cointegrated"; i.e., the levels of the variables (obtained by integrating the differences) satisfy certain long-run relation or relations.

To construct an error correction model to explain $\Delta \ln P$ by $\Delta \ln(M/y)$, we allow the short-run dynamics to be as complicated as in Eq. (16) and add an error correction term. The error correction term can be estimated as the difference between $\ln P_{t-1}$ and the regression of $\ln P_{t-1}$ on $\ln(M/y)_{t-1}$, i.e., as the lagged residuals u_{t-1} in the regression Eq. (6). Using annual data from 1954 to 1983, this model is estimated to be

$$\Delta \ln P = \ \ 0.00445 \ + \ 0.1364 \ \Delta \ln(M/y) + \ \ 0.0267 \ \Delta \ln(M/y)_{-1}$$
$$\ \ \ \ \ \ \ \ \ \ (0.00380) \ \ \ \ (0.0217) \ \ \ \ \ \ \ \ \ \ \ \ \ \ \ \ \ \ (0.0328)$$

$$+ \ 0.1415 \ \Delta \ln P_{-1} - \ 0.3086 \ u_{t-1}, \ \ \ \ \ R^2 \ = 0.7247 \tag{17}$$
$$\ \ \ (0.1447) \ \ \ \ \ \ \ \ \ \ \ (0.1478) \ \ \ \ \ \ \ \ \ \ s \ \ \ = 0.0195$$
$$\ \mathrm{DW} = 1.895 \ .$$

The coefficient -0.3086 of the error correction term has the correct sign and is statistically significant. The residuals of the regression do not show a significantly positive serial correlation. The lag structure, however, is more complicated than necessary in that both the coefficients of $\Delta \ln(M/y)_{-1}$ and of $\Delta \ln P_{-1}$ are not significant. If the weakest variable $\Delta \ln(M/y)_{-1}$ is dropped, the result is

$$\Delta \ln P = \ \ 0.00422 \ + \ 0.1430 \ \Delta \ln(M/y) + \ 0.2176 \ \Delta \ln P_{-1}$$
$$\ \ \ \ \ \ \ \ \ \ (0.00376) \ \ \ \ (0.0201) \ \ \ \ \ \ \ \ \ \ \ \ \ \ \ (0.1098)$$

$$- \ 0.3771 \ u_{t-1} \ \ \ \ \ R^2 \ = 0.7174 \tag{18}$$
$$\ \ \ (0.1209) \ \ \ \ \ \ \ s \ \ \ = 0.0193$$
$$\ \mathrm{DW} = 2.068 \ .$$

Equation (18) is a satisfactory error correction model. All three coefficients have the right signs and are statistically significant. The Durbin–Watson statistic indicates the lack of positive serial correlation in the residual. The equation explains about 72% of the variance of $\Delta \ln P$. Engle and Granger (1987) suggest seven tests of the null hypothesis that a long-run relation between the levels of the variable do *not* exist. One such test is to examine the DW statistic of the regression (6) and accept the null hypothesis if it is close to zero. Since the DW statistic is as high as 1.003, we reject the null hypothesis and conclude that a long-run relation between $\ln P$ and $\ln(M/y)$ does exist, as suggested by the quantity theory. The short-run dynamic relation between $\ln P$ and $\ln(M/y)$ is satisfactorily given by Eq. (18).

18.5. Comparable Analyses of U.S. Data

It is interesting to find out how well the statistical models of Secs. 3 and 4 can explain a comparable set of data for the United States. To do so I have selected a sample of annual data of the same length from 1922 to 1953, used in my study of the demand for money (1966), and estimated equations analogous to (4), (5), (6), (7), (8), (9), (17), and (18). The selection of this sample period is somewhat arbitrary. The period includes the Great Depression and World War II, providing variations in the data comparable to those occurring after the Great Leap Forward Movement in China. Our main purpose is to see whether the explanatory power of the theoretical framework is different and how different. For the U.S. equations, P is a price index of consumer expenditures, M is currency and demand deposits adjusted in the middle of the year, and y is net national product deflated by the above consumer price index, as referenced in Chow (1966, pp. 128–129). For ease of comparison, the equations are given the same numbers as before, except with an A added.

The demand for money equation corresponding to (4) is

$$\ln(M/P) = -3.912 + 1.241\ \ln y, \qquad R^2 = 0.9216 \qquad (4A)$$
$$(0.801)\quad (0.066) \qquad\qquad s\ \ = 0.1428$$
$$\mathrm{DW} = 0.4070\ .$$

After the lagged dependent variable is added, it becomes

$$\ln(M/P) = -0.5942 + 0.1908\ \ln y + 0.8487\ \ln(M/P)_{-1}, \quad R^2 = 0.9856 \quad (5A)$$
$$(0.4570)\quad (0.0954)\qquad\quad (0.0735) \qquad\qquad s\ \ = 0.0616$$
$$\mathrm{DW} = 1.141\ .$$

The similarities between these equations and the corresponding Eqs. (4) and (5) are striking. Equation (5A) is slightly less satisfactory than (5) in having a smaller t ratio for $\ln y$ and a lower DW statistic.

The equations explaining the $\ln P$ corresponding to (6) and (7) are

$$\ln P = 0.4699 + 0.6334\ \ln(M/y), \qquad\qquad R^2 = 0.7324 \quad (6A)$$
$$(0.1031)\quad (0.0699) \qquad\qquad\qquad s\ \ = 0.1239$$
$$\mathrm{DW} = 0.2381$$

$$\ln P = -0.7472 + 0.5385\ \ln M + 0.4493\ \ln y, \qquad R^2 = 0.7376 \quad (7A)$$
$$(1.6106)\quad (0.1437)\qquad\quad (0.2531) \qquad\quad s\ \ = 0.1248$$
$$\mathrm{DW} = 0.1806\ .$$

To test whether the coefficient of $\ln y$ equals the negative of the coefficient of $\ln M$, we compare the sum of squared residuals of (6A) 0.46026 with the sum for (7A) 0.45134. Their difference divided by the latter sum is 0.0198, not at all significant as an $F(1, 29)$ statistic and supporting Eq. (6A). However, the DW statistics of (6A) is very low, requiring further modeling of the dynamics of $\Delta \ln P$ as in (8) and (9).

The corresponding results from the U.S. data are

$$\Delta \ln P = \underset{(0.0443)}{0.1632} + \underset{(0.0442)}{0.1450} \ln(M/y) - \underset{(0.0632)}{0.1313} \ln P_{-1}, \qquad \begin{aligned} R^2 &= 0.2950 \\ s &= 0.0457 \\ DW &= 0.9079 \end{aligned} \qquad (8A)$$

$$\Delta \ln P = \underset{(0.0097)}{0.0116} + \underset{(0.1347)}{0.1773} \Delta \ln(M/y), \qquad \begin{aligned} R^2 &= 0.0563 \\ s &= 0.0520 \\ DW &= 0.8414 \,. \end{aligned} \qquad (9A)$$

Both equations are not as good as the corresponding equations for China, in terms of the lower t statistics for the coefficients of $\ln(M/y)$ and $\Delta \ln(M/y)$, higher standard errors of the regression, and less satisfactory DW statistics.

Attempts to construct a suitable error correction model using the residuals u_t from (6A) have produced

$$\Delta \ln P = \underset{(0.0073)}{0.0038} - \underset{(0.1144)}{0.0322} \Delta \ln(M/y) + \underset{(0.1144)}{0.0072} \Delta \ln(M/y)_{-1}$$

$$+ \underset{(0.1398)}{0.6886} \Delta \ln P_{-1} - \underset{(0.0622)}{0.1578} u_{t-1}, \qquad \begin{aligned} R^2 &= 0.5814 \\ s &= 0.0371 \\ DW &= 1.506 \end{aligned} \qquad (17A)$$

$$\Delta \ln P = \underset{(0.0068)}{0.0034} + \underset{(1.242)}{0.6758} \Delta \ln P_{-1} - \underset{(0.0548)}{0.1578} u_{t-1}, \qquad \begin{aligned} R^2 &= 0.5836 \\ s &= 0.0358 \\ DW &= 1.564 \,. \end{aligned} \qquad (18A)$$

For explaining $\Delta \ln P$ in (17A), neither $\Delta \ln(M/y)$ nor $\Delta \ln(M/y)_{-1}$ are significant. After both terms are dropped, we are left with $\Delta \ln P_{-1}$ and the error correction term u_{t-1} in (18A), both being significant. The long-run effect of $\ln(M/y)$ on $\ln P$ implicit in (18A) is still given by the coefficient 0.6334 of Eq. (6A). Equation (18A) is of the form

$$\Delta y_t = \beta \Delta y_{t-1} - \gamma(y_{t-1} - \alpha x_{t-1})$$

and can be rewritten as

$$y_t - (1 + \beta - \gamma)y_{t-1} + \beta y_{t-2} = \gamma \alpha x_{t-1} \,, \qquad (19)$$

which implies a long-run relationship $\gamma y = \gamma \alpha x$ or $y = \alpha x$.

By (19) we see that (18A) amounts to explaining $\ln P_t$ or $\Delta \ln P_t$ by $\ln P_{t-1}$, $\ln P_{t-2}$ and $\ln(M/y)_{t-1}$. By adding the variables $\ln(M/y)_t$ and $\ln(M/y)_{t-2}$ in the regression of $\Delta \ln P_t$ on the above variables, we have found them to be very insignificant, with t ratios of -0.097 and 0.083, respectively. Dropping these variables, the regression becomes

$$\Delta \ln P = \begin{array}{c} 0.0990 \\ (0.0430) \end{array} + \begin{array}{c} 0.4803 \ln P_{-1} \\ (0.1496) \end{array} - \begin{array}{c} 0.6357 \ln P_{-2} \\ (0.1405) \end{array}$$

$$+ \begin{array}{c} 0.1135 \ \ln(M/y)_{-1}, \\ (0.0412) \end{array} \qquad \begin{array}{ll} R^2 & = 0.5900 \\ s & = 0.0362 \\ DW & = 1.538 \ . \end{array} \qquad (18B)$$

Note that (18A) and (18B) are less satisfactory than Eq. (18) for China in having lower R^2's, larger standard errors of the regression, and DW statistics further away from 2. The DW statistic of (6A) is low, failing to reject the null hypothesis that a stable long-run relation between $\ln P$ and $\ln(M/y)$ does not exist.

In summary, we have found $\ln(M/y)$ to be a significant variable in explaining $\ln P$ in both China and United States, but the short-run dynamics are harder to model and the long-run relationship may be less stable for the United States.

18.6. Additional Issues

Two additional issues are addressed in this section. First, does total wage affect the price level? Second, does our Eq. (18) remain stable after the economic reforms from 1979 on and how well does it forecast for 1984? To answer the first question, a wage variable W is constructed as the sum of total wage of state enterprises (*Statistical Yearbook of China 1984*, p. 458) and total wage of collective enterprises. The latter equals the number of staff and workers in collectives (*Yearbook 1984*, p. 110) times their average wage rate, which is assumed to be the average wage rate in state enterprises divided by 1.2752. 1.2752 is the ratio prevailing in 1978 (*Yearbook 1984*, p. 455). Data for W are also given in Table 1. The addition of $\ln W$ to Eq. (6) gives

$$\Delta \ln P = \begin{array}{c} 0.5297 \\ (0.1221) \end{array} + \begin{array}{c} 0.2010 \ \ln(M/y) \\ (0.0266) \end{array} + \begin{array}{c} 0.0430 \ \ln W, \\ (0.0117) \end{array} \qquad \begin{array}{ll} R^2 & = 0.8786 \\ s & = 0.0305 \\ DW & = 0.9543 \ . \end{array} \qquad (20)$$

The coefficient of $\ln W$ is statistically significant, but the effect is small, having an elasticity of only 0.043. If $\ln W_t$ and $\ln W_{t-1}$ are added to Eq. (18), their coefficients have t statistics of 0.309 and -0.164 and the coefficients of the other three variables are hardly affected. It can be concluded that the effect of money supply on the price level is much more important than that of the wage bill, and that Eq. (18) remains valid in ignoring the possible effects of total wage.

To see whether Eq. (18) is subject to a structural change after 1979, we perform the standard F test by dividing the data into two periods, the first from 1954 to 1978 and the second from 1979 to 1983. The sum of squared residuals of the two separate regressions is 0.008217 with $30 - 8$ or 22 degrees of freedom. The sum of squared residuals of the pooled regression (18) is 0.009731 with $30 - 4$ or 26 degrees of freedom. The test statistic is the ratio of $(0.009731 - 0.008217)/4$ to $0.008217/22$, or 1.013, much smaller than the 10% right-tail critical value 2.22 for the $F(4, 22)$ distribution. We thus accept the null hypothesis that the four coefficients of Eq. (18) did not change after 1979.

If Eq. (18) remains valid after the economic reforms began in 1979, it can be used to forecast the retail price index P. The first post-sample year, 1984, provides a good opportunity for observing how well Eq. (18) can forecast since there was a rapid increase in the amount of currency in circulation M from 529.78 hundred-thousand yuan at the end of 1983 to 792.11 at the end of 1984, while the index of real national income increased by a much smaller percentage of 13.9 (see *Statistical Yearbook of China 1985*, p. 34). To perform the forecasting experiment for 1984, we rewrite Eq. (18) as an equation explaining $\ln P$ by $\ln P_{-1}$, $\ln P_{-2}$, $\ln(M/y)$ and $\ln(M/y)_{-1}$,

$$\ln P = 0.360428 + 0.840422 \ln P_{-1} - 0.217564 \ln P_{-2}$$
$$+ 0.143004 \ln \left(\frac{M}{y}\right) - 0.0416556 \ln \left(\frac{M}{y}\right)_{-1} . \tag{21}$$

Data for P_{-1}, P_{-2}, and $(M/y)_{-1}$ are given in Table 1. M is 792.11; y is 4342.79, or 13.9% higher than the 1983 figure given in Table 1. Using these data, Eq. (21) yields a forecast of 0.477928 for $\ln P$ or 1.6127 for P in 1984. The actual value of P in 1984 is 1.600 (see *Yearbook 1985*, p. 530). The error in forecasting $\ln P$ is -0.0079, even smaller than the standard error of regression 0.0193 for Eq. (18). Hence Eq. (18) stands up very well when it is used to forecast the retail price index in 1984.

In this paper I have found that the quantity theory of money provides a useful starting point in constructing a model to explain the index of retail prices in China. The ratio of money supply to real output is an important variable in explaining the price level, as the quantity theory implies. However, the elasticity of the price level with respect to this ratio is smaller than unity, suggesting that velocity is not constant. The assumption of constant velocity may serve as a satisfactory first approximation in explaining the demand for money, but not necessarily in explaining the price level. The success in one case does not carry over to the other. The theoretical framework suggested in this paper is somewhat more successful in explaining the Chinese data from 1952 to 1983 than the United States data from 1922 to 1953. The model for short-run changes in log price is more satisfactory, and the stability of a long-run relation between the price level and the money-output ratio is better established for China than for the United States. Total wage is found to assert little or no additional effect on price. The model for price change is stable after 1979, and forecasts well in 1984.

References

Chow, G. C., 1985a, A model of Chinese national income determination, *J. Polit. Econ.* **93**, 782–792.

————, 1985b, *The Chinese Economy*, New York: Harper & Row; 2nd edn., 1987 Singapore: World Scientific.

————, 1986, Chinese Statistics. *The Amer. Statistician* **40**, 191–196.

————, 1987, Development of a more market-oriented economy in China, *Science*, 295–299.

————, 1966, On the long-run and short-run demand for money, *J. Polit. Econ.* **74**, 111–131.

Engle, Robert F., and Granger, C. W. J., 1987, Co-integration and error correction: representation, estimation and testing, *Econometrica* **55**, 251–276.

Statistical Yearbook of China 1981, 1984 and 1985. Beijing: State Statistics Bureau, and Hong Kong: Economic Information & Agency.

INDEX

A